THE HOOP OF LIFE

A New Beginning

STEVE LAUGHLIN

Black Rose Writing | Texas

©2023 by Steve Laughlin
All rights reserved. No part of this book may be reproduced, stored in a retrieval system or transmitted in any form or by any means without the prior written permission of the publishers, except by a reviewer who may quote brief passages in a review to be printed in a newspaper, magazine or journal.

The author grants the final approval for this literary material.

First printing

Some names and identifying details have been changed to protect the privacy of individuals.

ISBN: 978-1-68513-139-5
PUBLISHED BY BLACK ROSE WRITING
www.blackrosewriting.com

Printed in the United States of America
Suggested Retail Price (SRP) $21.95

The Hoop of Life is printed in Garamond Premier Pro

*As a planet-friendly publisher, Black Rose Writing does its best to eliminate unnecessary waste to reduce paper usage and energy costs, while never compromising the reading experience. As a result, the final word count vs. page count may not meet common expectations.

"The building described in this book was designed in the form of our Sacred Hoop and represents the reunification of the body and spirit of the Dakota people. The resulting facility has been a great success and a significant source of pride for our community."
–Edward Red Owl, of the Sisseton Wahpeton Oyate, tribal advisor, historian & mentor

"Steve Laughlin, in his intriguingly-titled first book, *The Hoop of Life*, deals with sadness and tragedy beautifully. The opening of the chapter *Darkness* is very well done indeed. He also does comedy well and made me laugh out loud several times. The writing is witty and self-deprecatory."
–Malcolm Windsor, author of *Roving Mad: Odd Encounters*

"*The Hoop of Life* describes a portion of Steve Laughlin's life in a humorous, sometimes emotional but always special way. Prepare to laugh, cry and be amazed as he records a series of unusual events that happen in his life all at once."
–Hans Dreijer, film editor, sound & graphic designer

"Steve Laughlin is fearless in writing from the heart. His memoir of family life over several decades is at times laugh-out-loud funny and at others deeply moving. *The Hoop of Life* will delight readers with its authenticity and just plain good story telling."
–Pamela Shuttlesworth, educator, mother, grandmother

THE HOOP OF LIFE

Foreword

You go through life trying to break out of the dullness, do something special, or be something special. Usually, not much comes of it. Then once in a while, something really bad happens, or something really good, or really strange—so bad, so good, or so strange that it makes for a good story. These are some of my good stories, focused roughly on an eight-year period in my recent life.

Now... I'm an old fisherman from way back. One thing about us old fishermen is that every time we describe a nice catch, the fish gets bigger, the details about catching it get more exciting, and everything surrounding the event is embellished to the maximum. And after telling the story over and over again, it turns into a "whopper," which the fisherman himself begins to believe to be the absolute truth. To a certain extent, this is what I have been doing in the writing of this book. You could call it a "memoir," but now and then, when I sit down to write something, my old fish storytelling habits kick in. I have changed some names, dates, and places, and have filled in a few blank spots in my memory with some dramatizations. Just keep in mind that in all my "whoppers," deep down in there somewhere, is a dollop of truth.

Acknowledgments

I am deeply thankful for the memory of Sharon, who was my loving partner for 35 years, until her death in 2009. Her three-year struggle with her breast cancer had a powerful impact on our family and friends and is a major part of this story. Thanks are also due to our three boys, now young men, who have been a constant source of surprises, challenges, and entertainment in our lives.

Thanks and praise also to my second wife, Karen. High school classmates, we didn't see, or even think about each other in forty years, yet discovered love late in our lives. A French citizen, she has done a wonderful job of dragging me out of my recliner to travel and see the world for the first time.

My friends Hilary Kaiser, Catherine Monnet, Christine Rolland, and Malcolm Windsor over the past few years have been faithful companions in our Paris writer's group. Without their continuous encouragement and editing suggestions for quality, this writing experiment would have failed. For their support, thanks also to Mary Duncan and her group of American writers living in Paris. From their American west coast locations, Deborah Jayne (literary services), and Kristin Thiel (line editor services), were also of great help. Sincere thanks to all.

It is important that I give special thanks to Edward Red Owl and his Dakota people of the Sisseton Wahpeton Oyate, as well as the Lakota people of Pine Ridge. I came to know these two communities of Native Americans, their histories and present, while conducting the architectural design of a building for each group. I was deeply sorry to hear that my friend and mentor, Edward Red Owl, passed away in the spring of 2021.

Special thanks must also go to my workmates and friends at office of Leo A Daly, Architects and Engineers of Omaha: Dale, Mark, Sheila, Alissa, Ralph, Phil, Lloyd, Ardelle, Teri and all the other unsung heroes and heroines there, who every day, put their hearts, minds, energies, and talents into their facilities design endeavors, intent upon uplifting the lives of their patrons.

Finally, there would be no story to be told if it were not for my cluster of close friends, on and around 38th Street in Omaha, Nebraska. Not to forget our German friends, Hans Dreijer and Monika Haerle-Dreijer, as well as our friends Pamela and Jerry Shuttlesworth, and my brothers for their tolerance, encouragement, and support.

Thank you to everyone, Steve Laughlin

CHAPTER 1
Blue Jeans

Minnesota and South Dakota, June 2007

I was fishing in central Minnesota when I received a call from the office. One of my associates was asking me to join him for a meeting. It would be in Sisseton, South Dakota. He wanted me to stop there at the end of my vacation, on my drive back to Omaha.

"Jeez, Dale, I don't have any office clothes. I'm out here in the middle of a lake in my smelly blue jeans and a T-shirt."

"No problem, Steve. They're pretty informal people. You'll fit right in. Don't need a slick guy in a business suit."

I pondered his request and replied, "OK, OK. How about if I show up at noonish on Thursday? I can overnight in Fargo on the way in."

"Perfect!" Dale said. "Call me when you get to Sisseton, and I'll direct you to the council chambers. See you then."

Dale and I were both architects employed by a company in Omaha. His clients were the Sisseton Wahpeton Oyate. In the Dakota language, the word *Oyate* means "people." Using white man's terminology, these were Sioux Indians. The Sisseton Wahpeton reservation was a tract of land at the intersection of North Dakota, South Dakota, and Minnesota.

Dale wanted me to talk with the tribe's facilities committee to brainstorm some ideas for a new headquarters. At present, their offices were scattered here and there, in all manner of secondhand facilities: run-down stores, small-town office buildings, mobile homes, and dilapidated old houses. The new building was going to be as big as a city block, all on one level, serving a tribal population of some twelve thousand people. It was going to house twenty-eight tribal departments, kind of a city-county building, with everything from business offices and community services to historic archives, police HQ, and the like, all under one roof. The new facility would be in the far northeast corner of South Dakota, out on the open prairie, near the small town of Sisseton.

A few days later, I packed up my fishing gear and drove west. The two-lane blacktop snaked through the lodgepole pines, weaving around lakes and lily pad marshes. Near Fargo, as evening was coming on, the highway straightened out into farmland and rolling prairie. At dusk, I checked into a Fargo hotel and walked across the street to a Target. My plan was to buy paper, colored pencils, and markers. I wanted to use the evening to sketch some ideas that had been rolling around in my head for the proposed building.

The next morning, I drove to Sisseton, seventy-five miles to the south. Upon arrival, I parked in front of an old, one-story industrial building, refitted to serve as office space for the tribal council. I walked in to meet with the facilities committee.

Dale was right. The committee all wore blue jeans. They were Native Americans, nine big guys and two women, all with seasoned faces. There was a casual and natural look about the group. The room had a *U*-shaped layout of buffet tables, with three people at the head table and four on each side. After introductions, I told the group that I had brought some concept sketches for their proposed building. I explained I did not intend these to be solutions, but were options to get a discussion going.

I pulled out the sketches of my first idea and taped them to the wall behind me. It was my favorite concept. I explained that this scheme was inspired by a Sioux chief headdress. Departments would attach to a single long corridor, similar to the way eagle feathers attach to the cloth band of a headdress. I showed a view of the front of the building and was pretty happy with the way it looked. Turning to scan the committee and get a discussion going, it disappointed me to see that their faces were dull and disinterested. This idea had flopped.

I said to myself, "*Shit! I'm in trouble now.*" Reluctantly, I grabbed my second scheme, which was maybe an even bigger flop, owing to its spiritual implications. It was presumptuous of me, Mr. Paleface businessman outsider to talk to these people about their sacred things. A few years back, I had picked up a little knowledge of Sioux culture from my dormitory project for the Oglala Sioux in Pine Ridge. The Oglala were one of the farthest west Sioux tribes, located some 350 miles away, in the opposite corner of South Dakota. In contrast, the Sisseton Wahpeton Oyate were one of the farthest east Sioux tribes, and here I was, hoping that they had similar spiritual symbols. Expecting the worst, I put the second set of sketches on the wall and forced myself to spit out a sentence. "This sketch is a circular building in the shape of the Medicine Wheel."

The startling sound of a chair screeching across the linoleum floor immediately interrupted me. Filled with concern, I turned to face the committee. To my fearful surprise, everyone was looking at the head table, at Edward Red Owl, the facilities committee chair. He had bolted to his feet, knuckles on the edge of the table. Red Owl was an elderly man with a weathered face and deep wrinkles crevassing his cheeks. With scrunched-down eyebrows, he was serious looking enough to be scary. Holding the silent attention of everyone in the room, he walked around the table toward me. I froze with fear as he approached, thinking that I was about to be yelled at for proposing something totally inappropriate.

He stopped in front of the sketches on the wall and turned to face his committee. With a swooping gesture, he traced the curve of the circular building's plan in the air. In a slow, deep voice of absolute seriousness, he said, "The *Hoop of Life* is sacred to our people. It is fitting and right that we gather in such a way." This guy's voice was profound and patriarchal, sounding like FDR or Abe Lincoln. His words burrowed into my brain. "In winters past, our people followed the great buffalo migration to the south. Every spring we returned with the buffalo to our homeland, planting our crops and staying through the fall harvest. During this time, the seven tribes of our people placed our tepees in a great ring, camped around the sacred Hoop of Life. *Now is the time for our people to return to the Hoop of Life.*"

Surprise and relief swept over me. *Holy shit!* I thought. *That was the easiest pitch I ever made! Guess we are going to do a round building!*

Red Owl turned to me and asked, "Mr. Laughlin, how did this vision come to you?"

Now me, being an architect, I would have called it a concept or an option, or maybe design, a scheme, a sketch, or just an idea. This guy was calling it a "VISION."

Trying to figure out how to respond, I shuffled through my pile of papers and pulled out a wrinkly letter-size envelope. It had a chicken-scratchy sketch on the back, which I had made with a cheap ballpoint pen while on the road the night before. I held the envelope up to show the committee and said, "Well, I sketched this idea up as I was driving in through Minnesota yesterday." There it was—the *Hoop of Life*.

Red Owl sharpened his gaze and retorted with a deep guttural grunt, "Uhhh!" which was followed by a round of positive grunts, uh-huhs, nods and hmmms from the committee around the table. My reference to Minnesota was much more important than I had understood.

Red Owl spoke again. "Minnesota was the traditional homeland for our people, a homeland that was taken away from us a century and a half ago."

Now... not seeing myself as a spiritual man, I attributed arrival of this circle idea in my head to a dollop of luck and a sprinkling of serendipity. "Wow!" I said rather casually. "Guess I got lucky with this idea."

Red Owl responded, "No, Mr. Laughlin, *not* luck. That which is holy is that which moves by itself." I began to understand. Red Owl believed that as I drove through their homeland the night before, a spiritual intervention had given me guidance in the form of a *vision*.

Either way, for the rest of the afternoon, the committee proceeded with confidence that we were on the right track. We had a spirited back-and-forth discussion of ideas to be included in their new building.

Who knew? Maybe there *was* something to Red Owl's spiritual thing.

CHAPTER 2

Sharon

Nebraska 2007-2009

Sharon and I celebrated our twenty-fifth wedding anniversary in 2007, about the time that her troubles with cancer began. Our three boys had become young men, eighteen, twenty, and twenty-two years old, all off to college. She and I had shared a fairly normal life together—kids, house, cars, jobs, dog, cat, church, school. Surprisingly so, considering that we first met in 1970 in Lincoln. The '60s really didn't arrive in Nebraska until the '70s. We survived some pretty wild times, free love, drugs, keggers, the pill.

We were both twenty years old when we met at a beer party. It was at a house rented by my college buddies in an old neighborhood near the university. Sharon's first impression of me was not the best. Lying on my back on the bare oak floor, I was blocking the opening between the dining room and living room. I was chugging my second bottle of cheap Ripple wine when Sharon walked in with her girlfriend. The girls had to step over my body to get into the next room, and I reached up, grabbing Sharon's thigh. I remembered little else from that evening, but she did. Her comment was, "What an asshole." I passed out, and the guys carried me to one of their beds.

Awakening mid-morning, I stumbled to the bathroom. Looking in the mirror, I called my buddies in to see an amazing sight. I had thrown up in the middle of the night and the depression in my pillow had filled with puke. The nasty combination of pizza and cheap wine had dried completely, forming a halo of crusty hurl that circled diagonally around my head, looking rather like the great ring of Saturn or the brim of Maurice Chevalier's straw hat.

When not partying, I was living at home and attending the architecture college at the University of Nebraska. Sharon was from a small town in central Nebraska, newly arrived in Lincoln, having followed her older sister to town to take a job as a secretary. She wore miniskirts and calf-high white go-go boots. Meanwhile, I was turning from a nice, clean-cut kid into a hippie.

It took a couple extra years for me to graduate from college. Our inner circle of friends all graduated and scattered to jobs across the country. Sharon and I really didn't choose to spend our lives together. It was more like we were abandoned. In the absence of our closest friends, we clung to each other. Our companionship eventually grew into a comfortable love. After graduating, I took a job in Omaha, fifty miles away. Sharon followed me there. After five years of living in sin, we married. I wound up working with the same company, living in the same house, for thirty-five years. Staying put, Sharon and I developed a close-knit group of friends in our Omaha neighborhood, couples raising families together.

In the two and a half years that Sharon struggled with breast cancer, she endured an endless series of aggressive procedures. Months of chemotherapy were followed by discouraging test results, a double mastectomy, and the removal of lymph nodes. As she suffered through the pain and misery of her healing, our spirits drifted downward.

Judy, Sharon's older sister, also suffered from breast cancer. Both women had inherited "the bad gene." Judy's diagnosis was one year prior to Sharon's. During a lull between Judy's bouts with the cancer, she came to Omaha to stay with us for a few weeks, intending to help Sharon recover from her surgery. Unfortunately, Judy was too rickety and weak to help very much. It quickly became obvious that big sister was sliding back into trouble. Judy went home to discover that her cancer had returned. A year and a half into Sharon's extended struggle, Judy died, leaving Sharon under a blanket of grief and despair, with hope sliding away.

A few months after the mastectomy, Sharon's cancer reappeared on the suture line across her chest, requiring a second surgery and more healing time. The cancer returned a third time, again requiring surgery. Another round of chemotherapy followed this. Her desperation grew as she endured extended periods of suffering. Even so, we could not abandon our hopes for her recovery.

Eventually, Sharon received aggressive radiation treatment across her chest. The radiation burn over her sternum never healed. A month later, a hand-size chunk of dead flesh was surgically removed and replaced with a flap of living flesh that a plastic surgeon harvested from her back. More months of healing followed. The breast plate of relocated flesh recovered nicely, but the wound on her back refused to heal. It was like the back-pocket of a pair of blue jeans and was constantly filling up with fluid. Her pain would slowly increase as the quantity of fluid grew. Every two weeks, to relieve the mounting pain, the plastic surgeon drained the fluid with a big syringe that looked like a turkey baster. As her misery continued, Sharon's weariness and discouragement slowly changed to bitterness and despair.

During times of healing between procedures, Sharon was at home. On three different occasions, she stood up too fast and fainted. On her last fall, she hit her forehead hard on the floor and was briefly knocked unconscious. I was on a business trip to the East Coast. Our middle son, Mark, had to take her to the emergency room at the hospital. It was not the kind of thing you would wish upon your twenty-one-year-old. They couldn't find anything to cause the fainting spells, and after two days, she returned home.

The pocket of skin on Sharon's back continued to fill with fluid, prompting the plastic surgeon to perform an ultrasound. What he discovered, by accident, was fluid *inside* her rib cage, within the sack surrounding her lungs. They readmitted her to the hospital for a longer stay and yet another aggressive surgery. The procedure was to collapse her lungs, drain the fluid from inside the surrounding sac, and re-inflate them. In the process, they sprayed the outer surface of her lungs with an adhesive, then "glued" to the surrounding sack, so that the fluid would have no place to go. Well, that was the theory, anyway.

"Jeezuz," I asked. "Is she strong enough to go through all that?"

CHAPTER 3

Four Entrances

Omaha, October 2009

It was during Sharon's final hospital stay that I received a phone call from Dale at the office. I responded, "Jeez, Dale, this is really crummy timing. The damn Dakota project sat dormant for two years and now they want a room-by-room floor plan in three weeks? My wife is going through some pretty heavy shit right now. She needs me." I shifted in the recliner in the corner of Sharon's hospital room. The recliner was built like a Sherman tank and was about as comfortable as sitting on a plate of steel.

"I know, Steve. This timing really sucks. Guess we'll have to get somebody to stand in for you. Red Owl will be disappointed, but he'll understand. Hell, they'll all understand." Dale started to think about another architectural designer to pull into the project as my replacement.

"Bullshit!" I said. "I'm just sitting up here, bored out of my mind, waiting for hours on end for a fucking doctor to poke his head into the room and give us two minutes of input. I can't leave this place, but one thing I can do is sit here and do the building design. Sharon won't mind. She's just happy to have me in the room with her, especially when the test results come in. I'm coming over to the office now, and I'll pick up the stuff I need to get started. Print me out your latest room-by-room list of spaces. See you in a few minutes. Oh, and I really need a copy of the letter that Red Owl sent us last year." Wondering if I could pull it off, I was feeling naked without access to all the equipment and staff at the office. The drawings would have to be precise freehand, old-school, no computer.

I set up my makeshift mini design studio beside Sharon's hospital bed. It was not much more than my old drawing board from college days placed across the arms of the recliner. I used the windowsill for my papers, pens, and equipment. Surprisingly, once I got into the task, I discovered that there was a complete lack of distraction—no phone calls, no people walking by, no pesky "other" projects to pull my attention away, no staff meetings, no timesheets to fill out, no emails, no urgent requests from the VPs. Just me and Sharon. I couldn't have asked for a better situation to focus on the building design while remaining close to Sharon, as close as could be. The nursing staff and doctors were curious to see my architectural design unfolding, and they tracked my progress.

Edward Red Owl's letter was like a recipe book describing the Hoop of Life in Dakota spiritual lingo. All I had to do was to translate it into architecture. In his letter, Red Owl said, "The Hoop of Life has four entrances. The East is the place of the Eagle, new beginnings and the first light of day. The woman who brought the Sacred Pipe to the first council of our People came from the East." My interpretation of that comment was that "new beginnings" would happen as people came to the visitor's entrance. This would be the front door of the building, on the east side. It would also be the perfect place for the information display, reception desk, waiting area and gift shop.

Next, Red Owl said, "Our warriors enter the Hoop of Life from the North. It is the place of winter and the Kit Fox. The Kit Fox survives the winter using perseverance and strength." My assumption was that the "warriors," using present-day language, were the staff, Native American employees using their "perseverance and strength" to fight the day-to-day office battles. It followed that the staff entrance would be on the north side of the building. I placed the human resources department there, and the tribe's social services, as well as the break room and locker rooms.

"The West is the place of the Horse and the setting sun" was Red Owl's next comment. "All knowledge and prosperity of the Tribe resides here. It is the place of the Elders." My take on that was that the chief probably had the most horses. I located the offices of the tribal leadership on the west side, including those of the chair (the chief) and tribal leaders, the council chamber, the judges, and the courtroom and legal department. It gave these Elders their very own VIP entrance.

Red Owl continued, "The South is the place of the Buffalo. In the past, the buffalo would sustain and nurture the People. The buffalo herds arrived from the south in the great spring migration." We had discussed the buffalo entrance at the facilities committee meeting two years ago. I remembered being surprised by a strange gesture coming from one of the committee members. The man raised his chin high, rounded his lips forward and up into a circle, and made a deep grunting sound. Several people around the table smiled in mild amusement and nodded in agreement. Dale later explained to me that the gesture was mimicking a buffalo calf suckling its mother. The natural conclusion was to locate the fourth entrance to the building on the south side. This would be the service entrance, where all the deliveries would arrive, including food. The cafeteria would be there too, "to sustain and nurture the People."

As I worked on the building's design in the solitude and isolation of Sharon's hospital room, the serious nature of her situation enveloped me, bringing forward an elevated level of focus such as I had never experienced. As I sat there watching Sharon's life slip away, Red Owl's Hoop of Life was being born.

There was a profound irony in this. My guess was that Red Owl, with his spiritual perspective, would have said "No. There is no irony."

CHAPTER 4

Mark

Omaha, late October 2009

As Sharon underwent surgery for the "gluing" procedure, the doctors discovered that the cancer had spread into her lungs. Outside the hospital room door, the doctor pulled me aside. He quietly commented that there wasn't much more they could do other than to make Sharon as comfortable as possible, and that I should start preparing mentally for her death. He requested I bring a copy of her living will to be scanned into the hospital computer. They prompted us to decide that if Sharon reached the point when she couldn't breathe on her own, we would not request heroic measures to keep her alive—no artificial respiration, no resuscitation.

Sharon was getting more and more uncomfortable in her hospital bed. After having spent a month in it, she had developed ulcers on her bottom. Her recurring phrase was "I hate this damn bed." Eventually she said, "I want to go home to my lazy-boy chair." With the support of the hospice care people, we went home, oxygen machine in tow.

Our middle son, Mark, was in his final year of college and was temporarily living back home when his mother returned. In grade school and high school, Mark had been the all-American kid, athletic and self-confident. There was a vitality about him. But during his college years while living away from home, he picked up several bad habits, including beer, partying, junk food, smoking, chewing tobacco, drugs, and gambling. He neglected his physical health, and his mother noticed that he had lost his wholesome appearance. Mark had become thin, slouch-shouldered, dull-eyed, unkempt, and non-communicative. For a time, he had an on-and-off relationship with an older woman who was part of his casino gambling crowd. He lived with her for a few months, but she finally kicked him out. I was happy to have him back home. His mother's health was slipping away, and I needed the extra help.

Through his high school and college years, Mark worked part-time at a gas station near our home. This was one spot of stability in his life, and he eventually became the cashier, a position of trust. One early evening, I received a call from the night manager of the gas station, an older guy who was a buddy of mine. Sharon was resting in her lazy-boy recliner in the living room. I was in the kitchen.

"Hi, Steve. This is Rich, down at the station. We've got a problem. Our profits have been coming up short. We checked the surveillance tapes. Mark has been stealing from the cash register—a lot of cash. The big boss hasn't called the police yet. Can you come talk to us? The sooner the better." They had identified several thousand dollars that Mark had stolen, spread out over the last year. He had committed a felony crime. Mark was on the verge of being arrested and jailed.

I responded, "I'll be right over."

I went to the living room and told Sharon a lie. "I've got to go back into the office for a bit. See you later." With Sharon's health in decline, I would try to handle this without her involvement.

Mark had settled into a routine of going to the casino on Saturday nights. He was a regular at the Texas Hold 'Em table. It was a high-dollar game. He would play all night and into Sunday morning and was always a contender to win big. When he did, he would buy hundred-dollar meals and rounds of drinks for his inner circle of friends. As a result, no matter if he won or lost, chances were that he would go home with empty pockets. During the week, he was stealing a couple hundred dollars from the gas station's cash register to kick-start his Saturday night poker game.

Mark had become very competent at the thefts, with a dozen sly tricks to conceal what he was doing. He had worked out a deal with the young kid who handled tire repairs out in the garage. Often, tire repair customers would pay with cash, outside on the driveway, and not require a receipt.

Mark and the tire repair kid would split the cash. Mark became proficient at judging a customer's gullibility, often overcharging, and pocketing the difference. He would shortchange people, giving change for a ten-dollar bill when the customer had given him a twenty. The ten dollars that was overlooked by the customer would slide into Mark's pocket. If challenged, he would smoothly say, "Oops, sorry about that," and hand the customer a ten from the cash register. He would intentionally make mistakes so that he could open the drawer and grab cash. Mark used every method that he could get away with, including positioning his body to block the view of the security camera, or so he thought.

Here we were, locked in this strange knot in time. Events were piling on top of each other. During what would be the last few days of his mother's life, we were thrown into a desperate struggle to keep Mark from going to prison. This was not what a father-son team does every day. We sat down together in a confrontational meeting with Buster, the filling station owner. Mark's thefts were big enough to send him to the penitentiary. Buster was tough and verbally abusive, yelling at Mark throughout the meeting. We negotiated a settlement. I wrote Buster a $7,000 check on the spot. He demanded that Mark pay me back in full within the coming year, at $120 each week. Mark had to sign up for Gambling Anonymous and was formally barred from entering the casinos. He agreed to clean the bathrooms at the filling station every day at 5:00 a.m. for the next year, without pay. Under my supervision, Mark could not leave the house except to go to work or school for one year. He would be required to maintain a minimum B average in his classes at college. All these conditions were put into a contract that was signed by Mark, Buster, and me. I was to track the conditions and report to Buster on a monthly basis. Mark's failure to comply would trigger his arrest.

Throughout the meeting, Mark kept his head down, reluctantly mumbling short responses when he had to, "Uh-huh" or "Uh-uh" (meaning "no" and "yes" in Nebraska lingo). I broke down in tears several times. "What were you thinking?" I asked Mark. "Why didn't your conscience cry out, telling you that you were doing something wrong?" He had no answer. He just wanted to get out of there.

By the skin of our teeth, we had cut a deal with Buster, and we kept the police out of it. Mark would have no jail time, no lifetime label as an ex-con, no convicted felon disclosures on job application forms, no shit-canning of four years of college. He was lucky. But it left Mark and I with scars. There was a big wound that would not heal. It was the death of the joyful expectation that a parent carries when rearing a child. The vibrant and wholesome young boy, full of promise, was lost. The phrase, "Sorry, Dad," didn't work anymore.

Thankfully, we spared his mother all this.

CHAPTER 5

The Gathering

Omaha, November 9, 2009

"Mark, Mark... wake up. I need you to get up and watch your mother while I take a shower." Mark had stayed up late but crawled out of bed, came up to the living room and sat down in the corner chair across from his mother. It was sunrise, and I had been sitting with Sharon in the living room through the night. She was asleep in her morphine-induced slumber, lying comfortably in her favorite lazy-boy recliner. I went upstairs to shower and put on some clean clothes.

Nearly dressed when I heard the front doorbell, I came down the steps, barefoot, with socks in my hand. Our neighbor and close friend Gary stood at the door. "Hi, Steve, thought I'd drop in and see how Sharon is doing." Gary and I walked over to Sharon's chair. Mark was asleep in his chair.

Sharon's face had an off-white paleness. I laid my hand on hers and was surprised by the coolness of her skin. Dropping onto one knee, I lowered my ear to her mouth and discovered that she was not breathing. Placing my ear on her chest, I confirmed that her heart had stopped beating. I turned to Gary and in a broken voice said, "She's gone."

As the darkness of the moment swept over me, Gary phoned his wife. The news of Sharon's death quickly spread to our closest friends in the immediate neighborhood. It was an unusually warm, sunny Sunday morning in early November, seventy-ish. They were all close by, either in church or at the fund-raiser pancake breakfast or at home starting their day. In short order, people started arriving at the house. Sharon was lying in her recliner, an afghan draped over her body with her hands poking out naturally on the armrests. Her expression was as if she was napping. The morning light was filling the room with a warm glow.

Mark and I shared hugs and tears with our friends as they entered. Visitors spontaneously moved the dining room chairs close to Sharon's body. They sat and softly said their goodbyes, caressing Sharon's hands and forehead. After I regained some composure, I took the phone out onto the back porch, still barefoot, and called relatives. Eventually, some thirty people had gathered.

Mo, Sharon's best friend, went into the kitchen, put some coffee on, fried up a pan of bacon, and threw together a plate of finger food. Robyn, another close friend and neighbor, noted the heat leaving from Sharon's forehead, saying that in her home country, New Zealand, this is seen as the spirit leaving the body and rising to heaven. Suzanne, our neighbor three doors to the south, brought her seven-year-old granddaughter into the house. The young girl knew Sharon. Suzanne sat close to Sharon's body and invited the girl to sit on her lap. The two of them held Sharon's lifeless hand. Offering a comforting hug to the girl, Suzanne began to gently sway back-and-forth and softly sing a lullaby to her granddaughter and to Sharon.

Not long into the morning, I noticed Mark had retreated from the gathering. I sought him out, finding him sitting alone downstairs on the edge of his bed, elbows on his knees, head down. I leaned my shoulder against the doorjamb of his bedroom and prompted him. "You OK?" I asked, knowing that he wasn't.

His sadness was deeper than I expected. The twenty-two-year-old was breaking down, feeling guilt, thinking that he had failed at watching after his mother. Mark and I had agreed that if Sharon ran into difficulties, the plan was to call 9-1-1. In the hours before Sharon's death, under the spell of morphine, Sharon's breathing had sounded mechanical and rhythmical... breath in, *click*, breath out, pause, repeat. At the moment of her death, Mark heard the mechanical breathing stop. He misinterpreted this, thinking that she had returned to her normal breathing. With that, he relaxed, and he drifted off to sleep.

"I... I thought she was OK... breathing easier," Mark's voice was trembling and broken. "I didn't know... didn't know that she..."

Recognizing the reason for his despair, I interrupted him. "Stop, Mark. Stop. It's OK. If we'd called 9-1-1, strangers would have taken her away, poking at her with cold machines...." I fumbled with the words. "It's better this way. The people she loved—they're all here. You gave your mother a gift. She died peacefully. She's here, at home, in her favorite chair, surrounded by friends. Thank you, Mark. You didn't do anything wrong. It's all OK. You did fine. *You did just fine.*"

As I tried to find the words to comfort Mark, I began to realize the power of this gathering that was taking place around us. Death must have been like this in the old days, before 9-1-1 calls.

CHAPTER 6
Suspicions

Omaha, November 9, 2009

By midmorning on the day of Sharon's death, friends and family were leaving our house, with offerings of sympathy, more tears, and hugs. I called the hospice to let them know Sharon had died. Within thirty minutes, a mortuary vehicle pulled up to collect Sharon's body. The hospice nurse walked in with a clipboard and pen in hand. She inspected Sharon's body and took some notes. As directed by hospice, I had kept a log of the times and dosages of morphine I had given to Sharon. We walked to the kitchen, and I retrieved my log.

Sharon's routine had been to sleep for a few hours in a morphine-induced slumber. When she awoke and overcame her grogginess, she would have a few minutes of coherent conversation that would end when pain and panic returned. Terrorized, unable to catch her next breath, she would plead tearfully, "Can't breathe. Can't take it."

Sharing her panic, I would frantically prep another dose of morphine mixed with orange juice. Caresses and comforting words followed. "It's OK. It's OK, Sharon. It'll pass soon." As the morphine kicked in, mercifully, Sharon would go back to sleep.

The hospice nurse asked me to retrieve the vials of morphine that I had been saving, as directed. Upon her inspection of the vials, the nurturing, helpful, and supportive expression evaporated, changing quickly to sternness, suspicion, and coldness. It was an expression I had seen before.

My mind catapulted back to 1986, the day my father died, a sixty-eight-year-old man, overweight and worn out by life. His fingers were bent sideways from rheumatoid arthritis, and he had a nasty jack-o'-lantern mouth of missing, broken, and rotting teeth. Upon developing congestive heart failure, his heart was too weak to pump fluids around his body and his legs became dramatically swollen. Finally, in his weakened state, pancreatic cancer quickly finished him. For his final days, we transferred him to a nursing home where he received hospice care. On his last day, I sat at the foot of his bed, on a deathwatch. He stirred and opened his eyes.

"How you feeling?" I asked.

"Hurts like hell." His words were raspy and barely audible.

"I'll get the nurse," I replied. She came in and gave Dad a shot of morphine, and he drifted back to sleep.

An hour or so later, having become adjusted to the cadence of Dad's breathing during his morphine-induced slumber, I noticed that the time between his breaths had noticeably slowed. I sat up and listened intently. It grew even slower, with a long pause between breaths, then slower, pause… slower… stop. After another pause, I said to myself, "He's gone," feeling relief that his struggle was finally over.

I stood up and called the nurse into the room. Searching for words, speaking slowly and awkwardly, I tried to explain that I had just watched Dad's breathing slow and stop. She interrupted, barking out a question with urgency in her voice. "Do you want me to call in the resuscitation team?"

I was dumbstruck. I had just watched my father die a peaceful death, ending his horrific year-long battle with declining health. After another long, uncomfortable pause, I responded, "No. Let him go."

The woman's expression hardened, and she asserted, "He wanted to be resuscitated!" I hesitated, frozen by my instincts. Raising her voice again, she aggressively barked, *"Time is critical!"*

Reluctantly and sheepishly, against my better judgment, I said, "OK."

While waiting for the resuscitation team to arrive, I phoned my younger brother, Dean. He had just picked up our older brother at the airport. Larry had flown in from Denver in anticipation of Dad's death. They were on their way.

The emergency rescue team arrived laden with equipment. They ushered me into the hall as they entered Dad's room and closed the door. During those frantic minutes while the resuscitation effort was in progress, a uniformed police officer arrived in the lobby and took a position at the door to the room. Eventually, the resuscitation team exited and confirmed that Dad could not be revived. Immediately, the uniformed police officer announced I could not enter the room until he had conducted an inspection. He entered Dad's room and closed the door. A fog of emotions and confusion washed over me as I waited in the hall.

As my brothers arrived, I overheard the nurse whispering on the phone to Dad's primary doctor. By the tone of her conversation, I realized she had drawn a conclusion from my hesitation and my awkward response. She expressed to the doctor her suspicion that I had done something to stop Dad's breathing, ending his life in a mercy killing. She had called the police. My guess was that having expected my father's imminent death, the doctor was scolding her for overreacting. The police officer was called to the phone. After a brief conversation with the doctor, the officer expressed his condolences and exited. Finally, my brothers and I entered Dad's room and the process of our grieving began.

My thoughts wrenched back to the present, to the hospice nurse at my house as she measured the contents of Sharon's morphine vials. I could see what was coming. I was being accused, for the second time in my life, of a mercy killing. Suspecting that I had given Sharon an intentional overdose, she voiced her observation. "Half of the contents of this vial is missing."

"I know, I know." I nervously spat out an explanation. "At 1:00 this morning, Sharon woke up and was terrified. She stood up and tried to walk but fainted and fell forward onto the floor yanking on her hoses as she fell and toppled the oxygen machine. She was too heavy for me to move by myself. My son wasn't home yet, so I called my neighbor Mo to come over and help me. Together, we lifted Sharon's limp torso back onto her chair." As I spoke, I broke down, fighting back tears. "Mo comforted Sharon while I untangled the hoses and cobbled the oxygen machine back together."

"I ran to the kitchen to prepare a dose of morphine, but fumbled the vial, spilling it onto the counter. But I prepped a dose and left the damn vial lying there in a puddle. I had to get back to Sharon." Anger welled up in me as I spoke. "Those damn vials are so tiny. I came back later to clean up the spill. I used a butter knife. It was impossible to get the morphine back into that shitty little bottle. Anyway, I was more concerned about my wife."

The nurse coldly noted my response, her face awash with grim sternness. But, as I spoke, while observing my grief mixed with rage, her suspicions faded. Finally, her demeanor returned to one of understanding and compassion. "It's OK, Mr. Laughlin. I believe you. Now, let's get your wife's body taken care of."

CHAPTER 7
The Bench

Omaha, November 14, 2009

Four days before Sharon's funeral, the boys had all returned home. My three sons and I were raking the front yard in anticipation of visits from friends and family. The last time that we worked together on a task was over six years in the past, before the oldest boy, Dan, left for college in Cincinnati. Since then, the family unit had progressively disintegrated, with each young man becoming busy with college, work, and friends, and starting their own lives, while the attentions of Sharon and me became gradually more consumed by her illness.

Sharon had worked the last twelve years at Creighton University. Our home in Omaha was a mile and a half west of the campus. Thanks to their mother's job, we received tuition help and our two youngest boys, now young men, attended there.

As we raked leaves along the curb, the boys drifted toward the corner where the shuttle bus for the university was in the habit of stopping. The official stops were one block to the north and one block to the south. But my two youngest boys, Mark and Matt, and several other Creighton students in the neighborhood, trying to avoid a few extra steps, had cajoled the shuttle bus driver into regularly making an unofficial stop in the front of our house.

At the corner, my three sons had paused in their raking duties and were talking to two of their college buddies, who had walked into the yard to wait for the shuttle, backpacks over their shoulders. The bus arrived but stopped fifty feet ahead of the corner. The driver had chosen not to stop at the boys but to stop at me. He opened the door, leaned over, and said, "Hi there. Are any of those young men down there yours?"

"Yes, three of them are," I replied, expecting to be scolded about the boys not walking to the official bus stop a block away.

The driver introduced himself. "My name is Andrew. Andrew Gaines. I am so very sorry that your wife has died." He held out his hand through the open door of the bus and shook mine. "It's a pleasure to meet you."

"Thanks, Andrew. Call me Steve."

"Everybody down at Creighton is so very sad. We all knew Sharon. For as long as I've been driving the shuttle, Sharon was always there, down at the human resources office. We all had insurance issues, tuition issues and the like, so everyone talked to Sharon at one time or another. She was a big help and always had her happy face. I am so sorry."

"You know, Andrew, I hadn't thought much about the university people this week. I've just focused on family and friends. Good to know. This afternoon, I'll put in a call to the folks down at HR, maybe invite someone to say a few words at the funeral."

"I've been picking up your boys at this corner for several years now. Got to know 'em pretty well. They are great kids. Always seems to be a bunch of jabbering students here, halfway between my regular stops."

"Those kids! Look at 'em. They've worn a bare spot in my yard. You know what? We're gonna put a bench right there, give 'em something to sit on while waiting for your shuttle. It'll be an excellent project for us to do in memory of their mother."

"Great idea, Steve. If you run it past the facilities people down at Creighton, I bet they'll make Sharon's bench an official stop on the shuttle route."

A few months later, on the first Memorial Day weekend after their mother's death, the boys and I were together again, ready to install the bench in the front yard. A local artisan iron worker had built custom metal legs and frame for the bench. The design incorporated "S" shapes, borrowing from Sharon's first name and mine. Dan and I drove down to the ironworks to pick up the bench parts.

Everything was complete, except for one little detail. The artisan had been struggling to imprint Sharon's name onto a small metal plate, but it wasn't working as planned. He had constructed a contraption to pound the lettering into the hot metal plate. The assembly consisted of a chest-high metal tripod, which served as a guide for a heavy cylinder of steel, weighing about one hundred pounds, suspended from a pulley above. The invention completely failed to work. Worse than that, after several attempts to hoist the cylinder and dropping it, a large crack formed in the concrete floor.

The artist felt compelled to show us the one thing that the assembly was good for. He placed an orange on the floor below the raised cylinder and announced proudly, "It's a great air freshener." He then dropped the cylinder, which instantly atomized the orange. Mist shot out across the room, spraying our blue jeans with a wet, sticky band of aromatic orange juice. After a few surprised looks and giggles, we let him off the hook, saying we would figure some other way to add Sharon's name to the bench. Dan and I collected the metal bench parts, and we departed, smelling fresh.

At home, the boys and I cut several wooden slats and bolted them onto the metal frame, creating a backrest and seat. With some sanding, painting, and assembly, we had a sturdy and beautiful bench ready for installation in the front yard. We dug four holes, set anchor bolts in concrete, paved an area with cobblestones, and planted a half circle of lilies behind the bench. As a final touch, we carved Sharon's name into the wooden backrest.

In addition to the "*S*" shapes that were incorporated into metal bench design, there were two "*C*" shapes the artisan had added, necessary to complete the arm rests. A neighbor noted these, saying, "Those "*C*" shapes don't stand for *cancer*. They stand for *courage*."

I agreed with her. The bench installation was a meaningful father-and-sons team project and a pretty good remembrance of their mother, perhaps the family's all-time best example of the four of us guys working together. Sharon's bench became an official stop on the Creighton shuttle route.

As a joyful unintended consequence, the bench became a favorite spot for the young girls of the neighborhood to sit and watch each other scribble chalk messages onto the sidewalk and play hopscotch. Sharon would have liked that.

CHAPTER 8

Matt

Omaha 2006-2009

Of my three sons, Matt, the youngest, was the hardest hit by his mother's decline and death. In 2007, when his mother underwent chemotherapy and a double mastectomy, he was in his first semester of college, living on campus away from home for the first time. The quietest and least self-assured of the three boys, Matt, was the one most in need of his mother's guidance and support, two things that weren't available to him as Sharon's illness came on. And I paid little attention to him, as I was preoccupied with his mother's problems. I was glad to have him off to college so that I could focus on Sharon. Even though the campus was a short distance from our home, Matt was on his own to deal with his problems. But when things got out of hand and became *bigger problems*, I was called in.

Matt had trouble adjusting to the freedom of college life. There were too many opportunities for partying and late-night video games in the dorm. Without his mother telling him, "Do your homework," and, "Time to get up," he quickly ran into trouble. At the end of the first semester, Matt received a letter expelling him from school because of poor grades. In his mind, he had failed and was through with college. "Been there, done that."

Two days later, he was arrested for minor-in-possession. It's amazing how life doubles down on you sometimes.

My fatherly idea was that Matt needed to pick himself up and take another shot at college. He needed a jump-start to get back on track. I convinced Matt to talk to his counselor before giving up completely. We went together to the first meeting, though I was pretty much a fifth wheel, as the counselor wanted to talk to Matt, not me. Following the counselor's suggestion, Matt wrote an extensive letter of self-evaluation to the university, asking for a second chance and, identifying all those things that he had done wrong and what he would do differently. His counselor read the letter and complimented him on his thoughtfulness and thoroughness but pointed out that Matt needed to add two more sentences to the letter:

I will attend all my classes and *I will turn in all my assignments*. Duh!

What I had learned while sitting in on the meetings was that toward the end of the semester, Matt had fallen behind. When exams hit and term papers were due, he crumpled under the strain. He stopped going to classes, stopped doing assignments, and stopped taking exams. After counseling and Matt's promise to reform his ways, the university accepted him back into school, understanding that he would have to maintain a B or better grade average.

Upon his return to studies, Matt recovered and improved his routine, becoming more self-reliant. He straightened out, worked hard and kept his grades up, which provided much-needed comfort to his mother. Her death occurred during Matt's junior year at the university.

CHAPTER 9

Dan

Omaha, July 1995

My mission here has been to write about those situations in life that have been really bad, or really good, or really strange... so bad, so good, or so strange that they make for a good story. It is hard to find something to say about my oldest son, Daniel, who is in his mid-thirties as I write this. Dan's life has always been fairly level, somewhat better than normal, more or less. He was the smart, diligent student, never in trouble, having few serious difficulties, remaining constant in his upward trajectory through a wholesome life. No bumps, no bruises, no restarts. No drugs, no gambling, no car wrecks, no MIPs or DWIs, no pregnant girlfriends. He received the best student award as he graduated from eighth grade, continued his high marks through high school, and earned a full-ride scholarship to Xavier University, eventually receiving an undergrad degree in biology and a master's degree in hospital administration. He was a stabilizing force on the family and his brothers during the time of his mother's death, breaking away from his graduate studies for the week of the funeral, coming home the following month for Christmas and again for the first important Memorial Day. After graduating, he picked up a nice job in a Baltimore think-tank, eventually becoming a hospital consultant. In his first year of professional life, he earned double the salary that I earned in my last year before retirement. With all these positive things in Dan's life, it took some thoughtful reflection to remember something meaningful to write about him that fit my definition of "a good story."

Flash back to a lazy summer afternoon in Omaha when ten-year-old Dan was riding his bike along Cass Street, a half-block away from our house. As he pedaled toward home, a sizable bird swooped down onto him from behind. In a flurry of flapping wings, the bird clamped its claws deeply onto his right shoulder, piercing his shirt and digging into his skin. Terrorized by the attack, Dan dropped his bike to the pavement, screamed, and swatted at the bird to drive it away. The creature gripped his shoulder tenaciously and flapped its wings. Dan, in a fit of terror, raised both hands and grabbed the bird. He pulled it from his shoulder and threw it to the side. The bird flew to a large bush nearby. Dan could now see that it was a parrot.

Shaken by the aggressive attack, Dan hastily picked his bike up and pedaled down Cass Street toward home. Glancing back, it horrified him to see that the parrot was chasing after him, launching a second attack. Dan screamed again, this time pedaling his bike while swatting at the parrot to keep it from landing on his shoulder again. At our front yard, Dan dropped his bike into the grass and ran towards the front porch. The bird followed close behind, continuing his attack, trying to grab Dan.

I heard Dan's screams and caught sight of the parrot's attack through the front window. Bolting through the door, I was out onto the porch as Dan arrived. He collapsed into my arms. The aggressive parrot flew onto the porch, still attempting to land on him. I grabbed the creature out of the air and forcefully threw it into the front yard. The bird tumbled across the grass, rolled to a stop, and stood up. Dan and I stared at the parrot in amazement as it stood in the front yard, swiveling its head, looking left and right.

Dan was the first to spot the crows. Three large black birds glided towards us and swooped down onto the eave of the neighbor's roof and into the tree out front. The crows looked down malevolently at the parrot and peered over at Dan and me. The parrot took flight towards us and landed on the back of our porch swing. We were quick to understand that the parrot had not been attacking Dan but was terrified and desperately seeking protection from the crows. Dan held out his arm, and without hesitation, the bird hopped onto his forearm. The parrot had chosen Dan. I opened the front door, and together, Dan and the parrot entered our house.

We settled on a supposition that this was some young boy's pet and that the bird was accustomed to perching on his shoulder. Dan must have resembled that boy closely enough for the frightened bird to seek his shoulder as a sanctuary. Some young man out there, somewhere, was missing his pet parrot.

Dan and I spent the following week conducting a campaign to find the bird's owner. Meanwhile, our garage became the bird's temporary refuge. We stapled *Lost Parrot* messages with our contact information on telephone poles in the neighborhood and called the humane society. Dan circulated a flier throughout his school. We searched the want ads and placed a *Found Parrot* message in the newspaper. We went door-to-door through the immediate neighborhood and inquired about a missing parrot. All our efforts failed to locate the bird's owner. One neighbor, an elderly lady, asked us if we could use a birdcage. She brought one to her front door and gave it to us. It was a very comfortable fit for the parrot. I was rather suspicious that this old woman might have been the parrot's previous owner, but didn't press the issue. At this point, we had a new member of the family and a pretty cool cage.

Dan named the parrot Cassy, after Cass Street, which runs by our house, in remembrance of his first encounter with the bird. Dan's bedroom was on the lower level of our house, next to the family room. The family room was the hangout for Dan and his two younger brothers, who were often sitting cross-legged in front of the TV, playing video games. There was a perfect place to hang Cassy's cage in front of the family room window. This location, close to Dan's room, made it easy for him to look after his bird, give it food and water, and clean out the cage.

We had tried unsuccessfully to keep the bird in other locations. We allowed it to move freely throughout the house for a short while. This quickly became a hygiene nightmare. Cassy didn't settle into a roosting spot. Bird poop was to be found everywhere. It had a sticky consistency, like maple syrup, which sopped into our furniture and carpets. Drying to a concrete-like encrustation, the nasty white stuff was nearly impossible to remove. The other intolerable problem was that the bird was noisy. It had an extremely loud squawking fit every morning, starting at 5:00 a.m. and lasting half an hour. Better to keep the bird down on the lower level with Dan.

One Saturday afternoon, Sharon was on the telephone yakking it up with her sister for a good long time. On every third or fourth sentence, she would break into a classic Sharon laugh, "HAAH, Hah, ha, ha!" Her laugh was pretty obnoxious, starting loud and high pitched, then lowering as it trailed off. Her routine on weekends was to have long phone calls, embellished frequently by her laugh. On this Saturday, I was pecking away at my laptop at the dining table while Sharon talked to her sister. After her second or third laugh, I heard a sound coming from the basement, "ha, ha," and assumed it to be one of the boys. After a few more sentences, Sharon laughed again. Again, immediately after, I heard another giggle from the basement. "Hah, ha, ha," this time louder and more pronounced. More lady-chat ensued, and Sharon laughed again. This time, her laugh was repeated from the basement, precisely matched in loudness and pitch, "HAAH, Hah, ha, ha." My surprise revelation was that the parrot was imitating Sharon's laugh! I listened closely for Sharon's next laugh, and sure enough, Cassy repeated the exact same laugh, even matching Sharon's diminished volume at the end. That moment of recognition made me laugh, too. This evoked yet another "HAAH, Hah, ha, ha" from the parrot. I bolted from my chair, went to Sharon, and rudely interrupted her phone conversation with her sister.

"Sharon! *Sharon! Listen! Listen up! You gotta hear this!*"

Sharon gave me an irritated frown and told her sister to hold on. I blurted out a Sharonesque laugh. Cassy immediately responded, "HAAH, Hah, ha, ha." Recognizing the source to be Cassy, Sharon uncontrollably let out another loud laugh, "HAAH, Hah, ha, ha," followed by Cassy's "HAAH, Hah, ha, ha," followed by my "HAAH, Hah, ha, ha," and another from Cassy, and another from Sharon.

"*Oh my God!* We have a laughing parrot!" Sharon proclaimed to her sister. After that, regularly, Cassy did a pretty good job of lifting our spirits with laughter. In the process, the bird became an endeared member of our family. And with parrots often living to be over eighty years old, we accepted the bird into our family for the long haul.

The boys enjoyed having Cassy around and let her out of the cage regularly. Thankfully, after being scolded a few times, she became accustomed to pooping in her cage, and not on shoulders or furniture. She would happily flap around the family room, hopping from one boy to another, basking in their playful attention whenever it was offered, and cheering everyone up with an occasional laugh.

Fathers have been known to screw up once in a while. This comes as no surprise to their children. Sometimes fathers screw up *big time*. I had a big-time screw up related to Cassy. After a few months of Cassy's presence in the house, I became confident that Dan was doing a good job of taking care of the bird. I stopped paying attention, stopped coaching Dan, and stopped doing my fatherly task of checking on things. Dads have lots of excuses and distractions. There are plenty of examples of life getting in the way. Even so, this was a *big-time screw up*.

I came home from work one Saturday morning and pulled the car into the drive in a hurry to grab something out of the house and leave again. The boys were playing basketball in the backyard. I stepped out of the car as Dan walked over and spoke to me from inside the fence.

"Dad, Cassy died."

I immediately cut his comment short with a loud and brutal response.

"Good Riddance! No more squawking!"

I hustled into the house, grabbed something important, and drove off, leaving Dan leaning on the fence. Lost in my little hurry-hurry world, I completely blew him off.

At that very moment, Dan was in a dark place, overwhelmed by guilt and sorrow. As I drove away, I realized I had left him alone to deal with his feelings. Dumb Dad had ignored the boy, missing the chance to offer comfort. A short time later, I returned, anxious to reach out to Dan. I found him in the family room downstairs, blankly staring at the TV. Putting a weak apology together, I said, "Sorry I left you hanging, Dan. You OK?"

"Uh-huh" was his clouded response.

"What did you do with Cassy's body?" I asked.

"It's in the kitchen," he replied.

We solemnly walked upstairs.

Cassy's body was lying on a paper towel on the kitchen counter, her brilliant plumage on display against the white surround. Dan spoke.

"She was in her water bowl. It was empty." His voice cracked as he confessed, "I didn't fill it for a few days." Tears welled up in his eyes as he continued, "She was still alive. I brought her up to the kitchen and tried to give her some water." He braced his hand against the counter as he inhaled a shuddering, deep breath, his ribs heaving. His next ragged words were forced out in a half whisper and half cry. "That's when she died."

It hit me. "Jesus," I whispered, more to myself than to Dan. I now fully understood that Dan was feeling much more than sorrow at the loss of this creature we had all grown to love. The bird had died in his hands. Dan was racked by guilt, realizing that he had killed the bird out of neglect. The dark truth was that Cassy had died slowly from dehydration, over several days, while Dan had been in the same room, watching TV, walking by, playing video games and ignoring the bird's struggles.

And Dumb Dad had been too busy going about his business, too distracted to check on things. If only I had paid better attention, offered just a quick glance once in a while. If only I had shown a tiny bit of concern, I could have saved my son from this devastating tragedy. I searched for consoling words but couldn't find any.

"Too bad… Let's take Cassy outside and find a place to bury her."

I wrapped a shroud of white paper towels around Cassy's body and handed her to Dan. Outside; we found a place in the garden close to the window where her cage was hanging and solemnly dug a hole. Dan placed Cassy's body into it and we filled the grave with dirt.

"We should find a stone to mark the grave. Maybe we can chisel her name into it," was my somber suggestion.

Together, Dan and I scouted around the corners of the yard and found a right-size brownstone slab. We walked into the garage, set the stone on the workbench, and found a hammer and chisel. Dan held the stone while I chiseled Cassy's name into the surface. We returned to the grave and placed the stone.

"We'll miss you, Cassy," was my eulogy.

Sorry, Cassy, was Dan's unspoken message.

"It's OK," I said, pretending that it was, knowing that it wasn't. I had screwed up again. In my lame attempt to offer comfort, I missed my opportunity to accept some responsibility for Cassy's death, to say something to shift the blame from Dan's shoulders onto mine. But I missed it.

There we were, father and son, quietly standing, tears welling in our eyes, wrapped in our grief and guilt. We gave each other a hug.

A recurring, sad reminder of Cassy's absence was the noticeable silence after Sharon's laugh. Now, Sharon is gone too. I suspect that these feelings of loss and guilt remain seared into Dan's soul as they are into mine.

CHAPTER 10

Dean

Nebraska, November 2009

Dean was my younger brother by seven years. His doctors had temporarily released him from the hospital so that he could attend Sharon's funeral. He was being treated with some pretty heavy medications, and it had taken some serious consideration and counseling with the hospital staff before they gave him permission.

Dean and his wife, Cindy, sat with me at the funeral luncheon. While eating, Dean became light-headed, nearly blacking out, dropping his cup and silverware to the floor. He slumped sideways, on the verge of falling out of his chair. I stood up, grabbed his shoulders, and leaned against him, stopping his fall. He outweighed me by a hundred pounds, and it took some physical exertion for me to keep the big guy in his chair. Cindy immediately called Dean's doctor at the hospital and they dispatched an ambulance. I held him there, watching his head laze around on his shoulders, waiting for the ambulance to arrive.

Dean woozily attempted to talk. "Boy, sure feel dizzy."

My response was "Hang in there, Dean. Help is on the way." After several awkward minutes, the emergency crew arrived. While family and friends at the funeral luncheon looked on, the ambulance staff made their way across the cafeteria floor to Dean. After a quick evaluation of his situation, they strapped Dean onto a gurney and rolled him out to the ambulance. This was the second time in three weeks that I watched him being strapped into a gurney. Apparently, an imbalance in his medications had caused a dramatic drop in his blood pressure. That was not what I needed on the day of my wife's funeral, especially with all the other shit I was dealing with. Here it was again, this strange knot in time, events piling on top of each other.

The troubles with Dean started during my wife's last week at the hospital, ten days before her death. I had spent the day and evening in Sharon's hospital room, at her bedside, working late on the design of Red Owl's Hoop of Life. The building design was coming together nicely and I couldn't put the pen down. I went home tired after a long day. Just after 1:00 a.m., I had finally gotten to sleep when the phone rang. It was very unusual for Dean to be calling me at this time of the night. Something was wrong.

"There's a bunch of crackheads across the way."

I read the urgency in his voice. Dean and Cindy lived out in the country, off a two-lane blacktop highway between Lincoln and Omaha, on a small acreage surrounded by fields of after-harvest stubble. Dean's nearest neighbor was a half mile away, across the road, a farmhouse, barn, and outbuildings.

"They've got a meth lab going. There's a bad smell coming from over there. Some jackass druggies drove into my driveway a few minutes ago and thought my place was the neighbor's. I chased 'em off." Dean was talking frantically, much faster than normal. He was loud and the pitch of his voice was high.

I took him at his word. "You need to call the sheriff, Dean. Let him check it out."

Instantly, Dean agreed. "Yeah, gotta do that," and then he abruptly hung up.

This was strange. Dean made no inquiry into Sharon's ongoing battle with cancer or her declining health, which was the usual intent of his calls, and he had given me no chance to update him. But I wasn't totally awake, so I rolled over and went back to sleep.

At 2:30 a.m., Dean called again. He started talking as soon as I picked up. "The county sheriff drove over there, checked out the neighbors and talked to 'em. He says the place is quiet, nothing suspicious going on. He's gone now. I don't believe it. Still smells bad. I'm gonna keep watch." There was that frantic, high-pitched voice again.

"OK, Dean. But if you see anything, call the sheriff again. Let him handle it."

He agreed, "OK," and hung up.

The tone of his conversation was completely weird, but I went back to sleep, thinking that he would let me know how it all turned out.

At 4:00 a.m., I received another call. This time, it was Dean's wife, Cindy. It was the very first time that she had ever phoned me directly. I groggily answered, "What's up?"

Her voice crackled as she whispered a frantic message. "Steve, it's Cindy. Something's wrong with Dean. Can you come here?" A loud noise in the background interrupted her. "Can't talk."

Her words jarred me fully awake. Understanding that she was in the middle of an emergency, I blurted out, "On my way. Call 9-1-1."

"OK. Hurry." She abruptly hung up. Her quick acceptance of my 9-1-1 suggestion was a confirmation to me she was in some sort of serious trouble.

It took me twenty minutes to drive there. I arrived at what looked like a scene from *The Fugitive*. Police lights were flashing in the predawn darkness. Several black-and-whites were on the grass in front of Dean's place, arranged in a half circle, keeping their distance. Spotlights were shining on the house. Police officers were crouching behind their vehicles, guns drawn, pointed at Dean's front door. More cruisers and emergency vehicles were arriving. I pulled over onto the shoulder, parked and cautiously approached on foot.

The sheriff, a longtime friend of Dean's, was talking on his loudspeaker. "Dean, this is Sheriff McDermott." Pause. "You are scaring these officers. You need to put your gun down." Pause. "We have the situation under control." Pause. "It's OK. We are here to help." Pause. "Put the gun down and come out with your hands in the air." Pause.

Dean walked out of the front door with his empty hands raised. From their hidden positions on either side, four officers grabbed him and forced him to the ground, face down on the sidewalk, shouting commands. They placed his hands behind his back and restrained him, while Dean frantically tried to explain, "No, no, no... you don't need to do that."

Another officer, with his gun drawn, peered into the open door, offered a hand signal, and then entered, cautiously followed by two others. After a pause and an "all clear," they reappeared, escorting Cindy through the open doorway. She appeared unhurt but visibly upset. The sheriff moved quickly to her side and calmed her down. She fearfully looked over the scene in the front yard. Dean was being strapped onto a gurney and rolled into the back of an ambulance. Cindy moved close to the gurney and offered comfort to Dean. "It's OK. It'll be all right. It's OK." They retracted the wheels and slid Dean and the gurney into the vehicle. Four officers entered the ambulance with Dean and the doors pulled shut.

I explained to an officer on the perimeter that I was Dean's brother, and he escorted me to the sheriff. Cindy was talking with him as I arrived. She saw me and collapsed into my arms, breaking into tears. They introduced me to the sheriff, and he immediately barked out a hurried message. "The emergency vehicle is leaving now. We need to get Dean to the hospital." The sheriff asked me to give Cindy a ride in my car and follow him. We were quickly out on the highway, part of the police caravan headed for the hospital in Omaha.

Once the line of vehicles was underway, Cindy attempted to calm down and tell me what had just happened. "Something's wrong…" She paused, her words choking to a stop. She tried again. "Something is wrong with Dean. He shot out all the windows in the house."

"What the hell?" I responded. Shock and confusion swept over me. "You OK?"

"I'm OK. I was standing next to him as he did it. He was shooting at something outside the windows. He said it was Bigfoot."

"Jeezuz!" Questioning what I had just heard, I repeated, "Bigfoot?"

"He said that it was trying to get into our house."

"What?" I tried to wrap my mind around her words. "You gotta be kidding!"

"I didn't see anything out there. He shot maybe twenty times."

"Jeezuz!" I said again.

"He reloaded as he ran through the house, shooting out the windows in the living room and family room with his shotgun. Then he grabbed his hunting rifle and shot the kitchen window out, then shot several times into the front door."

I prompted Cindy again as to her condition. "You hurt?"

Cindy responded, "No. I wasn't in any danger. Dean was trying to protect us. I was standing beside him, holding on to his arm, trying to get him to stop. He kept shooting, yelling out strange things, like 'There you are, you son-of-a-bitch,' and, 'I'm not letting you get in here.' I told Dean that I didn't see anything, but he wouldn't listen."

As I listened to Cindy's struggle to describe the scene, I imagined her senses being battered as Dean fired his guns inside the house... the deafening sound of the blasts, the shattered glass, blue gunpowder haze filling the room, shotgun pellets ricocheting off the walls...

She continued, "Right after I called you, I called the sheriff. He heard shots over the phone and came pretty quick."

Strangeness and confusion settled into my thoughts. I voiced a question, addressed more to myself than to Cindy, "What was going on in Dean's head?"

Cindy responded, "I don't know... Something's wrong." Cindy wilted into the seat and whimpered, lowering her face into her handkerchief.

"We'll be there soon," I said, trying to offer some measure of reassurance. "And can get Dean some help." Together we followed the ambulance and police caravan towards Omaha, the emergency lights flashing as the dim light of early morning was coming on.

The ambulance crew and police rolled Dean's gurney through the emergency entrance at the hospital. We followed them directly to the elevator and up to the psychiatric ward. They held an on-the-spot briefing in a secure room. Dean, the sheriff, Cindy, and I sat around a table with the psychiatric staff. They adjusted Dean's wrist restraints to the front so that he could sit with his hands in his lap. Two husky patrolmen took up flanking positions behind his chair.

After introductory comments, a doctor prompted Dean to describe what had just happened. Dean immediately started talking, trying desperately to explain his actions. His words were in that weird, frantic, and high-pitched voice again, speaking at twice his normal speed. "I been trying to get these guys to listen to me... Bigfoot was trying to get into my house. I shot him... several times. I saw him walking around outside, so I grabbed my twelve-gauge shotgun and some shells. He tried to come in through the dining-room window, so I shot him three times. Cindy stayed close to me... She'll tell you. Then the *son of a bitch* tried to break in through the family room window. I reloaded, and I shot him again, but he just wouldn't go down! He moved to the other side of the house, so I grabbed my thirty-aught-six... Figured *that* ought to stop him. I shot him again as he tried to break in through our kitchen window. Then the *cock sucker* tried to smash the front door down, so I shot him several more times. That's when the sheriff arrived. He asked me to put my rifle down and walk out with my hands in the air. These officers tackled me and roughed me up. They didn't need to do that. They should have been chasing down Bigfoot."

After listening to Dean's comments and further discussions, my instincts took over. I laid my pen and pocket notebook on the table, open to a blank page and blurted out a question: "Dean, can you draw a picture of the creature you saw?" Reaching out with his wrists bound, Dean quickly grabbed the pen and drew an outline of the monster. The image was of a big, barrel-shaped body with rounded shoulders and a slouching, retracted head, seeming to be without a neck. To my surprise, I immediately recognized the shape. The outline matched the profile of Dean himself. A strange explanation for his actions popped into my head. "Dean, is it possible that you were shooting at your own reflection, moving around in the windows of the house?"

Dean barked back at me, "Nah! It was Bigfoot. I saw him. I shot him several times. Go look around the house. If he got away, there's sure to be a blood trail."

They interviewed Cindy. She explained Dean had not slept in the last four days and had progressively become more agitated and irritable. He had been sick with the flu. The psychiatric doctors asked her which medications Dean had been taking. She named the drug that Dean was using for his flu and what he was taking for his asthma.

Dean had been taking two different steroids in fairly high dosages. The doctors arrived at the prognosis that the medications had driven him into hyperactivity, leading to sleep-deprivation, eventually forcing him into a psychotic episode. The powerful drugs had caused him to drift into a delusional state, hallucinating that the nightmarish monster was trying to get into his house. Dean was mixing his dreams with reality.

The following night, I was back in Sharon's hospital room, watching her health further decline. I sat down in my make-shift design studio in the corner, seeking to understand my *vision* of Red Owl's sacred *Hoop*.

They confined Dean to the psychiatric ward at the hospital for the upcoming month. He quickly returned to his senses after the drugs were purged from his body. During his second week of his confinement, my wife died.

The human mind works in strange ways. Dreams, delusions, hallucinations, and visions are on the edge of our consciousness, waiting to be seen and paid attention to. To this day, years later, Dean still believes that his vision was true.

And, to this day, Red Owl believes that the vision of his Hoop of Life was given to me by a spiritual intervention as I drove through the homeland of his people.

CHAPTER 11

The Horse in the Kitchen

Nebraska, Christmas 2009

Five weeks after Sharon's funeral, my three sons were home together for our first Christmas without their mother. Dan was in his last year of graduate school in Cincinnati and had driven back during the Christmas break. Mark was in his fourth year at Creighton University and was temporarily living home with me. Matt, in his third year at Creighton, was within walking distance from his rental house, a few blocks away. We had been invited to drive out to Kearney, Nebraska and spend Christmas Day at the home of Sharon's brother and his wife, the aunt and uncle of the boys. Several cousins would be there, offering some relief from the darkness surrounding their mother's death.

But before that, like every Christmas of the past, we had a sharing of gifts at our house in Omaha on Christmas Eve. Without their mother around, the four of us guys were not sure if we could still behave like a family, but we were about to try it. It was late morning on Christmas Eve, and living up to the reputations of men, none of us had done any Christmas shopping. After a huddle and brainstorm of gift ideas, we headed out in two cars to conduct a frantic half day of shopping. The weather was not cooperating. A huge storm was moving in, which would blanket Omaha with six inches of snow by the end of the afternoon. But we were not to be deterred. We armed ourselves with windshield scrapers, bottles of deicer, brooms, and shovels. With the defrosters and windshield wipers on full, the two cars slipped and plowed through the gathering snow in the streets and parking lots of the big-box stores to complete our task. We all arrived back at the house at about the same time at the start of the evening. After sloshing their way through the front door, the boys dusted the snow off their shoulders and removed their coats, gloves, and soggy tennies. We piled our boxes and bags onto the living room floor and quickly came to a consensus that there was no time or necessity to wrap the presents. The store bags were concealing their contents, enough to evoke some sense of Christmas surprise.

I had the foresight to bring home a couple of large pizzas, so we left all the bags in a disheveled heap in the center of the living room floor and moved to the kitchen. It was a memorable, all-guys, weirded-out family Christmas pizza dinner. We laughed and joked about the harrowing experiences out in the snowstorm as we foraged. These were our first joyful moments together after their mother's death. After the pizza, we returned to the living room to have a guy version of opening the Christmas presents that were piled on the floor, wrapped in bags from Target, Walmart, and the like, while continuing our talk about our afternoon of fighting the storm. We proved that, yes, we could still behave as a family, albeit an all-man family that was rough around the edges. But, noticeably absent from our chatter were references to the recent death of their mother.

On Christmas morning, my three young men and I piled into one car and headed off to Kearney. The interstate had been cleared of snow, and the three hour-drive was uneventful, except for the four of us trying to sing along to a Lady Gaga tune on the radio. We arrived before noon. After a round of family conversations, we sat down to the big Christmas dinner their aunt had prepared and enjoyed a lazy, overstuffed break after the meal.

In the midafternoon, the boys and I drove over to visit their grandmother, Doris, who was at a local nursing home. She was my wife's mother. Doris was in declining health, but she perked up when her three grandsons and I arrived. Another carload of her grandkids followed us to the nursing home. Their parents were cleaning the dishes and would be along a bit later. After greetings, sharing of Christmas cards, and some small talk with their grandmother, my three boys and their cousins drifted off to hang out in the lounge around the ping-pong and pool tables.

I sat alone with Doris in her room. It didn't take me long to realize that Doris was grieving the loss of my Sharon, her youngest daughter. Doris had been too frail to attend the funeral in mid-November. We shared tears and hugs. She had lost both of her daughters to breast cancer. Judy, Sharon's older sister, had died just eleven months before Sharon. Both of her girls had suffered from the same genetic flaw. Doris, broken by grief, was declining toward her own death. In the past, whenever we visited Kearney to attend family gatherings, Doris was always chatting with Sharon. Very often, Judy would be there too. During these family visits, the two girls would talk to their Mom, all day, every day. Doris never talked much to me, being of lowly son-in-law status. But now, with both of her girls gone and just the two of us alone together in her room, something remarkable happened. Doris talked to *me*, and I started talking to her.

The snowy weather brought memories of storms in the old days. She described to me her life on the farm as a young girl, out on Coal Chute Road, east of Kearney, back in the late '20s and during the Depression. She had four brothers and sisters. The farm family raised chickens and cows, harvesting eggs and milk. The children were busy farm kids, getting up early to help mom and dad gather eggs and milk the cows. Their parents would make daily deliveries to the market at Kearney, ten miles to the west. Every morning, the children would go to the one-room schoolhouse a mile away, walking with their five dairy cows on the gravel county road. The cows would graze in the pasture behind the school while the children were inside. Then, when school let out, Doris and her four brothers and sisters would walk the cows back to their farm.

Doris remembered one Saturday on a summer day when her mother and father had gone to town and left the kids alone at the farm. Doris, the oldest of the children, was to take care of things while the parents were gone. Unlike today, back then there were no distractions like TV, video games, or cell phones. But there were other ways to get into mischief. Doris and her oldest brother decided it might be fun to bring the family's horse into the house. The youngest kids went along with the idea. Too nervous to bring the horse in the front door into the living room, they decided to bring it into the kitchen through the back door.

The kitchen door had a screen and a single wooden step. Doris orchestrated the event. She had one of the young ones hold the screen door open. She and the oldest brother backed into the kitchen and coaxed the horse through the kitchen door, while gently pulling on the bridle and using voice commands on the animal, "Come on, Daisy." Two of the youngest kids were given the duty of pushing from behind on the horse's bulging butt cheeks. The horse had to lower its head to clear the top of the kitchen door. It entered the room, clomping its front legs onto the wooden plank floor covered by a loose sheet of linoleum. As the hind end of the horse approached the door, it became clear that the animal was wider than the opening by a few inches. Its big butt muscles pinched in a little and popped out again as the horse slid into the room.

Once the horse was completely inside the kitchen, Doris became painfully aware that she had underestimated the size of the animal and overestimated the size of the kitchen. The room was quite a bit smaller than Daisy's horse stall in the barn. Cupboards lined the kitchen on each side, with only four feet of space between, which the huge animal completely filled. Dry goods, pots and pans, and the family's glassware and dishes filled the cupboards. Doris and her brother jammed up against the blank end wall of the kitchen with the horse's muzzle between them. The animal could not fully raise its head without hitting the ceiling.

Immediately, the animal became fidgety and nervous. It stomped its feet and jerked its head up and down. Doris and her brother could not calm the animal with the soothing command of "Easy, girl, *easy*." The horse was having a panic attack and was on the verge of bucking. Doris's mood instantly changed from mischievous and amused to terrified. The horse was going to bust the kitchen apart. Doris shouted a command: "Back her out!" The youngest kid opened the screen door again, and the other two youngsters, who had been peering in through the screen with wide eyes, backed out of the way. The two oldest kids in the kitchen knew what to do next. Doris and her brother, each holding on to a side of the harness, grabbed a big ear of the horse and pulled down hard. The animal submitted, lowering its head to waist high while shuddering in panic and stamping its hooves on the floor. Doris yelled another command, this time at the horse: "Back up,

Daisy, *back up*." The horse retreated, backing out the door in a nervous tizzy. Its hind quarter pinched down again at the door opening, but pushed on through. The animal's hind legs stomped wildly, struggling to find solid footing as it encountered the drop-down onto the back step into the yard. Steadily, Doris and her brother, holding down the animal's ears, pushed the horse backward out of the kitchen. Upon clearing the door, the two older kids released the ears of the animal, and the horse popped its head up wildly into the summer sky. Instantly, as fast as the crisis had arrived, it was over.

Amazingly, the screen door was undamaged, the wooden step hadn't broken, there was no horse poop or pee in the house, and the kitchen floor was intact, as were the cupboards, dishes, and ceiling. The only evidence was some dirt on the floor, which Doris quickly wiped away. What had started out as a funny prank had turned into a frightening struggle to avert a disaster. When their parents arrived back home, Daisy was back in the barn, and it was as if nothing had happened. The five children were feeling rather guilty but had agreed not to tell.

The horse-in-the-kitchen incident would remain a secret of the children, never to be talked about with their parents. Eventually, the story was lost over time. Now, eighty years later, Doris was explaining the details of the event to me. We giggled and laughed like a couple of schoolkids as she told the story, completely releasing ourselves momentarily from the grief that we shared at the recent loss of her daughter, my wife. I suspect it was the last time in her life that Doris giggled. I felt blessed to repeat this story to her grandchildren at Doris's funeral two months later.

During the drives between Omaha and Kearney for the Christmas visit and later for their grandmother's funeral, my three sons and I had plenty of opportunity to talk to each other. Jokes, sports chatter, and small talk filled our conversations on the road. Words regarding their mother were noticeably missing. Sharon's death was too close, only months in the past. Fearful that the pain might show itself again, we guarded our thoughts and words. We'd had our fill of grief and tears. Crying was not a manly thing to do. We hid our feelings away, kept them to ourselves. *Don't go there.*

We were in that strange knot in time surrounding Sharon's death. Our lives were changing. My three sons, young men in their early twenties, were scattering to pursue their new lives. Even after the passage of time, comments remained short, sideways, and shallow.

"Your mother would be proud of you."

Responses were truncated, "Uh-huh," and thoughts suppressed.

Best to keep it in.

CHAPTER 12
Lakota

Pine Ridge, South Dakota 1995

In the months following Sharon's death, I returned to my office routine and continued to work on Red Owl's Hoop building, in anticipation of breaking ground in the spring of the following year. As I worked, memories from my first encounter with the Sioux Nation fifteen years earlier echoed in my mind.

In 1995, my office gave me an architectural assignment to design a dormitory on the Pine Ridge Indian Reservation. Pine Ridge is in the middle of no-where, out on the prairie at the far southwest corner of South Dakota, on treeless rolling hills of prairie grass broken by a ridgeline of limestone bluffs, a shallow canyon, and a small stand of pines. Pine Ridge is the home of the indigenous people called the Oglala, who are part of the Lakota people, on the western edge of the Sioux Nation. It is a place of powerful names from the past: Red Cloud, Sitting Bull, Crazy Horse, and Wounded Knee.

I was knowledgeable about how to do a dormitory design, but I knew very little about these Native American people, even though I had been born and raised in the land of the Sioux. My perceptions had been formed around legends, weirded out by a youth filled with "cowboys and Indians" stories and exaggerated Hollywood myth. The open prairie of 150 years ago, once vast grasslands roamed by giant buffalo herds, is completely obliterated, transformed into the landscape of the white man, with corn and bean fields as far as the eye could see, speckled by herds of cattle standing in stubble.

Nomad villages were gone, replaced by small towns. Tepee enclosures made of hide stretched over a gathering of poles became hip-roofed houses clad in lap siding. Warriors riding bareback on painted horses had morphed into vehicular traffic on Interstate 80.

But there was a deeper truth. The Sioux were still here, scraping out a living on their small tracts of reservation land while trying to hold on to their culture from another time. Through my face-to-face involvement with these people, working as their architect, I was being introduced to something beyond the norm, gaining a deeper understanding, filling gaps in my knowledge that were not visible to me before, out there in the white man's world. While going about my task, I began to connect with the present-day truth about these people and better understand their history and ongoing culture.

I remember a verbal conflict that I witnessed during one of our planning meetings held in the city of Pine Ridge, just north of the Nebraska border. There were six of us at the meeting, a mix of men and women, all Lakota except for me. We were sitting around the glossy-blond laminated wood table, standard issue for a '60s school library.

One participant became furious. "This is a bunch of bullshit!" He was a big guy, Native American, well over six feet tall, sixty-ish. Shouting loudly and aggressively, he stood chin forward, knuckles on the table, in your face.

The other man, fortyish, an administrator and the one on the receiving end of the harsh words, was sitting in a student chair. It was undersized, holding his adult frame. He rested his forearms on either side of his notes. "We have to make some changes," he replied. "There've been too many problems."

The aggressor spouted more angry words. "Screw the funding, you suck-up!" He wore blue jeans with a big, silver cowboy belt buckle. His western-style shirt with the curvy shoulder seams pulled taut at the pearly snap buttons of his slightly bulging midsection. He was wearing a cream-colored cowboy hat with a molded plastic look, its broad brim swooping upward at the ears, and displaying a crescent array of colorful pheasant feathers on the forehead. It seemed odd to be wearing this big hat indoors. The tall heels on his old, weathered cowboy boots and the hat made him tower over the seated administrator. All he needed to complete the menacing image would have been a large hunting knife, sheathed in a beaded leather holster, hanging from his belt. He probably had one in his pickup truck parked outside.

The school administrator, also a Native American, was not budging. He held his ground against the verbal onslaught, maintaining his calm. He dressed casually, a white dress shirt open at the collar, his sport coat draped over the back of his chair. "The safety of the students is at stake." It was apparent that he had been through this type of confrontation before. His calm demeanor was in stark contrast to his adversary's, who continued blowing a gasket, spewing more angry words.

As I witnessed the verbal conflict unfold, I was becoming uncomfortable with my presence, Mr. White Man Outsider, dressed in my black pinstriped suit and tie. I wilted away from the conversation, doing my best to disappear into my chair.

The conflict ended as quickly as it started, when the big guy clomped off in a huff. The administrator apologized for the disturbance, and the rest of the group settled down to address the task at hand. It took me some time to put together the meaning of what I had witnessed.

The young administrator probably had a master's degree in education from Oregon State or some such. He was easy to talk to, as if I was jabbering with one of my college buddies. He nurtured a powerful bond with his people, with a deep desire to improve their situation, and a mountain of problems to overcome. Pine Ridge had a reputation for difficulties, with extremes of poverty, alcohol, drugs, violence, and abuse. It was a tough place to run a school program.

The big angry guy was the other type of tribal leader. My guess was that he probably was a Vietnam veteran who dropped out of high school and joined the Marines at the minimum allowed age. I had noticed the monument that was proudly displayed in the park in the middle of town, front-and-center, listing the Native American soldiers from this community, fallen warriors. I imagined this man's struggle as a young man to overcome alcohol and drug abuse, his history of connections to AIM (the American Indian Movement) and Wounded Knee. He was all about rejection of the white man's ways out in the modern world, all about reaching out to the past, revering the path of the warrior, his bowed legs revealing his time spent saddled on a horse, time spent gazing across the rolling sea of grassland, time spent seeking sweat-lodge visions. This man, committed to the greater good of his people, was equally a leader in his community, a traditional man.

It was impossible for me to avoid stereotyping these two extreme adversaries. Even though a century had passed, the long-standing roles of the "assimilated" and the "warrior" seemed to persist, the modern person and traditional person. One was seeking ways to tap into the resources of the modern world and use those resources to uplift his people and the other focused on the proud past, wanting a return to "the good life" that was lost. My guess, and my revelation, was that this schizophrenic extreme of opposite ideals must exist, to some degree, in the minds of all the people of the Sioux Nation. And for the rest of us out in the white man's world, this conflict of mindsets was just not on our radar.

I had two all-day work sessions to develop the space needs and design concept for the proposed new dormitory building, working closely with the two Lakota women who were running the current dormitory program. They were presently operating the existing dormitories out of old buildings, institutional looking, three-story red brick, built at the turn of the century, seeming more like grim prisons than residences for kids. Like everything at Pine Ridge, they were making do with limited resources and tough challenges. The dormitories were serving a portion of the reservation's population of school children. Kids were being bused to the school from remote locations and would stay for the week in the school dorm, arriving early Monday morning and leaving Friday afternoon. The homes for these kids spread out across a vast expanse of prairie grasslands, some in small neighborhood communities. Some houses were in small, isolated groups, and there were individual trailer homes located out in the middle of nowhere. It took some time for me to realize what I was working on. This building was a present-day version of the infamous boarding school.

In the late 1800s, the United States federal government forced into existence the boarding school concept on Indian reservations as a tool to "deal with the Indian problem." The goal was to impose a cultural change from "Indian" ways to "white man" ways, to outlaw Indian culture. The traditional Sioux languages of the Lakota, Nakota and Dakota people were forbidden, and they enforced the teaching of English in the boarding schools. Indian students were required by law to cut their hair, discard their traditional clothing and wear white man's clothing. Traditional Indian religions became outlawed, and Christianity imposed. Farming replaced nomad hunting and foraging. It was to be the end of the Indian way of life. The future would be white man's religion, language, dress, and way of life. The "Blanket People" were to become "Cut-Hairs." Cultural change and the teaching of English became willfully imposed and strictly enforced. The boarding school concept was an essential tool for implementing the process of this assimilation.

Now, more than a century later, echoes of the boarding school concept still existed, and my task was to design a new dormitory for the school. Their school system had changed over the years. It was now filled with dedicated Native Americans of good intentions, wanting to provide the best possible situation for their children. Yet the ghost of the boarding school and the dark legacy of assimilation remained. It was impossible for me to measure the effect of these kids being pulled away from their families for the entire week, only to be returned on weekends. But it wasn't my job to judge the system. My job was to design the best possible dormitory that I could.

It was during the planning sessions for the new dorm that I was introduced to the Medicine Wheel. The new dorm was to accommodate boys and girls from kindergarten through twelfth grades. A hundred kids were to be housed. As we organized the requirements for the new building, we shuffled scraps of tracing paper and sketches with torn edges around on the table. We identified four hallways to divide the dorm rooms into four manageable groups: younger boys, older boys, younger girls, and older girls. The four halls seemed to work the best when they radiated from a central hub of communal functions, which included a cafeteria, living rooms, laundry, and control desk.

As the building layout took shape, there was a moment of recognition. One Lakota woman said, "The Medicine Wheel," almost under her breath, followed by an obvious lifting of her spirit. Turning and pointing at the graphic symbol that was framed and hanging on the wall behind us, she repeated the phrase, this time with more assertion, wanting me to pay specific attention, "The Medicine Wheel!" The image was that of a circle with a cross in the center. She described to me the image, the four quadrants, the four sacred directions, the four colors red, white, black, and yellow. She explained her excitement that the four hallways of our building concept were like the four sacred directions of the Medicine Wheel. At the conclusion of the design session for the new dormitory, the two ladies and I integrated a Medicine Wheel design into the patterned flooring in the central commons for the new dormitory. It was to hold a prominent location at the hub of the facility, with the four hallways radiating out from it.

During my stay at Pine Ridge, the recurring circle image was further revealed to me by two teenage boys, both Native American, both fourteen-ish, both wearing blue jeans and T-shirts, their rather long, straight, black hair revealing glimpses of ear. My interactions with the boys were in two separate places, on separate days, in totally separate situations, but the same.

The first boy was sitting on the low wall beside the back entrance steps of the old brick dorm building, next to a weathered door that was chained shut. We were alone as I walked by. He sat in a relaxed posture, one leg up a step, with an elbow on his knee. It was a lonely setting, with the prairie off in the distance behind me. It seemed weird to have this building sitting next to nothing. He was selling silk-screened T-shirts out of a cardboard box. The image on the T-shirt was powerful. It was of a Sioux warrior on a Paint horse, with a version of the Medicine Wheel graphic as a backdrop. The design was striking because one quarter of the circle was a field of blue with white stars, and another quadrant had red and white stripes. The American flag integrated into the traditional Native American symbol. "Wow! Neat graphic," I said.

"Want one?" was the simple response. We shared some words about the artist located somewhere on the reservation, and I bought a T-shirt.

The second boy was leaning against an old weathered upright at the gate of the Wounded Knee Cemetery. A cardboard box was lying on the dry ground next to him. Worn-out blue jeans and T-shirt, again, seemed to be the uniform for these school kids. The cemetery, located some miles northeast of the town Pine Ridge, sits on top of a hill, surrounded by a rolling landscape of grass-covered hills and shallow valleys, devoid of trees except for a sprinkling of sunbaked cedar bushes struggling to survive. No one else was there. It was just the boy and me. There it was again, this windswept, lonely feeling again. The boy held up a small 'dream catcher' talisman to show me. "Wow! That's neat!" I said.

"Want one?" was the request. The boy explained it was handmade by an artisan on the reservation, his words like those of the previous boy. They were simple words, incomplete sentences, devoid of salesmanship; soft words, level, unpretentious, with something haunting about them. The dream catcher consisted of a circular hoop about three inches in diameter, sized to hang nicely on your rearview mirror inside your car. An asymmetric spider-web design of netting stretched across the middle of the hoop, with two small feathers and some beads hanging from the bottom.

"I'll take one," was my reply. There it was again, this powerful circle symbol.

I hadn't really known much about Wounded Knee before my visit to Pine Ridge. Thinking back to my college days, I vaguely recalled news reports of a conflict that happened in the early '70s at Wounded Knee, with members of AIM riding around in pickup trucks, waving their hunting rifles in the air and confronting federal agents. At the time, my interest in the event was lost in the many other Vietnam-era social upheavals going on.

The Wounded Knee Massacre of December 29, 1890, happened here, signaling the end of the Indian Wars. This is where Big Foot and his people were buried in a mass grave. In the nearby village of Red Cloud, there was a small rural structure converted into a museum and shop. Inside was a photographic display at that brought me clarity and understanding. As I walked around and looked at the photographs hanging on the museum walls, I felt like someone had slapped me in the face. A shockingly brutal record was on display.

The photographs recorded US Army soldiers standing over frozen stacks of human bodies. The soldiers were smiling with their long guns in hand, posing like trophy hunters with their slain big game in the foreground. Big Foot, the chief of this band of Lakota people, was among the dead in the photographs. They had rolled his frozen body over and propped it up in a death pose, his stiff arms defiantly raised in the air. Narratives of the photographs described how the exhausted and hungry band of Sioux, under Bigfoot's leadership, had walked down into a bitterly cold encampment in a valley at Wounded Knee. Their intent was to surrender to the US Army, give up their guns, and take up internment on the reservation. A hilltop perch of US soldiers with their guns and cannon surrounded the cluster of tepees. As I understand it, a Lakota man, reluctant to surrender his gun, struggled with a trooper. A shot was accidentally fired into the air. The soldiers of the US Army reacted, unleashing a massive attack of gunfire upon the Sioux encampment. Men, women, and children were slain indiscriminately. The photographs recorded the dead bodies of the Lakota people, lying in the snow where they had been shot, dark lumps reminiscent of buffalo carcasses after a kill. One hundred and forty-six frozen bodies lay in one large trench grave. This was the Wounded Knee Massacre, December 29, 1890. This was the end of "the good life" for the Sioux Nation.

Over the few days of my stay in the city of Pine Ridge, I saw variations of the Medicine Wheel everywhere. I saw colored imprints of the image on the sidewalks. Customized variations of the circle design were on the letterheads of official correspondences, integrated into departmental logos. The circle image was visible on glossy covers of the local magazines at the convenience store, on banners hanging on walls, on decorated purses hanging from teenagers' shoulders.

Slowly climbing out of my naivety, I began to "get it," to understand that this Medicine Wheel was a sacred image, engrained in the minds of these Lakota people located here at Pine Ridge, in the southwestern corner of South Dakota. To the Lakota, this symbol held powerful spirituality.

Fifteen years later, having spent all this time back in the white man's world, I had my first meeting with the Dakota people, in Sisseton, some 350 miles to the northeast, in the opposite corner of South Dakota. At that meeting, I made a discovery. Like it was for the Lakota, a similar circle symbol had powerful spiritual meaning for the Dakota people, comparable in some ways, I suppose, to my Christian cross. Red Owl referred to it by a different name, "The Hoop of Life."

CHAPTER 13
Darkness

Omaha, February 2010

In the months after Sharon's death, I drifted into and out of the darkness of grief. I was sixty years old. My father was dead by sixty-eight. This would be my fate. I was overweight, like my father... the Laughlin way. He died of remote-control disease—a gruff, old, fat man, retired to his lazy-boy recliner. No hobbies, no joys left in his life, only the television. Like father, like son, my life was in the past. I was a widower. My kids were now young men, starting their own lives. I said to myself; *It was a good run. It's over.*

Late one cold winter evening, the house was deathly silent, except for the sound of the water splashing around in the kitchen sink as I rinsed some dishes. A simple memory of Sharon doing the dishes flashed into my brain. Grief hit me, like a glass shattering on the floor, deep, hard, crashing into despair. Cup in one hand, towel in the other, face contorting with anguish, tears aggressively squeezed out, washing across my cheeks. I fell to one knee, with my hands still dangling over the sink, wrists on the rim, head down, the anguish worsening, darkening. I dropped farther onto the floor, releasing the cup into the sink, dragging the towel with me. On all fours, head dangling, relentlessly sliding into darkness. Lifting back onto my knees, I rocked forward and back, heaving with the pain of grief, slouching forward... on and on.

On a similar dark winter evening not long after that, my doorbell rang. "Hi, Steve. Saw your light on. Got a minute?" Gordon came in, removed his hat, gloves, and coat and rubbed his shoes against the rug before we sat down together in the living room. He was a neighbor from down the street, a few years older than me, a friendly acquaintance, but not one of my close friends. "Steve, as you know, I lost my wife a year ago. I think I know what you are going through, and I have some things to tell you... things that have helped me get through it. Maybe they will help you... maybe not. Either way, there are some things you might think about." Gordon had a simple bag of tricks to help him handle the grief.

Gordon presented his first idea. "If you are feeling depressed, go to your doctor and get some happy pills. They helped me."

"Easy enough," I replied. "I haven't tried that yet."

Gordon went on to say, "Sometimes my house feels like a dark and empty place. I dread walking into it... haunted by memories of her... and so terribly quiet. What I do, Steve, is just get the hell out—visit someone, take a four-day weekend and go to Denver, or go to a movie. Anything to get away from the place."

"I know what you mean, Gordon," I replied. "Good idea."

Gordon continued: "Here is one idea for you that took me a while to figure out. Frequently, my closest friends, wanting to comfort me, invited me over to their home for dinner. A typical dinner would be attended by two couples and me. I call it 'the two-and-a-half couples effect.' Halfway through the evening, someone would say something like, 'What a beautiful dinner. Too bad Elvira isn't here to share it with us.' That simple comment would instantly trigger the entire group falling into grief. Several evenings crashed. 'Thank-you, can't stay, goodnight,' fighting off tears, dark ending." He went on to say, "I stopped accepting their invitations. Too much pain. They needed some time to grieve, too. Maybe I'll try again later in the year, but not right away."

I agreed with Gordon. "Yeah. It's already happened to me."

"Another good course of action that helped me, and that might help you, Steve, is that I started inviting new people, new friends, into my life." I listened intently to Gordon's words of wisdom and took them to heart.

I didn't know it but Gordon's last comment would profoundly change the trajectory of my life. He suggested, "And I started looking up old friends I had lost track of... friends from way back before I met my wife."

CHAPTER 14

Trout Ranch

Central South Dakota, spring of 2010

One of my old friends called from his home in Sioux Falls. "Hey, Steve. It's Jeff. Next weekend, I'm going to a trout fishing resort with a couple of my dad's buddies. Dad can't make it, and we have room for one more person. I wanted to invite you to come along if you are interested." I guessed Jeff saw this as an opportunity to get me out of my house and cheer me up considering my wife's recent death.

I responded without hesitation. "I'm interested, Jeff. Fill me in on the details."

Next thing I knew, Jeff and I were on the road together, driving west to spend a weekend at a trout ranch out on the prairie in central South Dakota. We were going to rendezvous with two older gentlemen from his hometown of Rapid City. I had done little trout fishing, and my tackle was a little heavier, intended to handle bigger game fish, but I was willing to give it a go.

We pulled into the resort at the end of the afternoon and checked in at the "office," which was a converted double garage. It had a couple of freestanding racks of shelves in the middle of the floor, filled with snack foods, flashlights, paper towels. One wall had a pegboard full of fishing tackle for sale. There were freezer and refrigerator units against another wall. The checkout counter also served as the reception desk for the resort. A stocky, middle-aged lady was behind the counter, one of the owners of the resort. "Your party of four is in cabin number three. Two older guys arrived about an hour ago." After grabbing a key, Jeff walked out to the lakeside to find the others. I said I'd join him in a minute, wanting to check out the fishing gear that was for sale.

I turned to the lady behind the counter and asked, "What's the best setup to catch these trout?"

"Night crawlers," she said as she looked me over. Once she saw I was waiting attentively for more information, she rattled off a detailed answer. "Tie one of those small number ten hooks on your line and set a bobber at about two feet deep. Then tear a bit of worm off, about a half inch, no more than that, and put it on your hook. Don't need a sinker or split shot, just a hook and a little piece of worm. Make sure the hook is hidden inside the bit of worm, so the fish can't see it. The night crawlers are over in that refrigerator."

Without pause I said, "I'll take a dozen, and a pack of those hooks. I've got bobbers." My next question to her was, "Where's the best place to catch 'em?"

She squinted her right eye and looked out the window over her shoulder. "You see that cottonwood hanging out over the water? It's right across from your cabin. There." She pointed through the window. "Now, you go sit down right under that tree and put your bobber about ten feet out from the bank, in the tree's shadow, and you'll catch a few. It's the best spot on the property. I'll put this stuff on your tab." I thanked her, and she wished me good luck as I headed out the screen door.

The trout ranch had, at one time, been a fish hatchery for the state of South Dakota, but it had closed, and the property sold to the resort owners. There were several small ponds in a row, formed by earthen dams built across a gentle stream that carved a shallow valley. The ponds were edged with grass meadows and a few majestic cottonwoods, making it a picturesque setting out on the prairie at the top of the Missouri River Valley. There were six nice little log cabins near the water's edge.

I spotted Jeff talking to one of his people who was fishing, a tall and stately looking older gentleman. The other man was not far away. The two older guys were duded up with all the proper trout fishing attire, including flop hats with flies attached, tan fishing vests with three pockets on each side, brand-name outdoorsman shirts, rubber boots, and ultralight spinning tackle. We had our introductions, and I commented I hadn't done much trout fishing. The one old guy standing close to Jeff looked me over and decided that I needed some serious coaching, assuming me to be one of those city-slicker types who didn't know which end of the pole to hold. He proceeded to give me the rundown on the proper trout fishing methods, everything from the line weight, the proper light spin-casting gear, the best little spinner lures to use, and the proper technique of letting it settle down into the water before you wind in. He promised, later, to show me his secret lucky-seven knot, which worked best on this light monofilament line, but right now, he had to get on with the prime-time fishing as evening was coming on. I was feeling a bit out of place with my baseball cap, Hard Rock Cafe T-shirt, and tennies. Introductions over, Jeff and I walked back to the cabin to unload the car and grab our tackle.

By the time Jeff was ready for fishing, he was making his own fashion statement, with a cowboy hat, big fancy belt buckle and beat-up old cowboy boots. We were the two "young" rebellious guys, me at sixty years old and Jeff at fifty-two, who just weren't fitting the trout fishing stereotype. I told Jeff that I was going to start fishing across from the cabin "under that cottonwood." Jeff joined up with the other two gentlemen, who were fishing on the next pond farther down the valley.

Precisely following the directions given me by the lady behind the counter, and intentionally ignoring all the directions that the old trout "pro" had given me, I sat down under the tree, tied a number ten hook on, set my bobber at two-feet depth, tore a piece of worm off, placed it over the hook, and lobbed the setup ten feet out into the lake, under the shadow of the cottonwood. The bobber floated motionless for ten seconds and then aggressively jerked down under the surface of the water. I set the hook and fought a nice-size trout to shore. For all you non-trout fishermen types, these trout really are fun to catch because they fight hard and fast, often jumping into the air. After placing the fish on my stringer, I pulled a small length of rope out of my tackle box, attached one end to the stringer, and tied the other around the cottonwood before stealthily lowering the fish and stringer into the water at the shoreline. Happy with the arrangement, I cast out into the lake again and immediately caught another nice trout, followed by a third, a fourth and a fifth fish. After about an hour's time, I had filled my stringer, which had eight loops on it, and had to double up fish on five of the loops, to total thirteen nice, pan-size trout. *Not bad for a city-slicker*, I said to myself.

My three companions walked toward the cabin, having completed their first evening of serious fishing. The third member of our party, the stand-off-ish one, Neil, was the first to arrive and see me sitting under the tree across from the cabin. "How'd you guys do?" was my loaded question.

"No good, nothin' yet," Neil replied.

Jeff and Leo were a few steps behind. "Nope, skunked," Leo yelled. "How about you? Any luck?"

I held up a finger, as if to say, "Just a minute," and got up from my seated position against the tree. Saying nothing, I grabbed the rope and followed it to the edge of the water. All eyes were on me when, with a big-ass grin on my face, I lifted the flopping stringer of fish out of the water. "I got thirteen."

Neil opened his eyes wide and proclaimed, *"What?"* with alarm in his voice. He then broke into a fast walk, bordering on a run, toward me around the edge of the pond while vocalizing a command that was half whispering and half yelling, *"Put that back in the water! Back in before someone sees it!"* His request dumbfounded me, but responding to the anxiety in his words, I eased the stringer of fish back down into the water. He got very close to me before he spoke again. In an aggressive whisper, he pointedly said, with arrows coming from his eyes, *"That is over the allowable daily possession limit! You are breaking the law! Leo, here, is the attorney general for the state...the highest law enforcement officer in South Dakota! Do you realize what will happen if this gets out to the newspapers? It will ruin his reputation! Release those fish right now! And be discrete about it!"*

I was afraid that this guy was going to stroke out right here on the spot, but I wasn't too excited about letting these nice fish go. I lowered the stringer back into the water, out of sight of prying eyes, while Neil continued his nervous tizzy. *"You've got to release them... right now!"*

Now, me... I have been known to break a few rules when it comes to fishing. There was the time when I had just caught a nice four-pound bass, which was a "slot fish." The slot rule is that any bass between fifteen and twenty-one inches long must be immediately released. This one was about twenty inches long. The game warden was walking down to me from the road. It was dusk, dark enough to make it hard to see. As he approached, I removed the bass from my stringer and discretely slipped it head-first into one leg of my hip waders. The fish wiggled and squirmed all the way down my leg inside the boot, to where the rubber near the ankle cinched tight around him like a girdle. The fish stopped his flipping around, except for jabbing me a few times with his fins on the way down, while I was doing my best to pretend that I was a law-abiding fisherman.

Back at the trout ranch, Jeff approached, with Leo not far behind. Jeff reluctantly agreed with Neil, "Yeah… the daily limit is a maximum of three trout in your possession. You've got too many fish there, Steevie."

Judging that Jeff was not acknowledging the gravity of the situation, Neil assertively whispered another comment. "And let's not forget that *you, Jeff,* are an advisor to the governor, sitting on the Fish and Wildlife Committee!"

Jeff scratched his chin. "Yeah, Neil's got a point there. I didn't tell you before, Steevie, but Neil here is Leo's chief legal counsel." Jeff was buckling under the pressure.

I dried my hands on the untucked bottom of my T-shirt and lifted the brim of my baseball cap to the top of my forehead before attempting to defend myself. "Now, let me get this straight. I'm fishing with the *attorney general* for the state of South Dakota, his *chief legal counsel,* and an *advisor* on *the governor's Fish and Wildlife Committee*! Boy, Jeff, you sure did a piss-poor job of introductions. And why did you invite me on this trip? You know I don't pay much attention to these *Gah-dam* rules when it comes to fishing."

Neil injected a nervous whispery yell, *"Please, keep your voice down. Someone might hear us!"*

Jeff spit out a side-ways apology. "Sorry, Steevie. I didn't do a very good job of explaining things to you. But how was I to know that you would catch *every fricking fish in the lake in the first hour?*"

Leo had been holding back, wanting to keep his distance in case his counsel was correct and a game warden or a CNN reporter was within earshot. This gave him a chance to calmly think things over before he spoke. Leo walked to water's edge, lifted the stringer, and looked at the fish with envy. "That's a damn nice stringer of fish! I might be wrong, Neil, but we aren't on state property. This is private land. I don't think that state possession rules apply when you are on private property. Am I right about that, Neil?"

Neil scrunched his eyebrows down over his eyes, and two big vertical wrinkles appeared in the middle of his forehead. "Ahhh, well, uh… I'm not completely confident that…"

Leo cut in, "Now, hold on there, my friend. Look at it this way. Thirteen fish are on that stringer. There are four of us, and each of us can have three fish in our possession. If my math is correct, that makes twelve as our legal limit. Isn't that right, Neil?

Neil's neck turned purple, which matched nicely the colors of the sundown sky. "I don't think that will hold up…"

Leo interrupted again, this time stating a directive, voiced with a sense of authority, "All you need to do, Steve, is let one of them go, and we can divvy up the rest between us. Besides, it's about suppertime, and I'll bet we can have these all cleaned and fried within an hour."

I chimed in, "Hell, yes… We'll eat the evidence!" I threw the smallest fish back in the lake while Jeff gut-giggled and the brim of his cowboy hat wobbled.

The attorney general lifted his squared jaw into the fading colors of the evening sky and flashed a broad, tight-lipped smile, looking for a moment like Charlton Heston or John Wayne at the end of a heroic Hollywood saga where the forces of goodness had just defeated evil.

Neil had a concerned and confused look washing across his face, convinced that what we were doing was illegal. He nervously rubbed his forehead and scanned the shoreline left and right to see if there were any witnesses standing around. We were in the clear.

It was a nice meal that night. I had a chance to entertain the attorney general by telling several of my true-to-life fish stories, just ever so slightly embellished. He had a couple whoppers of his own. And we had two more days of fishing ahead of us, with a cup of night crawlers at the ready.

CHAPTER 15
The Knot in Time

While a building is molded into the shape of the sacred HOOP, while a wife's health declines towards her death, while a son grapples with the dark forces upon him, while a boy leans against a weathered upright, while a brother fends off a monstrous intruder, while trying to understand the OYATE, while soldiers stand over stacks of bodies, while an old man breathes his last breath, while a nurse suspects murder, while young men leave home to start their own lives, while children keep secrets, while the "Blanket People" become "Cut-Hairs," while an older guy is duded up with all the proper trout-fishing attire, while the spirit world and the real world intermingle, while a house is haunted by memories of her...

 VISION: evoked by a dollop of luck and a sprinkling of serendipity.
 VISION: evoked by a spiritual intervention from the HOMELAND.
 VISION: evoked by a sleep-deprived mind that intermingles the real world and the dream world.
 VISION: evoked by a psychotic episode, delusions brought on by powerful drugs.
 VISION: evoked by the remnants of the good life that was lost.

CHAPTER 16

Karen

Paris, France and Lincoln, Nebraska 2007-2009

Karen was calling from her apartment in Paris to check on her mother, who was drifting into Alzheimer's. Karen had been living in Europe for the past thirty years while her mother, Peg, remained in their family home in Lincoln, Nebraska.

    Her mother's friend, Melva, was on the line. "Peg's place is getting messy, Karen," Melva said. "There were several bags of rotting garbage piled up on the landing at the top of the steps to the basement. I cleaned them out for her. And it's been several months since the fire in the kitchen. She was lucky to put it out herself, but she still has done nothing to fix the damage. She's not grooming herself the way she used to. Thank goodness your mother invites me into her place once in a while, so that I can snoop around."

    "Thanks so much, Melva," Karen replied. "It's not the first time she let the garbage go rancid. When I was there last June, I found she had packed the trunk of her car with sacks of garbage and then forgot about them. They'd all gone rotten, with flies and maggots. If you weren't checking in on her once in a while, taking care of things, I don't know what I would do. I can't leave my life here in Paris and I'm only good for a visit or two each year back home. It's obvious that she can't take care of herself anymore. I guess it's time for me to get her out of her house and into a nursing home. That'll be my task for next month when I arrive. Mom's not going to like it, the hardheaded old German biddy that she is. And she's definitely not going to like the fact that it is me dragging her out of her home."

Karen grew up in a military family. Her mother, a young lady in postwar Germany, had fallen in love with an American military man. She worked as a secretary in the military office where the two met. Her name, Irmgard, was too hard to pronounce, so her future husband started calling her Peg, considering her tendency to peg office supplies at him whenever she was mad about something. The nickname stuck. They were married in Frankfurt in 1948. The couple would have two children, girls, both born in Rapid City, South Dakota. The family jumped around on military assignments, spending years on air bases in Germany, South Dakota, England, Montana, and back to England again. Finally, the family moved to Lincoln, Nebraska, with the two young girls settling into their permanent home on Holdrege Street. Karen was thirteen and Diana was ten. Their father retired from the military in Lincoln and took up a job running the local drive-in theater. Karen and her younger sister helped at the concession booth on weekends. Now that the girls were to spend a good portion of their formative years in one location, Lincoln would become the place they called home.

Karen was the smart older sister, and Diana was the darling little sister. Their mother favored Diana, showering her with pretty clothes, attention, forgiveness, and love. Karen was the less cute, more willful child, always butting heads with her mother, two females with attitude and differing opinions on everything. Her childhood dance teacher dismissed Karen from her class, partly because she wasn't graceful enough but also because she wasn't taking direction well. Karen was a bit of a tomboy. Boys were the only children of her age to play with during several grade school years living in England, and she had missed out on girl things. She gave up playing with dolls at an early age. It followed that she was her father's child. She adored him deeply and was loved in return by him. It devastated Karen when he died midway through her college years at the University of Nebraska. Karen's sister, Diana, died fifteen years later in middle age, after a struggle with aplastic anemia and a lifetime of alcohol abuse and heavy smoking. Diana, who had married and was without children, had lived in a house near her mother's home in Lincoln, seemingly forever connected by her mother's umbilical cord, the favorite child to the end. But now, after Diana's death, only Mom and Karen remained.

At an early age, Karen was impressed by the idea of medicines helping and healing people and decided that she was going to be a pharmacist. By the age of twenty, she had left home and was married, partly to get away from her mother. Her marriage did not fare well. After a time, there were no children, no love, and a husband who did not value her successes in her college and professional life. The marriage lasted ten years but became an empty shell halfway through. By the age of thirty, she was divorced, had earned her Doctor of Pharmacy degree, became the president of local and statewide professional organizations and was a well-respected clinical pharmacist. Shortly thereafter, she discovered she could not bear children, which explained failed attempts in the early years of her marriage. Free to pursue her life as she saw fit, she took a job in Germany, hoping to see some of the world and to find herself. After twenty years living in Nebraska, she had moved to Europe, eventually became a French citizen. She returned to the USA only for occasional visits to her mother. Karen took a research position with a large pharmaceutical company and joined their international team, adding French, German, and Spanish fluency. Her job took her to Vietnam, the Philippines, Mumbai, Istanbul, Sao Paulo, and other far-flung destinations, where she would audit clinical drug tests and live her life as a successful single professional woman of the world.

Now, living four thousand miles away, Karen had to confront her headstrong mother, living alone in Nebraska, declining into Alzheimer's. Peg knew she was losing her memory and having difficulty taking care of herself, but she would never be convinced to leave her home. Karen hatched an audacious lie to get her mother into a nursing home. Upon her arrival in Lincoln, Karen told her mother that she had arranged a temporary stay for her, "a few days at a medical facility," to receive some physical evaluations, promising that Peg would return home after she was feeling better. The ploy worked. Karen moved her mother into the nursing home. Once there, with the help provided by the staff, Peg quickly became comfortable with her surroundings. As luck would have it, Peg rather smoothly accepted her new situation. Willful woman that she was, her time at the nursing home was not without the occasional incident of head-butting with the staff. Most memorable was the time that the nurse was slow to get around to changing her diaper, so Peg, living up to her nickname, decided to peg a turd at the nurse as she entered the room.

Peg's health continually declined over the next two years, and she died in June 2009. A small group attended the funeral, and Karen delivered a eulogy. With the death of Karen's mother, all family ties to her home were broken. She had two cousins on her mother's side living in Germany, but no longer had an American family. Father, sister, and mother… all gone. No husband, children, nieces, or nephews. Alone. No one to love or be loved by. Her next step would be to sell her mother's house, the house of her childhood. At sixty years old, it was now possible for Karen to close the Nebraska chapter of her life completely, to uproot… and never again be home.

CHAPTER 17
Reunion

Nebraska, July 2010

Six months had passed since the death of my wife, when I opened an e-mail inviting me to attend my high school reunion. They dubbed it "The 60th birthday party for the Northeast High School Class of 1968." There were some 530 students in our graduating class. These were people I had paid no attention to for over forty years. Then I remembered the suggestion of my neighbor, Gordon, that one way to combat my grief and loneliness was by looking up old friends, so I thought to myself, "*Now here is a bunch of old friends from way back*, people from the time before I met Sharon." and decided to attend the reunion, scheduled for midsummer. They had opened a new website dedicated to our class of '68 which prompted me to write a short bio on myself and post it. My last comment on the bio was "*Recently widowed.*"

They flagged my bio as a new entry on the website and, in short order, I started receiving emails from old classmates. The first one was a surprise—from Paris, France... and from a lady I didn't recognize; her picture on the email or her name didn't ring a bell. The message was short and sweet: "*So sorry to hear about the recent loss of your wife. I hope to see you this summer at the reunion,*" signed Karen Levorson. My dusty old yearbook was on the shelf in the basement. I hadn't looked at it in twenty years, not since we moved to our new house in '89. But now I recognized that high school girl. We had been classmates in Mrs. Krause's Latin class in 1967, sitting across the aisle from each other. She got straight 'A's, and I nearly flunked that class. We hadn't seen each other, or even thought about the other for forty-two years. In high school, she was not one of the in-crowd beautiful people. She was more on the periphery, like me. I was a skinny string bean, a self-conscious kid, afraid of girls, sixteen going on fourteen, and stepping on my tongue every time I tried to talk to a girl. I remembered her as an Amazon, towering over me in the halls, sixteen going on eighteen. She was a bit of a bookworm, with a pleasant smile and a friendly voice. We were not close friends, me hanging around with my buddies, and her with her clique of smart girlfriends. We knew each other enough to say hi and share a few words in the hall. When we talked, she slightly cocked her head, and was always attentive and inquisitive.

We had our reunion in June. I was apprehensive and nervous considering that I had been through a lifetime of getting old, fat, and ugly. I hadn't attended previous reunions and didn't track any classmates through the years. Old high school anxieties were welling up in me. I was a heavy guy now, 255 pounds, twice as big as I was in high school, not the skinny little guy that these people would remember me as. As all reunion preparations go, I threw a couple weeks at dieting, and peeled a few pounds off, but it really had little effect on my appearance or self-consciousness.

I drove in the fifty miles from Omaha to my old hometown of Lincoln. Randy's Bar and Grill was pretty easy to find, it was in the stomping grounds of my youth, on the northeast side of town. There were fifty or more people attending, classmates and spouses. As I walked into the bar, I scanned the room, looking for familiar faces from the past. I didn't recognize anyone. They all looked older, heavier and uglier, dramatically different from the kids I knew. But a few recognized me, and we began reintroductions. I had brought my yearbook, and we started flipping through the pages.

Karen was easy to spot in the crowd. She was tall, head held high, shoulder-length dark hair, with a vibrant smile, full of joyful confidence. She flitted around the room like a colorful butterfly, sharing small conversations, drink in hand. Everyone knew her. She had been coming to Lincoln from Paris with some regularity to visit her mother and had specifically scheduled some trips to coincide with high school get-togethers in the past. In contrast with her Nebraskan classmates who were in blue jeans or casual dress, she was wearing a tight one-piece, designer dress with some sexy French cleavage. The way she carried herself gave her a kind of Jane Fonda look.

I was feeling old, ugly, and fat by comparison. I didn't have the nerve to approach Karen, being content to spend the evening reconnecting with a couple of old buddies. But she came up to me and introduced herself. She suggested we sit down together to catch up with each other. We talked, one-on-one, for thirty minutes. She inquired whether I received her email she sent last spring. I apologized for not getting back to her. I had difficulty tracking her conversation, as my hearing was not the best, compounded by the noisy bar setting. But we became reacquainted after forty-two years of leading totally separate lives. There was something comforting about having known her in high school. Deep down, we knew each other. We exchanged contact information, and she invited me to come to a barbeque at her mother's house the following weekend. She explained that her mother had recently died, and she was here for another six weeks before returning to Paris, wanting to get her mother's house ready for sale and take care of estate issues, go through family things, and do a yard sale.

I came to a conclusion. I liked this lady. Here I was, sixty years old, having stirrings of interest for another woman. And, I was free to pursue them, for the first time in thirty-five years. This wasn't just any woman down the street. If I were to get serious about this lady, it would be a dramatically different life than the one I had expected for myself, reclining in the lazy-boy chair, drifting into my senior years with a remote control in my hand. This would be a long-distance dating game conducted across the four thousand miles between Paris and Omaha. It would definitely drag me out of my recliner. But I had accepted the challenge. I had locked-on to this babe. Karen was *the one*! The only problem was that she hadn't locked-on to me.

CHAPTER 18

Spare No Expense!

Lincoln and Omaha, summer of 2010

If I was going to get Karen interested in me, I needed to overcome my negative self-image as that "old, ugly, and fat guy." At the reunion, I imagined my classmates whispering to each other, "Oh my God... Have you seen how fat Steve Laughlin is?" This was not the impression I needed to make.

The day after the reunion, in anticipation of Karen spending the next six weeks in Lincoln, I embarked on a dramatic weight-loss program. I changed my eating habits. For breakfast, I ate a plum. Lunch was a small aluminum pocket of tuna and a squeeze of lemon. Supper was a cup of Cheerios and milk. I felt hunger! Always, all day, all night. Also, I needed abs! You know, those rippling bumps you see on a young man's tummy. Membership in one of those trendy new gyms was required. I went there, three days a week, Monday, Wednesday and Friday evenings, for an hour each time, mostly doing crunches. I started fast-walking three miles each day, between 6:00 a.m. and 7:00 a.m., eventually jogging for an extra mile before and an extra mile after. My program had a name. I called it The Joy of the Pain of Hunger and the Joy of the Pain of Exercise program. Once my routine kicked in, I started peeling off weight at, believe-it-or-not, a pound a day. Oh, the things we do for the prospect of love.

GYM MEMBERSHIP..$300

The following Saturday, I drove the fifty miles to Lincoln to attend the BBQ at Karen's place. I was a bit rusty at woman chasing. My bag of tricks was pretty old and worn out. It had been thirty-five years since the last time I "dated." But I thought that a few of the old tried-and-true tactics still ought to work. *"Flowers!"* seemed to me to be a brilliant plan. I arrived in Lincoln at six o'clock and was lucky to find a florist's shop that was still open. I definitely did not want to resort to a cheap handful of flowers that you would find near the exit doors of your typical grocery store. In the shop, there was only one employee frantically trying to pull together a series of flower arrangements for end-of-day delivery. He invited me to look around while he continued to work. My goal was to impress Karen, exhibit my interest in her as a female candidate, display my refined visual selectivity skills, and present my discerning eye for quality, elegance, beauty, and the goodness of life. Also, I needed to divert her attention away from my true objective, which was *wild sex*. What I needed was a nice bouquet of flowers, not too fancy, not too expensive, and not too presumptuous. It was surprising to me how much thought one could put into the simple act of purchasing flowers. A tall vase of long-stemmed lilies was waiting for me, deep in the back corner of the store. The orange petals were speckled with deep red, and long, arching leaves lined the stem of each flower. A handful of these would do nicely. I paid the clerk thirty-five dollars for the flowers. Two-fifty apiece seemed high, but I was on a mission to impress this hot babe. The attendant reassured me that these were a special lily.

Arriving at Karen's place, before exiting the car, I pulled the flowers out of the box. I didn't need the box, the tissue paper wrap, or the frilly green accents. I wanted the flowers to have an elegant, natural, hand-picked look. Feeling a bit like a teen on a prom date, I walked up to the side door of the house. Through the screen door, I could see Karen in the kitchen. I knocked. Karen answered the door, pulling herself away from some cooking. With a quick glance, she said, "Hi, Steve." I was deflated that she didn't immediately beam with girlish excitement upon seeing my offering of flowers. Adding to my disappointment, she said, "Oh, did you grab those out of my yard? Those damn things grow like weeds." She nodded her head sideways toward the backyard. "I'm thinking about ripping the whole mess of them out," she said as she turned her attention back to the stove. I glanced at a planter bed in the backyard that was some ten feet wide and running one hundred feet down the property line full of orange lilies. There must have been a thousand lilies out there, all looking the same as the ones in my hand. Well, apparently, some fine-tuning of old Steve's courtship skills was needed.

Karen did take notice enough to say, "Cut a little off of the stems," as she slid a pair of scissors across the kitchen counter to me. "And put them over on the table, would you, dear? I think there is enough room for them in the vase with the others." She already had a vase of the orange lilies in the center of the dining room table. So much for the tried-and-true flowers method. The bouquet purchase wasn't a total loss, though. That evening, it made for some entertaining conversation and a few gut chuckles from the gaggle of plump and seasoned ladies sitting around the patio.

FLOWERS..$35

At Karen's patio party, I found out that she enjoyed bicycling. Seizing an opportunity for a "date," I suggested we go bike riding together the following Saturday morning, during the day before the next patio party. Now, truth be told, I hadn't ridden a bicycle in a very long time. I didn't even own one. My ability to balance on a bicycle had been seriously compromised fifteen years before in a white-water boating accident that destroyed my right-side inner ear. Now, with thoughts about a certain woman weirding out my ability to make proper judgments, this handicap seemed to have slipped my mind. In fact, there was the distinct possibility that I couldn't even ride a bicycle anymore. But, at this moment, I was lovestruck and trying my best to come across as a biker expert from way-back.

On the following Friday, the day before our bicycle outing, I took action to enhance the illusion. I bought a brand-new bicycle, complete with car carrier, helmet, pump, locking cable, water bottle, and saddlebags. I didn't purchase a spandex racing outfit, but probably would have, if it had occurred to me. Besides, I didn't need to call attention to my bulging gut. My purchase wasn't just any bicycle picked from the rack at the big-box store. It was a Bianchi, made in Italy, purchased at a serious bicycle shop from a dude with zero body fat. If I couldn't display much in the way of riding skills, at least I would exhibit my material cool and a refined appreciation of quality.

Karen had asked where we were going to go biking. I said, "I have a place in mind," thinking I would impress the hell out of her with a cute little lake I knew along the Platte River that had a quiet ring road and a canopy of cottonwood trees. (No hills!) "Pick you up ten-ish in the morning." With my brand-new bike on my brand-new bike rack, I showed up at Karen's house in Lincoln on Saturday morning. While I was lashing her bike to the rack, Karen asked again where we were going. "There's a place out on the Platte that I know," I said, coyly trying to add some surprise mystique to the destination. We headed out of town, east on Interstate 80.

As I took the Mahoney Park exit, turning south, Karen said, "Are we going to the lake at South Bend?" As it turned out, she had been at this lake the weekend before, spending the day at a friend's cabin for a Fourth of July barbeque bash, with fireworks and a keg. OK, OK, so much for impressing her with my surprise mystique destination.

Karen had two separate buddies living there in their lakeside homes, in fact. As we rode our bikes around the lake, we stopped by each guy's place and spent a lot of time talking to my competition. One of them was out front in the driveway as we rolled up, polishing his red Corvette, convertible top down, with a white leather interior. This pretty well trumped the high-end impression I was trying to make with my brand-new Italian designer bike, which I had pulled from the rack on my Honda Civic. In truth, I appreciated the visits with those lake-house guys, because it reduced our riding time, with me struggling to keep up the illusion that I knew how to ride the damn bicycle. I had a few challenges, such as trying to figure out how to shift gears, nonstop wobbling left to right because of my balancing issues, relearning to stop using the brake for the rear tire and not the front one. Luckily, I didn't flip.

NEW BICYCLE... $900

Mid-afternoon, we drove back to Karen's house in Lincoln. Plans were for another Saturday night barbeque with friends on Karen's patio in the backyard. As we pulled into the driveway, one of Karen's ex-lover-boys was sitting on the front porch. Karen invited us in. She made a beeline to the cupboard and pulled out a bottle of Balvenie single malt Scotch whisky, twelve years old, and some glasses. Karen and Rick had had lots of scotches together in the old college days and considered themselves to be connoisseurs. I had tried scotch maybe twice in my forty-two-year history of drinking. To me, drinking scotch was comparable to drinking turpentine.

After listening intently to a series of refined comments about "peaty-ness" and "oaky-ness" and, "smoothness" and "floral bouquet," I was dismissed and sent off to the grocery store to perform the lowly task of buying ice and potato chips for the evening's party. But I was not to be outclassed by this Rick dude. As I walked out of the store, I passed by the rollaway door of the liquor store. Just inside was a rack of bargain bottles. Sparing no expense, I snatched up what was, in my mind, a fairly pricey bottle of scotch, listed at $150, and on sale for $125. Back at Karen's pad, I proudly deposited my purchase on the kitchen table. It seemed to me to be pretty cool looking. Inside the glossy royal-blue box, the bottle was wrapped in a sexy deep-blue velvet cloth sack, cinched with a braided white rope with tasseled ends. I stepped back with a smirk, thinking, *"What a good boy am I."* Immediately, both Karen and Rick had disturbed looks on their faces, as if there was something smelling funny on my shoe that I had brought in from the barnyard. *"Eauuh! It's a blend!"* Karen said. Now, scotch snobs apparently don't go for *"blended"* scotches. Single malt is *preferable*. They made it precisely clear to me I was in the presence of two people with better taste than me, and that my purchase was shit. They singled me out as a lowly beer drinker with no class. This was turning out to not be my best day of babe hunting.

BOTTLE OF SCOTCH..$125

A week later, for my second attempt at a "date," I invited Karen to come to my home in Omaha to have a Saturday lunch out on my patio. The problem was that my cheap, white, plastic patio furniture had been sitting outside in the weather for twenty years. The plastic that hadn't cracked was so badly weather-worn that it felt like sandpaper and was permanently stained by black mold. Colonies of what looked suspiciously like brown recluse spiders had built their nests in the niches on the undersides of several chairs. So, on the morning of her luncheon visit, I launched another last-minute campaign to create a good impression. I purchased an $800 patio set with table, chairs, cushions, canvas canopy, and the heavy round thingy that sits on the ground and holds the pole, whatever that thing is called.

To bring my new purchase of patio furniture home from the nearby hardware store, I had time for just one trip. All this stuff had to fit into my Honda Civic, with emphasis on the word *stuff*. Luckily, the hardware store offered me all the twine I needed.

Now, you lady readers will probably not be too interested in the rest of this paragraph, which focuses on car-packing strategies, which is definitely not going to be as much fun as watching the old episodes of Desperate Housewives. Therefore, you have my permission to skim through this part or maybe even skip it altogether. You guy readers, though, will be thoroughly impressed with my skill, savviness, and creative genius regarding my solutions to the challenging task at hand.

The six new metal chairs stacked nicely together, but with the trunk lid fully open, I could fit only the back legs into the trunk. I lashed the chair backs to the trunk lid, fearfully wrapping the rather wimpy twine fifteen times around the assembly, with the front legs precariously hanging out into the air behind the license plate on the rear bumper, defying gravity. Table legs laid across the back seat, inside my car, but the door on one side wouldn't quite close. I ran twine through the car interior and tied the elbow-rests of the two back-doors together, thus securing the partially open door. The thing-with-no-name sat on the front seat, passenger side, squashing the air out of the cushion. I laid the tabletop onto four fluffy outdoor chair pads placed on the roof of the car and cinched it down with twine laced across the interior of the car through the windows, cracked open. The roof made a buckling oil-can sound as I tightened down on the twines. The umbrella canopy thrust through the trunk and pierced into the interior of the car, thanks to the back seat that flopped down. Impaling the entire interior of the car, back to front, the umbrella's crown rested on a cushion placed on top of the dashboard to the right of the steering wheel. It hovered above the center console, so that I had just enough room to operate the stick-shift while sliding my hand through the draping cloth folds of the canopy. I stuffed the remaining chair cushions into the car wherever I could find any room, filling all the voids. By the time the Civic was fully loaded, it looked like Jed Clampett and the Beverly Hillbillies were moving to Omaha.

Luckily, I had to drive only a mile from the store to my home. Creeping through the neighborhood at about ten miles per hour, I expected one of the speed bumps to break my twines and cause the entire load to be strewn onto the street. Upon arriving home, I squeezed two hours of required assembly time into one. I threw the old plastic furniture into the corner of the backyard and draped a tarp over the pile. Stressed out and sweaty, I took ten minutes to shower, shave, brush my teeth, and slip into some casual clothes. Finishing just in time for Karen's arrival, I successfully pulled off the illusion of myself as a carefree and leisurely guy, ready to enjoy a casual lunch. Ahhh! The things men do behind the scenes to impress the ladies.

PATIO FURNITURE...$800

In the weeks following the Rockets reunion, in contrast to my interest in Karen, Karen was not especially interested in me. After all, how stupid would it be to become involved with an old guy who lives four thousand miles away from her home in Paris, and a chunky one to boot? Eventually, I became aware of Karen's plan to pawn me off on one of the many available Nebraska ladies. I imagined her idea to sound something like, "Steve's nice enough, but he's too fat for me. I'll set him up with one of my heavier lady friends." At her mother's place, she had scheduled a patio party for every Saturday evening, BYOB potluck, spread out over the entirety of her stay in Nebraska before returning to Paris. Karen invited me to all six of them and I attended them all.

It was rather surprising to me the number of unattached sixty-year-old ladies there were from our high school class of 530 kids, including divorced, widowed, and otherwise single women. Add to that all the other "friend of a friend" female attendees. Unlike all those skinny men dressed in black walking the sidewalks of Paris, these Nebraskan ladies were used to old guys like me that were more than filled out. At one of Karen's patio parties, there were twelve unattached women... and me... the only guy. I should have felt like I had my very own harem, but it was more like I was a toy boy to be auctioned off to the highest bidder. I had to fend off several advances. Whenever I received the chatty attentions of a lady, one defense mechanism usually worked. I proclaimed to be hard of hearing. This gave me the excuse to ignore her advances and invitations while keeping my focus on Karen.

PARTY FOOD AND DRINKS.. $300

For my third attempt at a "date," I invited Karen to a steak dinner. *This should be a safe choice for a date*, I told myself. Karen and I were to meet on a Wednesday evening at Round-the-Bend Steak House, near the small town of South Bend. It was halfway between Omaha and Lincoln, and we drove separately to the rendezvous. Dinner for two.

When Karen arrived at the steakhouse, unbeknownst to me, she had brought along our mutual friend, Linda, one of those unattached classmates of ours. Contrary to my goal of hooking up with Karen, Karen had decided that I was a good match for Linda. "*This isn't good, Steve,*" I said to myself. Dinner for three wasn't what I had planned. *The team is losing. It's halftime. Need to change the game plan.*

The dinner didn't turn out to be a total waste of time and money, though. One good thing came from it. Linda and I got to know each other better. When Karen went to the restroom, Linda confided in me. Linda was savvy enough to see that I wasn't interested in her and that my attentions were focused on Karen. Linda wasn't interested in me either, and she said so. "You're not my type, Steve." She gave me some coaching on how to warm up Karen. "Now, look, Steve, you know that French double-air-kiss thing that Karen does?" Karen was in the habit of greeting everyone in the French way, with two cheek-to-cheek kisses, which had become an exaggerated ritual and a source of awkward amusement when greeting all her clueless Nebraska friends. Linda said, "That Frenchie double-cheek-kiss thing just doesn't cut the mustard. If you are interested in her, you've got to get a *Front and Center Kiss* out of her... *Full body! On the lips!* If you don't get that before she leaves for Paris, you've got nothing. *Do you understand me?"* I agreed. Linda's comments were reminiscent of the old Ronald Reagan movie where the Notre Dame football coach gave "the Gipper" an inspirational speech at the end of the game, five points down, with thirty seconds remaining on the clock: "You can do it. Now, get out there and *win!*"

Front and Center Kiss! Full body! On the lips! These words became my mission statement and mantra. Unfortunately, as ladies do, Linda chatted about my situation with our mutual friend, Lynn, who proceeded to lay a kiss on me at the next patio party: *Front and Center Kiss! Full body! On the lips!*... ambushing me as I walked through the kitchen door at Karen's house. The problem was that she was not the woman I was in hot pursuit of.

THREE STEAK DINNERS AND DRINKS........................$240

During Karen's stay in Nebraska, it was hard for me to make a favorable impression and maintain the illusion of my good taste, considering that I hadn't been shopping for new clothes in many years. And, when I found some decent clothes in my closet, they were pretty baggy and droopy, looking rather tent-like, considering my recently successful crash weight-loss program. My reentry into the dating game required a new wardrobe of super-cool casual clothes: $125 tan penny loafer shoes, $110 khaki deck pants, $55 Hawaiian shirt, $10 beige casual socks with a subtle stripe, and $30 for alterations to reduce the waistline of my three pair of shorts from forty-two inches to thirty-six.

Then there were all those charges for long-distance phone calls, emails, snail mailings of thank-you cards from Hallmark with the cute messages. And, let us not forget the money spent on gasoline (round trip from Omaha to Lincoln = 100 miles @33 miles per gallon = 3 gallons of gas x $3.33 per gallon = $10 per trip x 10 trips = $100).

OTHER EXPENSES..$430

On her last weekend before returning to Paris, Karen had scheduled yet another backyard party for Saturday night at her place. I would drive to Lincoln from Omaha again. Karen phoned me and invited me to stay overnight. "Bring your jammies," she said. After we hung up, I repeated the phrase out loud, *"Bring your jammies?"* presenting it to myself as a question. Now, any red-blooded guy would assume that *THIS IS IT! D-DAY! STORM THE BEACHES! FULL SPEED AHEAD! LOCK AND LOAD! ASSAULT THE HILL!* (The testosterone surging in my blood didn't allow my rational self to consider the possibility that Karen was innocently offering the option to sleep over to save me from driving home drunk or to consider that the offer had gone out to others, too.)

Unfortunately, I had been sleeping in my underwear ever since I left home for college forty-two years ago. I didn't even own a set of "jammies," having somehow missed out on twenty-five years of Father's Day gift opportunities. Intent on making the most of the situation, I decided to buy some pajamas. But nooo, I didn't want to buy just any pair of cheap plaid cotton pajamas that you could purchase at Target or Walmart. I needed some pajamas that were top-notch. After all... *THIS WAS IT!* So, I walked into the Von Maur store for the first time in my life and headed for the men's clothing department. They had the cheap plaid cotton jammies, too. But in anticipation of my upcoming *ENCOUNTER WITH DESTINY*, I asked the clerk: "Got anything fancier?" Now, this clerk was one of those prissy, sensitive guys you always find in the men's clothing department, with his measuring tape draped around his neck. Over the top of his glasses, he took a minute to look me over. With reluctance, he decided that, even though I was dressed like a clodhopper, he would show me the fancier pajamas. (You city types would like to know that "clodhopper" is derogatory slang meaning "farmer.") The special pajamas were behind the glass counter, not to be touched by just anyone who walked in. They were black, made of silk, and had a delicate white cord that trimmed the edges of the collar, seams, and cuffs. The clerk raised one eyebrow and scanned my reaction as he presented them to me, folded in his hands.

"Hmmm. How much?" I asked.

"Before tax," he said, "$149.99." he said. As I pondered the price, he elongated his neck, moved his chin forward and slightly tilted his head.

"Got my size?" I asked. At this moment, I felt like I had just crossed some territorial border and was about to be shot for trespassing.

"Well!" he said hesitantly. "We'll just have to take a look." He eyeballed me, again, top to bottom, this time to estimate my size, then turned and made his selection from the elegant stack of black silk pajamas. "These will probably fit you, but I recommend you try them on to be sure. The dressing rooms are just over there." He daintily unfolded them and handed them to me. "Be careful," he cautioned in a rather effeminate voice. "Rough hands can snag the silk."

The fit was fine. *Yeah, baby!* I said to myself as I stared at the dressing room mirror. *Move over, Hugh Hefner.*

SILK PAJAMAS..$155

The fifty-mile drive between Omaha and Lincoln was taking way too much time. On this Saturday, I had gotten another late start, having had another full day in at the office. And the purchase of the black silk pajamas took longer than expected. I was hurrying to get out of town, in hot pursuit of a babe who had just invited me to stay overnight at her place. It was after dark when I crossed the Platte River Bridge on the interstate, which was about halfway between Lincoln and Omaha. I was on the cellphone to Karen, explaining that I was running a bit late, when I noticed the flashing red lights in my mirror. I glanced down at the speedometer, and I was cruising at about eighty-five down the interstate that was posted at seventy-five. "Shit!" I said. "Got to go. Have a police car on my tail. Call you later." I was cussing myself, because they had ticketed me at this same location in the past. The Cass County Highway Patrol had a routine of staking out this stretch of highway. After I set the phone down on the seat, I noticed I was cruising past a bunch of yellow blinking lights. "Shit... SHIT!" I was in a construction zone which was posted at "fifty-five," and "Fines Doubled." I pulled over to a stop.

As the officer walked toward my car, I mentally ran through the plausible excuses for my speeding. The first one was: *I was running late for a date with this hot babe.* This might have scored some sympathy points with an older guy like me, but not with this young woman who was approaching. My second excuse: *I was on the cellphone and...* I quickly dismissed that idea. Luckily, the legislation outlawing the use of phones while driving was still in the discussion phase at the Nebraska State House. Then, remembering an incident from my past, I considered telling a bald-faced lie: *Well, Officer; I lost track of my speed when I picked a big booger out of my nose, which had a long, gooey tail, which sagged across my lap and onto the steering wheel...* By this point, the officer was at my window. I decided that my best option was to fake a sad look of regret, apologize, and hope for some sympathy. "Sorry, Officer, I wasn't paying attention to my speed."

She issued me a ticket for $250 and offered the parting refrain: "Slow it down, buddy." As I drove away, while carefully signaling my lane change, I realized that her words of wisdom applied to both my driving and my dating expenditures.

SPEEDING TICKET.. $250

All this "dating" added up to, let's say, a round figure of $4,000 spent over six weeks that summer in 2010 in hot pursuit of Karen. This was dramatically different from the last time I was dating, back in 1972, when the cost of taking a girl out for a burger and beer was six bucks and promised a much higher likelihood of "getting lucky."

GRAND TOTAL.. +/- $4,000

CHAPTER 19

The Moment

Nebraska, August 2010

Don't forget that all during Karen's six-week stay in Nebraska, I was on my *"The Joy of the Pain of Hunger and the Joy of the Pain of Exercise"* weight loss program. By the end of her stay, I had lost some fifty pounds, down from 255 to 205. If I stood at just the right angle in the bathroom light, I could see those youthful ripples showing through my tummy fat. I had a few other attributes to flaunt too: college educated, architect, *recently widowed*. And now, with my weight problem melting away, I was becoming a "good catch" for any of the patio ladies. And in the last days of her stay in Nebraska, Karen was taking notice.

In my mind, up to this point, I had been out with Karen on several dates. You know: a guy and a girl... *dates!* As it turns out, Karen had considered none of these to be "dates" at all. Not the bike ride, not the steakhouse dinner, not the Saturday lunch at my place, not any of our other get-togethers, outings, or parties. She had been thinking that all these were just casual meetings between good friends, nothing serious.

It finally came down to Karen's last weekend and her very last patio party before returning to Paris. I arrived a bit late, delayed by my pajamas purchase and speeding ticket. It was an evening similar to previous ones, with a flock of available women chasing me around the patio. It was 1:00 a.m. when the party ended and everyone finally had gone. Karen and I had been drinking all night and were both pretty blotto'd. We were now alone together in her house. There was some cleanup and put-away work in the kitchen that we did together, and we talked casually. Earlier in the evening, I began to understand that she had expected others to stay over too. Her invitation had been open to anyone who didn't want to drive home drunk, and it was not specifically directed at me. I was the only one to accept the invitation. I was definitely not capable of driving home safely. Karen prepared a bedroom for my stay, and I helped her make the bed. She returned to the kitchen to check her emails one last time. After carefully removing all the sales tags and stick-on labels, I slipped into my new black silk "jammies" and put on my best impression of Hugh Hefner. *THE MOMENT OF DESTINY* had arrived.

Then, *THE MOMENT* vanished. In her emails, Karen received news from Paris that her best friend's husband had just died. Karen had to reach out to her people in Paris. She was about to shift into email mode that would last several more hours into the night. I understood. There we were, standing in the kitchen, barefoot, in my new pajamas. We gave each other a big hug, and I said something like, "Look after your friend, and I'll see you in the morning."

With tears welling up in her eyes, and perhaps with some sort of appreciation for my having released her to pursue her emails, Karen responded with something completely unexpected. She said, "I love you, Steve." We hugged again and said good night.

I turned and took several steps down the hall toward the bedroom. The gravity of Karen's words took a few seconds to sink into my soggy brain. At the moment of realization, I did an about-face and returned to the kitchen. Karen hadn't moved. I said, "I think I like you too." She stood there, dumbstruck and speechless.

I turned and walked away again, then kicked myself for saying the wrong thing. "*I think I like you?*" I thought. *You dumb shit! TRY AGAIN!* I turned and walked back into the kitchen, this time saying, "I mean... I think I *love* you too."

Karen was standing motionless, like a tree trunk in the kitchen, with a concerned and confused look on her face, which I assumed to result from a desperate search for a graceful way to retract her statement. It was too late.

I turned and took three steps toward the bedroom again, thinking, *No, no, you stupid ass, get it right.* I did a quick about-face again, marching back into the kitchen for the third time and said, "Karen, I meant to say I love you too." We hugged again, said good night again.

As I started down the hall toward the bedroom in my black silk pajamas for the fourth time, I thought, *That wasn't fair. She scooped me. I was in love first! I should have been the first to say it.*

My guess was that, as Karen sat down to start her emails, she was probably going through a painful process of questioning her choice of words and concluding something like, *"What have I done? Stoopid woman!"*

I crawled into bed, realizing that an opportunity had passed. SHIT! *That was the perfect time for a "Front and Center Kiss! Full Body! On the Lips!"* But I was too tired and too drunk to walk back into the kitchen again.

Sunday morning, Karen and I acted like nothing had happened the night before. That was then; this is now. She had done her emails into the early morning hours and slept downstairs on the couch in the family room. It was shaping up to be a beautiful summer day, and I had no urgency to return to Omaha, so we decided to take our bicycles on a ride down the trail along Highway 77 to the south. At about forty-five minutes out, we stopped at a picnic shelter to sit down, take a break, and have a drink from our water bottles. There were two picnic tables under the shelter. Karen sat on the bench of one table, and I sat on the bench of the other table, facing each other. There was a beautiful sunlit backdrop of trees and hills behind Karen. So that she could see the beautiful view better, I invited her to move over to my bench. As she sat down next to me, she snuggled up close, and I put my arm around her. We sat together for some time, Karen talking softly about her friend in Paris and losing her husband. She laid her head on my shoulder. We sat, not saying anything, floating in the comfort of each other's company. At this moment, we knew that our fumbling around for words in the kitchen the night before was sincere... even though in Karen's mind; we had never had an official *date*, and I had not accomplished my mission of having a *Front-and-Center, Full-body Kiss on the Lips*.

Karen was scheduled to fly out midday Wednesday to Paris. I had to get back to Omaha to take care of a few things at the start of my workweek. Before parting company on Sunday evening, Karen and I had dinner, our first official date, and when we said goodbye, we kissed, finally accomplished my mission. We agreed I would come back to Lincoln Tuesday evening, and I would stay over, taking a day off work on Wednesday to get Karen to the airport.

On Tuesday evening, Karen invited her four closest lady friends over for a small goodbye gathering. It was necessary for me to work late again, and I wouldn't arrive until the end of the evening. I called Karen to let her know I was on my way, ETA 10:00 pm. The ladies later revealed to me they knew something was up when, immediately after my call, Karen abruptly made an announcement to them. "Steve is arriving shortly. You all have to go now." I arrived as they were all out in the front yard saying their goodbyes, each receiving a French air-kiss on each cheek from Karen. Each lady filed past me, giving me a quick hug and goodbye, along with a sly wink, a whispering of "Congratulations!" in my ear, or a sly sideways smile. Linda, the last of the ladies to leave, put on her best May West look and said, "Way to go, big guy." With the ladies gone, Karen and I went into the house together.

Now, sex between two sixty-year-old people is not what sells tickets to the Hollywood blockbusters. Besides the age issue, factor in that "old, tired and ugly" Steve had not been much of a sex-meister in recent years and that I hadn't had fresh new sex in decades. You could say I was a bit rusty. Also, you need to visualize a lady who considers herself to be the preeminent queen of multi-tasking, who, in addition to a night of taking care of her man, had several other things to accomplish. She wasn't coming back to Nebraska for six months, and she needed preparation before her departure. This included packing for her trip, getting out a last-minute batch of emails, resetting the furnace and humidity controls, shutting down the water heater, locking all the doors, cleaning dishes left by the ladies, pouring bleach into the drains, and printing a boarding pass. The lockdown of her house included sliding shut all those crummy storm windows from the '60s that break your fingernails, taking the garbage sacks over to the neighbors' bins, making sure all the lights were off and the electric appliances unplugged, and, after a few episodes of *A-Roll-in-the-Hay*, showering and taking care of personal hygiene, then cleaning the towels and putting them away. I probably have left a few things out, but you get the idea. Let us not forget that superimposed on top of all of that, she spent a good amount of quality time with her man! Luckily, she was going to have plenty of time to rest once she was on the plane for the twelve-hour flight to Paris. Now, me, I go to bed... I sleep. Karen, on this night, was jumping around between me and those other tasks, all night long, like a jackrabbit on a hot asphalt parking lot in Phoenix in the middle of the summer. Needless to say, I had a long night of brief naps between "activities" and was pretty tuckered out by the time we got her to the airport.

After all that, the good news was that we had found each other. And we both knew it as we said our goodbyes.

CHAPTER 20
The Bach

New Zealand, December 2010

Through the late summer of 2010, Karen and I kept in contact by email and phone. Karen's phone service in France was inexpensive, with unlimited overseas calling, so we spent a lot of time talking to each other. The *L* word was pretty regularly used, both ways. It seemed easy to talk about our newfound love from a distance. I remember that, as a young man, this word, *love*, left a pasty aftertaste in my mouth. But now, I had outgrown my youthful resistance to it. I could freely talk about it with Karen. I was happy to be in love again. Joy had returned to me, and a long, dark spell had ended. In contrast to my gloomy perspective from the previous year, I now had a new vitality. My life was not over. A future was there for me to reach out to.

Karen's employer had recently given her a buy-out package, and she officially retired. With her free time, she planned to do some traveling and had scheduled a six-week trip to New Zealand, Australia, and Tasmania in November and December 2010. She asked if I wanted to travel with her for part of the trip. I could swing ten days of vacation time and said yes.

My close friend and neighbor, Robyn, was born in New Zealand and raised on an apple farm northwest of Nelson. Her family owned a cabin on the ocean, on the northernmost tip of the South Island, which I rented for ten days. In the early history of New Zealand, the first settlers were sheep farmers, most of them being unmarried men who lived out in the hills in their little bachelor cabins. Over time, the two-word term *bachelor cabin* shortened to *"bach,"* which now had become a contemporary reference to any small cabin. In my case, the American term *bachelor pad* would more precisely describe my intentions. This was a rather experimental rendezvous, considering that Karen and I had been intimate only one night, and it had been four months since we had last seen each other.

Karen had been touring the north island of New Zealand for a few weeks prior to my meeting up with her at the Nelson airport on the South Island. She and I had continued on our weight loss routines through the summer and were both as slim and trim as we had been in many years. I was down to 180 pounds, which was a weight that I hadn't seen in thirty years.

My flight in from Los Angeles arrived late, and I missed my scheduled short flight from Auckland to Nelson. Karen was waiting for me at the Nelson airport and looked at all the male passengers as they exited from my scheduled flight. I had lost so much weight (seventy-five pounds!) that she was fearful that she could not recognize me in that group of passengers. She frantically inspected the arriving male passengers several times before she could convince herself that I had not been on this flight. After she calmed down, she could confirm at the desk that I would arrive on the next flight a couple of hours later.

She recognized me immediately as I stepped off the plane. In fact, I was looking more like the high school kid she knew forty-two years ago than the sixty-year-old that she had become reacquainted with last summer. We tentatively hugged and greeted each other, sizing each other up, not wanting to create a public scene in the airport's lobby. Karen, in fact, had a fairly strong dislike of PDA (Public Display of Affection) whereby young couples would wrap around each other like wrestlers, proudly practicing their smooching skills while intentionally standing on the busiest sidewalk corner so that everyone passing by got an eyeful. We waited for my bags to arrive, calmly chatting, fighting off our hidden desires to grab each other and smooch. Then we headed out the door.

The Nelson airport is fairly small and has only one main set of doors into the lobby. Ironically, as we were leaving the building, we ran into a Nebraska acquaintance of mine, precisely fitting the phrase *it's a small world*. It was Ducker, whose wife was from my neighborhood in Omaha. They were living in retirement here in New Zealand. After introductions and a quick description of our situation, I concluded with a phrase that would be repeated many times, to become the motto for Karen and me: "We're two old people having fun." At the end of our chat, Ducker gave us an open invitation to visit him and his wife in Nelson sometime while we were here, and we parted company.

Karen and I hauled my bags out to her rental car in the parking lot. The car was located a discrete distance away from the front door of the airport. By this time, Karen and I had shed our tentativeness about each other. We dropped my bags on the ground next to the car, and capitalizing on the private location, came together in a *Front-and-Center, Full-Body Kiss on the Lips*. Lingering in the embrace, perhaps a little too long, we leaned up against the car. We didn't know it, but as Ducker returned to his car, he caught sight of us in the middle of our over-extended smooch. He kept himself hidden and watched, soaking up the view of these "two old people having fun." With a few choice words of embellishment, he turned the scene into a dramatically exaggerated storyline to be repeated regularly and exuberantly to our mutual friends on his annual holiday visits to Omaha.

The bach at Golden Bay was a little, white cabin with a black shingle roof. It was long and thin, stretched out along the ocean frontage. There was a wooden deck along the sea-side yard. The bach nestled into thick shrubs and small trees, which effectively isolated the cabin from its neighbors up and down the beach. A big crescent of ocean frontage stretched for miles, with a beautiful sandy beach that was a soft beige color, wide and flat. Chest-high vegetation separated the cabin from the beach, covering a barrier hump of sandy soil. A single footpath led through the vegetation up and over the hump, down and out onto the vast and empty beach and seascape that was surprisingly devoid of people or boats.

It was early December, one of the first days of summer for the southern hemisphere. Upon our afternoon arrival at the bach, we found the cabin to be uncomfortably hot inside. There was no air-conditioning. We threw open the windows and slider doors to let the breeze waft through. But it was a hot day, and there was not much of a breeze. Karen and I had been talking about our love long-distance, using phone calls and email, over the past four months. We had shared only the one night of physical intimacies prior to that, in late July, and to use movie lingo, that night was a *rough cut*, dramatically needing a *retake*. We had both waited for this moment to arrive with great anticipation.

Now, the hot weather was not cooperating. But we were not to be denied. We threw our attentions at each other. We began tearing each other's clothes off and dropping a trail of them onto the floor as we shuffled through the cabin toward the bedroom. Hot or not, this was going to happen. We were both naked by the time we plopped onto the bed, immediately discovering that there were not enough wooden slats under the mattress. The slats bowed and popped loose, one after the other, in a dominos effect, slapping onto the floor with a loud clatter. The mattress sagged dramatically under our weight into a deep bowl, touching the floor in the middle. After recovering from our surprise, we hopped up and reinstalled the slats. By this point, we were two old naked people, drenched in sweat in a boiling hot bedroom, imagining more of the same over the week ahead.

As luck would have it, I had seen that there was a ceiling fan in the living room. It was the only fan in the cabin. "Karen, hold on a minute. I've got an idea." Stark naked, I bolted to the living room, found the controls on the wall, and tried to start the ceiling fan. "It works!" I said, as I turned the controls to the fan's highest setting. Without further words, Karen came into the living room to help with the next obvious challenge. Sweaty, naked, and old, the two of us lifted the coffee table and moved it across the room, out of the way. The coffee table was made from the stump of a tree, cut to coffee-table height, and weighed about 150 pounds.

Now, we had an open patch of floor under the ceiling fan. We raced back into the bedroom and, like two seasoned moving-and-storage guys, we lifted the mattress off of the bed, turned it onto its side, set it onto the floor, and slid it out the bedroom door. We plopped it down onto the living room floor under the fan, fitted sheet intact. Finally, our *MOMENT OF DESTINY* had arrived. With both of us covered with sweat, head to toe, and with the fan blowing full speed down onto us, we cooled down pretty fast, becoming a living example of how evaporative cooling really works.

The mattress stayed there on the floor of the living room for all ten days of our stay. Although we had to hastily get our clothes on and slide the mattress back into the bedroom on Wednesday late morning when the neighbor showed up to loan me some fishing equipment. Luckily, he came to the front door, and *not* around back to the open screen doors on the ocean side of the cabin, where he would have gotten a view to the inside worthy of late-night HBO. (I should say... I *hope* he came to the front door first!)

Keeping true to our new motto, "two old people having fun," our typical New Zealand day consisted of late-morning adult entertainment and afternoon hikes. My friend, the owner of the batch, had given me a list of wilderness hikes in the area. Karen and I walked one each day. The landscapes along the northernmost tip of the South Island were exhilarating. Giant sand dunes lapped against rugged cliffs. Ocean overlooks, tidal pools, and mussel-encrusted water caves exposed themselves to the air at low tide. An occasional lazy seal pulled up onto one of the endless beaches. Cold mountain streams cut through steamy, hot, subtropical forests. Grazing sheep spotted rolling grass pastures. There was a distinct lack of people. We walked alone for hours on end, surprising ourselves with our stamina.

Exhausted from a long day of hiking, a late dinner and a bottle of wine would finish our evening. The wines in New Zealand were top-notch. We drank a bottle a day, stacking the dead men in a row across the fireplace mantle like trophies. We would sleep late in the morning. Brunch with poached eggs, bacon, orange juice, fried potatoes, toast, and coffee would re-energize us to a point of recognition that the person sitting across the table was waiting to be played with. In the future, Karen and I would refer to our stay in New Zealand as our honeymoon, although it was premature for either of us to see it.

CHAPTER 21

Love

Omaha, Christmas 2010

The easiest thing to say is that this is a love story. But love is supposed to be for young people embarking together into an unknown future, not for two over-sixty people, set in their ways, comfortable in the rhythms of their lives, at the tail end of their existence, only to be knocked off track, discombobulated, giddy, weirded out by the discovery of another person. Love is some sort of insanity. Common sense is thrown out the window. What the hell. The math doesn't work. "Illogical," as Spock would say. Two people who have lives four thousand miles apart, on either side of the Atlantic. Why would you even consider trying to put a relationship together? How was it that Karen, a French citizen living in Paris, a person who had lived a life as a single professional woman of the world, childless, hooked up with me, a family guy in Nebraska who had raised three kids and lived in the same house and kept the same job for thirty-five years? You worked your whole life and put something of value together, only to throw it all at a stranger in the fourth quarter? Insanity.

Immediately after our blissful ten days in New Zealand, I returned to Nebraska, and Karen extended her tour with a visit to Australia. During my long flight home, I handwrote a note to Karen. Surprisingly, at sixty years old, there I was, writing my first ever love poem. I sent it to her attention, at the address of the friends she was visiting in Australia, arriving just before Christmas 2010.

Dear Karen:

I love your zest for life, your joyfulness, the ease with which you offer your friendship.

I love the way you helped me find my way through the darkness, into the light.

I love the way you seek and enjoy the beauty of the natural world surrounding us.

I love the time we shared in New Zealand, the bach, the beach, the sea.

I love our physical closeness, the bicycle rides, our hikes and walks, our joyful intimacies.

I love the soft beauty that lays across your face as you sleep.

I love our long phone calls, our talks on the porch and patio, the emails and texts.

I love your touch, your scent, the silky warmth of your skin against mine, your kiss.

I love the physical changes in me, the return of my youthful physical self, brought on by you.

I love being in love. What a surprise it is to find love at this time in my life.

I love that you have helped me find a future life that can be as meaningful as my past life.

I love your funky hair that has to be clamped down into submission.

I love your intellect, your purposefulness, your willful and zesty attack on life.

I love that we are searching for a way to find a place for each other, to share each other's life.

Steve

Did I really write this mushy crap? Ugh! In another fit of insanity, I sent Karen a second love note. I can't recall exactly what it was for... either Valentine's Day, or our reunion anniversary, or perhaps a birthday card. But I do recall that it was important! It had to be special and had to be mailed that day! *Let me think... Aha! A butterfly! OK!* I banged the closet door open and grabbed colored papers. Orange and yellow, cut and glue, a message scribbled onto the wings. I stuck it into an envelope while the Elmer's was still wet and rushed off to the postal box. *Damn, I'm late for work again*!

Karen:
Before you entered my life,
I was old and tired, weighted down by life, slowly crawling through the undergrowth, heading toward my cocoon.

When you entered my life, I was reborn, youthful, energetic, joyful, flittering about on colorful wings, seeking the sweetness of life.
Steve

Yuck! More gobbledygook. Like I said, love is some kind of insanity. It has happened to me twice. There were many brushes with love, near misses, false starts... but only two *big ones*. When Sharon and I were young and in love, there was no conscious attempt to understand it or talk about it. It just happened. But with Karen and me, we recognized it for what it was, chatted about it, texted, sent emails.

Meanwhile, Karen had returned to Paris, and I remained in Omaha. And, in the middle of all this love chatter, I still had a job to do at the office. As I put the final touches on the design of Red Owl's Hoop of Life building, I wondered how falling in love might have been for young Dakota people, a century and a half ago, out on the open prairie...

CHAPTER 22
The Cottonwood Limb

Central Minnesota 1856

One of the older Dakota boys walks towards the horses through the tall grass along the river's edge. It is the task of the boys bordering on manhood to watch after the herd during the daylight hours. The wealth of the people resides in the horses and watching the herd is of high importance. It is no small effort to keep the herd intact. The horses are not tied up or penned in but free-range. They graze close to the encampment and are naturally bonded to their people. Ojibwe raiders, intent on stealing horses, will come under the cover of night, making the task of watching the horses in the darkness fall to the young men of the tribe who have achieved warrior status. Horse raid conflicts are violent and brutal, requiring necessary acts of bravery. But during the lazy sunny afternoons, watching the horses is fairly safe. It is a good duty for the older boys who are at that in-between age, not children anymore, but not yet men. Even so, this boy is prematurely harboring the idea that he already is a warrior. He is the stereotypical warrior-wannabe.

Late summer reduced the river to a narrow flow in the center channel. As the boy walks through the undergrowth, he catches sight of a girl down at the riverbank. He recognizes the girl, who is about his age, but he doesn't really know her very well. He stealthily approaches and stops behind a thick tuft of tall grass, hidden from view.

Of necessity, young people of the camp have naturally fallen into two separate groups, with boys supporting the hunting, horse, and warrior duties and girls helping with the in-camp routines of cooking, caring for the children, and making clothes. One result of this division by gender is the perpetuation of a profound inability to understand the mysterious inner workings within the minds of the opposite sex. A second result... love.

A wide band of nasty green slime and mud runs along the edge of the river. The girl is thinking about how best to retrieve clean channel water without getting her deer-hide skirt soiled. The encampment is new to this location and day-to-day routines have not yet adjusted to the features of the unfamiliar landscape. Her assignment is to scout the river and find the best place to collect water. She has two water sacks to fill and bring back to the camp. The girl had fashioned the sacks and their shoulder straps from the stomachs of deer. She finds a low-slung cottonwood limb that has split away from an old mother tree and fallen. The large limb has dropped straight out into the river, its heavy trunk resting on dry soil. The trunk arches out over the muddy embankment and separates into smaller limbs and branches as it reaches out to the clear, flowing water of the center channel.

The girl sees this fallen limb as her chance to avoid the mud and retrieve some clean water. As the boy watches from his hidden vantage point behind the tall grass, she bends down to remove her moccasins. Beautifully crafted by her own hands, a colorful design of beads adorn the moccasins. Holding a moccasin in her hand, she gazes deeply at it with pride.

The boy was dumbstruck by the sight before him. He follows with his eyes the frilly seam of her skirt as it gracefully rolls over her hips and down to her bent knees, then folds back to reveal her bare ankles. He stealthily watches from his hiding place as the young lady pulls her skirt up over her knees. She raises one leg up and over, mounting the limb like you would a horse. The boy studies the lines of her youthful legs as she saddles out onto the limb, her bare feet dangling just above the slimy surface of mud.

As she inches ever closer to the clear water in the center of the channel, she is confronted with the log separating into smaller branches. Placing her hands and feet onto separate branches, the girl crawls further out. The boy watches the girl's crab-like movements and catches tantalizing glimpses of a raised skirt. She finally positions herself, standing barefoot on a rather small-diameter branch at the waterline. While holding on to an overhead branch with one hand, she leans forward to fill the bladder bags with water. As she hoists the full bags up and slings their straps over her shoulder, the added weight causes the supporting branches to break.

The girl descends in slow motion into the water, frantically grabbing at smaller branches which break off in her fingers. As she drops into the shallow water, her feet touch bottom and sink ankle deep into the mud. She desperately sloshes her way towards shore, while attempting to climb back up onto the branches. Unable to lift herself back onto the tree trunk, she wallows through the mud at the river's edge. Finally, stepping out onto stable ground, she looks down at her mud-splattered skirt, sloshes, raises her hands into the air, and releases a long groan of frustration. As her voice trails off into the air, she spots the young man standing behind the thick tuft of grass.

The boy steps out from his hiding place and giggles at the girl. Embarrassed, the girl blurts out, "Stop laughing! It isn't funny!" The boy brings his giggles under control. After an awkward silence, she yells again, "Go away!" The boy turns and walks off, giving an amused glance over his shoulder as the girl cleans herself.

Fifty yards down the river, the boy encounters a dry gully that he needs to cross. In wet weather, the gully flows with water and feeds into the side of the larger river. Now, the gully is empty, its floor dried to hardpan. Large flakes of dried mud and cracks create a pattern on the dry surface. The flakes are hand-size, with edges curled upward, like large dry leaves.

The boy quicksteps down the embankment and out onto the floor of the gully. As he reaches the mid-point of the crossing, the seemingly hard surface of the stream bed cracks open under his weight. He immediately sinks to his waist, into a quagmire of thick, brown-black mud. He tries to move toward the edge of the gully but sinks farther into the mud. Now, up to his chest, he tries to lean forward and swim through the mud, but his struggles only cause him to sink more. With only his head, neck, shoulders, and arms above the mud, he stops struggling, spreads his arms out flat on the surface of the quagmire and becomes filled with fright. He will not get out of this! His thoughts return to the girl nearby, and he screams to her, *"HELP! HELP ME! I'm SINKING IN MUD! PLEASE! COME QUICK!"*

He pauses, listens, then yells again at the top of his lungs, *"HELP ME! HELP!"*

The girl stops her scrubbing so that she can hear better. Recognizing the seriousness of the boy's screams, she bolts to her feet and runs barefoot toward him. She yells in response, *"I'm COMING!"* She arrives at the gully to see the boy who has nearly disappeared into the black sinkhole.

"Can't move!" His words are brief and frantic. "I'm stuck!"

The girl scrambles down the embankment and takes two steps out onto the mud flat before she realizes that she herself is about to break through the crust. She stops and carefully retreats onto the edge of the gully. "Hold on! Don't move! I'll get a branch and reach out to you!"

The boy screams, "Hurry!"

She scrambles up the embankment and scans the surroundings, finding a sturdy fallen limb tangled in the underbrush. After forcefully yanking it out of the brambles and snags, she drags it down the embankment and lunges it out onto the surface of the mud flat toward the boy.

The boy stretches out with one hand. "Not long enough! Can't reach it!"

The girl pushes hard on the branch, attempting to slide it farther out onto the surface, but it is bogged down in the mud. She steps out farther, her leading foot breaking through the hardpan, slipping into the mud. She is lucky, though, sinking only to her shin before hitting solid footing. Straining with both arms, she lifts the mud-laden branch into the air, flopping it down again, farther out, this time within the reach of the boy's outstretched hand.

"Got it!" he yells.

Slowly, strenuously, the boy drags himself forward, exiting the muck amid sucking sounds. The girl yells, struggling to hold on to the branch, leaning backwards. "Keep coming!" Finally, hand over hand, the boy extracts himself.

The two young people, caked in mud, drop side by side onto the embankment. The terror subsides, and the girl gazes down at her dress, then at the boy. He is completely covered in black goo, except for the whites of his eyes and his teeth. After a pause, she giggles.

"Stop laughing," the flustered boy blurts out. "It isn't funny."

She brings her giggles under control and exclaims, "You know, don't you? Those are the same words that I screamed at you a little while ago. Don't you remember?"

The boy fingers the mud away from his eye sockets, looks at the girl, and joins in with the giggling. "Your dress is muddy" is his teasing response, as he flicks a handful of drippy goo, adding it to her already mud-splattered skirt.

After sharing a few more giggles, the two young people climb up the embankment. "I think the best place to clean up is back at the big log," the thoughtful girl suggests. "We can climb out to the clear water in the center of the channel." The two return to the overhanging cottonwood limb.

The sure-footed boy climbs up and stands on top of the cottonwood log. He reaches down and helps the girl up. While continuing to hold each other's hands for balance, the two walk out onto the limb, stepping over the thinner branches as they go. Once over the center channel, the boy lowers the girl down by one hand. She finds sturdy footing on the sandy bottom in waist-deep clear water. The boy plops into the water next to her. A milky trail of dirty water wafts away from the two and drifts downstream. As they wash the mud from their clothes in the cool, clear current, the two young people giggle, splash, and muse about their experience.

They devise a clever way to get back to dry ground and avoid the mud along the river's edge. The boy locks the fingers of his hands together to form a stirrup, which the girl steps into. Placing one hand on the top of his head, she rises out of the water, grabbing a sturdy overhead branch and stepping onto the main limb. She then turns, reaches down, and hoists the boy up out of the water. Together, hands clasped, with the girl leading, they scamper back across the hovering cottonwood log to dry land.

After a few parting comments and a twinkle in his eye, the boy turns and sloshes off to find the horses and his companions.

"Watch out for the mudhole," the girl snickers as he walks away.

The girl finds her moccasins on the dry shoreline, and the bladder bags where she left them, hanging on a branch. She sits down on the cottonwood log to dry her clothes in the afternoon sun and breeze. Afterwards, she heads back to camp in her clean skirt and moccasins, with two bags hanging over her shoulders, bulging with fresh water.

The two young people keep the afternoon's events to themselves. It becomes their secret, the girl not wanting to be scolded by her mother, and the boy not wanting to be teased by his warrior-wannabe companions. Through this experience, these two young people find each other. As affirmation that love works in mysterious ways, their muddy encounter is the beginning of a bond that will eventually blossom.

CHAPTER 23
Paris

France, spring of 2011

The world perceives Paris to be the City of Light and the City of Love, the center of art, culture, style, and beauty. People everywhere cherish their impressions of the city's grand landmarks: Notre Dame, the Louvre, the Arc de Triomphe, and the Eiffel Tower. Markets, sidewalk cafes, galleries, street musicians, and beautiful parks... these are impressions that visitors to Paris hold dear to their hearts.

My first visit to Karen at her home in Paris was in the spring of 2011. Despite all the hype, I was inclined to give Paris a more critical eye, having a good measure of skepticism in my nature and considering myself to be a no-nonsense guy. I took some time off and planned to stay for two months. My objective was more about being with Karen and less about experiencing her place of residence. But despite my intentions, metropolitan Paris would present itself to me as a wildly different place compared to salt-of-the-earth Omaha... Duh!

As a young man, some forty years before, I had been in Paris on short a visit, but my impressions had been dulled by the passage of time and by other mind-altering influences, considering that back then I was a fully loaded hippie, wearing bell bottom blue jeans and a rope instead of a belt. On this visit, I was experiencing Paris for the first time all over again.

During the first week, I was completely disoriented. We regularly walked to our destinations. Karen was totally familiar with her city, having lived there for twenty-five years. She led the way, zig-zagging through the backstreets, avoiding the grand avenues and landmarks, always taking the most direct path. She discouraged me from pulling out my map, complaining that it marked me as a tourist. My self-perception as a fairly intelligent man in control of my world quickly dropped to that of a faithful companion, not unlike a golden retriever, happy to be following along on my imaginary leash, stopping to be petted every once in a while, and wagging my tail.

Part of my disorientation in Paris was because of the singularity of the city's architecture. Upon stepping away from the Seine River onto the side streets, it was as if I had walked into an endless maze of narrow limestone canyons. There were no tall buildings and no short ones. It seemed that they had cut the entire city from a giant block of cheese, seven stories tall and fifteen miles across.

The buildings all were so similar in design, their beige limestone facades adorned with an overabundance of carved garlands, ogee curves, floral displays, wreaths, stone faces, and the occasional cherub. For my taste, which was a mixture of easygoing rural unfussiness and modernism, these Parisian building facades were way too fussy, as if the Beaux Arts offered a dual college degree in architecture and wedding cake design. Everything looked the same to me, an impression reinforced by the repeating regiment of windows reminiscent of *Hollywood Squares* (minus the gut giggles provided by exchanges between Phyllis Diller and Mel Brooks).

Then there were the throngs of people. A typical neighborhood city block in Nebraska would have a dozen homes, counting those on both sides of the street. Assuming an average of three people per household, the total population of that single block in Omaha would be about forty people. An equal stretch of neighborhood in Paris would have a solid wall of housing on both sides of the street, stacked seven stories high, holding 130 apartments. That is equivalent to four hundred Parisians living on the same acreage as forty Nebraskans. That's right, ten times as many people on the same plot of land! And superimposed on that were the throngs of tourists! No wonder good ol' Nebraska Steve was feeling a little uncomfortable, craving the wide-open spaces of home.

When this mass of humanity spills out onto the narrow sidewalks at rush hour, Parisians very often resort to territorial displays to defend their sidewalk space. "This is *my* sidewalk, and you other people don't exist." A repeating occurrence would involve an approaching female assertively marching straight at me from the opposite direction. Her gaze would be into the distance as if she had X-ray vision, and I was invisible. Not breaking stride, she would march forward, causing me to dodge to the side at the last minute, not unlike that '50s American movie where two guys in white T-shirts and duck-tail hairdos "play chicken" in their cars.

One complication is that Parisian sidewalks can be very narrow, often only three feet wide, just barely having enough shoulder room for two people, assuming there is no signpost or garbage can in the way. A properly trained Nebraskan would pause, lift his cowboy hat, and say, "Pardon me" *before* passing a lady too closely on the sidewalk, in a manner of asking permission to pass. A Parisian, in contrast, would use the word "Pardon" *after* banging into your shoulder, then continue walking away, too consumed by personal issues to be concerned about the carton of broken eggs in your grocery sack.

At first, I perceived this as an exhibition of arrogance, believing that all Parisians were insensitive snobs. It took me a while to realize that this behavior was a natural reaction to hordes of people jamming onto the sidewalk at the same time. My guess was that this was not just a Parisian characteristic, but one common to all major metropolises. If all these urbanites were to adopt the Nebraskan version of sidewalk politeness, entire economies would grind to a stop. After my first few weeks in Paris, I began to use X-ray vision to cause people to disappear and adopted my own version of sidewalk snobbery. "This is *my* sidewalk and you other yahoos don't exist."

Certain Parisian women have adopted another method of sidewalk ownership. This method has a fairly long descriptive title. It is the "Don't you hear me clomping my fancy shoes behind you?" method. The noise of their clomping heels is effectively used to move slower pedestrian traffic out of the way. It also is a good way to exhibit a supreme sense of balance, one's sidewalk dominance and elevated pride of shoe. The more elite Parisian shoe stores have a hard surface floor in the sales area, where the clomping noise can be tested for tone, volume, echo, decibel level, and reverberation time, prior to purchase. An occupational hazard has been documented that salespeople in Paris shoe stores are prone to an early onset of deafness.

Another alien experience that I had to adjust to resulted from my Boy Scout training in Nebraska. I had been taught the four points of the compass: north, south, east, and west. I'm guessing that Thomas Jefferson was probably a Boy Scout, too. He laid out the entire United States like a gigantic tic-tac-toe grid that aligned with the four points of the compass. As a result, a typical housing block in Nebraska has streets on four sides. Streets running north-south are numbered *First Street, Second, Third,* on up to, say, 268th Street. Those that run east-west are identified using *A Street, B, and C,* followed by the names of the Presidents in alphabetical order, and then, if needed, the names of trees. Therefore, one might live on Twenty-Third Street or F Street, Washington Street or Pine Street. Having exhausted these, one might find other creative street names out there in Nebraska, like York Street or Zanzibar Street as there are no trees or presidents that start with the letters Y or Z." (Ok... I suppose Yew Street and Zachary Taylor Street may be legitimate candidates.)

Now, the layout of streets in Paris is not so regimented, one could say. It seemed to me that, as he designed the layout of the Paris street system, the famous planner, Monsieur Haussmann, was using the game of pickup sticks. A block of apartments in Paris might have three, four, or five surrounding streets, and maybe more occasionally. If you are walking north and you turn left, there is a good bet that you are not going west. More likely, you are going 12.3 degrees north of west, and after your next turn, your new direction can only be determined by a calculus equation.

This streetscape is complicated by the closeness of the canyon-like walls on either side and the often-overcast French sky, which makes it difficult to see the sun. Parisians don't know N-S-E-W. They only know G-P-S. When asking a Parisian, "Is the Eiffel Tower south of here?" a Midwesterner would expect a quick answer like "It's down that away." In Paris, if you don't witness an immediate brain seizure, you might be given verbal directions comparable in length to the Gettysburg Address. "Walk down this way

THE HOOP OF LIFE | 105

along Rue de Monbel to this very next corner, then veer to the left onto Rue de Tocqueville for only a few steps, maybe five meters, and then turn right onto Rue de Cernuschi, which is a fairly small street, and proceed for some two hundred meters until you get to Boulevard Malesherbes, which is more of a main street..." You get the idea. Now, a savvy Parisian direction-giver will taper off before reciting the entire Gettysburg Address to you, assuming that you will find another direction-giver a little farther along.

Another metropolitan phenomenon is the abundance of cellphone zombies. Like in *Night of the Living Dead,* masses of slow-moving semi-conscious bodies walk through the sidewalks of Paris, moving rather stiffly, cellphone in hand. The only perceptible difference between a cellphone zombie and regular zombie is that the latter has fewer functioning body parts and its complexion seems to be a bit worse. Occasionally, one might see one of these semi-conscious subhumans riding an electric scooter, steering with their one fully functioning body part, while chatting on the phone and zigzagging through heavy traffic at high speed.

I was disoriented by another detail that is part of the Paris street system. In Nebraska, Washington Street has the same name along its entire length, no matter if you are in the center of town or six miles away, out in a new suburb. In Paris, as you walk along Boulevard Berthier, unbeknownst to you, the street name changes to Boulevard Bessieres, then five or six blocks later, the street changes its name again, to Boulevard Ney, and farther on, to add insult to injury, its name changes to Boulevard MacDonald. When one street changes its name four or five times along its path and you multiply that by the thousands of streets in Paris, the result is a very large number of street names, which is complicated by the relatively small number of names of past French Presidents to choose from.

To acquire a map of Paris, you must choose between the three types that are available. One has very teeny-tiny street names printed on it. Another map has bigger lettering but doesn't show all the streets. Or you can get a map booklet that is the size of a paperback novel that shows every street and every name. Just for fun, I grabbed Karen's booklet map of Paris, flipped to the index, and counted 361 street names that start with the letter *B*. This approximately matches the *entire* number street names in Omaha, even though the two cities are about the same footprint in size.

Because of my background in architecture, I noted another odd thing about Paris. There are lots of naked people carved into the stone building facades, resulting in a veritable plethora of bare boobies on buildings. If I were to go to the City-County Building in Omaha and ask for a permit to build a new facility that featured carvings of females with exposed boobies plastered all over the front of the building, they would take my license to practice architecture away and put me in jail for the crime of indecent exposure or public lewdness.

What is it about the acceptance of nudity in Paris? It's everywhere, on signage, on TV, on public monuments, in museums and store windows, in paintings... *everywhere!* This rather uninhibited display of the human body translates into Paris clothing too. Women all across Paris wear really tight pants... skin-tight. There must be some female tool that I haven't seen yet, equivalent to a shoehorn, for getting into them. Even the guys wear tight pants. I'm not too excited about seeing a bunch of bony men's knees, but maybe that's just the Nebraskan in me.

And there are those sexy, high-heeled shoes. I imagine that if a lady wears them around long enough, her feet permanently deform to a point that she must walk on her tippy-toes when going barefoot to the toilet in the middle of the night. Common sense flies out the window when it comes to matters of style in Paris. Who in their right mind would pay 4000 euros for a purse? And what is so special about the color black? Black pants, black coats, black socks, black hats and gloves, black motorcycles, black helmets, black cars, black, black, black.

What about all those cute little beige dogs? They are everywhere in Paris, being led around by cute little old ladies in beige overcoats. You know, the dogs that are about the size of a loaf of bread with legs. My guess is that for every ten apartments in Paris, there is one of these pesky little critters. This means that for a typical hundred-meter stretch of street, lined by 120 apartments, there might be a dozen dogs. And two or three times a day, where do they all go to piddle and poop? In the absence of yards, they go on the sidewalk. The result is the stork-like one-legged stance of the tourist, propped against a building by one hand and resting one ankle on the knee of the other leg, while trying to scrape the underside of his or her shoe with a stick. Akin to wearing night-vision goggles, long timers on the sidewalks of Paris have developed enhanced poo-vision to avoid stepping into difficulties.

Sports shoes leave very interesting tread marks in the doggie doo. A result of metropolitan living, the cleaning of poo off the sole of a sports shoe is best accomplished in the kitchen sink with a fork, which generates to some unresolved questions regarding food preparation.

Doggie piddle is less devastating, but also leaves an impression on visitors. Piddle puddles are common. Also, the little doggies always walk right next to the buildings, checking with their noses for evidence of their other doggie buddies. A twelve-inch-tall band of mold blooms along the base of the stone buildings of Paris, thriving on the nutritious doggie pee that has been regularly deposited there over the last century or two.

In addition, a large percentage of young Parisians chew gum. Thousands of squashed chewing gum blobs can be found on the sidewalks, especially noticeable in front of schools. After the gum has been stepped on a few times, these blobs bond with the darker sidewalk surfaces to become permanent white spots, creating a polka dot visual effect that the typical tourist often confuses with pigeon poo.

This plethora of sidewalk booby traps leaves a negative impression on the visitor to Paris who is constantly forced to look down to avoid the poo, pee and doo. *Oh, my God! Did I just stumble onto the origin of that famous song: "Poo Poo Pee Doo?"* (The author apologizes, here, for inserting the previous distraction into the storyline.) It took me about a month of accidents to develop my own poo-vision. Now, I can use my enhanced precognitive skills to avoid stepping in doggie doo like a longtime Parisian.

I had a few other first impressions of Paris. Karen has this tiny elevator with the maximum weight limit equal to one and a half Nebraskans. And there was the time I saw a big black Mercedes in front of Karen's apartment, using its front bumper to nudge a Fiat a half meter forward to make an empty parking stall big enough to fit the sedan. There were these gigantic traffic snarls occurred at every rush hour, with cars and busses jammed together, looking as if a tsunami had just receded. Elegantly purported beautiful people flowed around homeless people asleep on sidewalk grates, as naturally as water sliding around boulders in a mountain stream. The first time I went grocery shopping, I recall my acute anxiety and stress caused by the lack of stacking space on the tiny countertop at the end of the check-out booth. Then there were all those language issues, exemplified by my visit to an audiologist who spoke Parisian English and did not pronounce the letter *H*, causing my constant confusion whether he was referring to my *hearing* or my *earring*.

After my first visit to Karen in her City of Light and City of Love, this good ol' boy was definitely in need of some serious down time in his lazy-boy recliner back in the wide-open spaces of Nebraska. But upon my return to Omaha, the entirety of my first week was devoted to pulling weeds, mowing, edging sidewalks, trimming bushes, sawing limbs, and cleaning Ace Hardware out of its stock of yard waste bags. I raked, mulched, spaded, pitchforked, and hoed. It didn't take me long at all to reconsider that there might be advantages to living at Karen's place in the limestone canyons of Paris.

CHAPTER 24
Red Owl

Sisseton, South Dakota, June 2011

Toward the end of my first stay with Karen in Paris, the tentativeness of our relationship faded away, and we decided to spend more time together. Karen had recently retired and now had the freedom to return with me to Nebraska. She would stay at my place in Omaha through the summer months of 2011 while I continued with my full-time job.

During her stay, Karen took up an interest in my architectural work. She was especially attentive to the project that I was working on in South Dakota. It was Red Owl's Hoop of Life, the headquarters project for the Sisseton Wahpeton tribe, which was now under construction near the town of Sisseton. Karen felt some connection to this project, as she had been born in South Dakota and had lived there as a child. She prompted me often for updates.

Responding to Karen's growing curiosity, I invited her to come with me on a visit to the construction site. We took the five-hour drive together from Omaha to Sisseton to walk through the project. At this point, the building was about a third of the way through its first year of construction. The site was muddy. We wore rubber boots and hard hats. Karen, who was an avid photographer, had brought along her camera and began to take pictures. No concrete floors had been laid down yet, and no roof decks were installed, but the basic skeleton of the building was coming together. The exterior walls were rising out of the mud and form a ring around the perimeter. An open framework of steel hovered above the circular community space at the center of the building. The new building, in the shape of the Hoop of Life, was starting to be visible.

The four entrance corridors were being built. Large hand-peeled logs, like telephone poles, formed a colonnade that lined roofless corridors. The tall wooden columns reached upwards into the blue sky and billowing white clouds of the Sioux-land summer. Two bronze-skinned Native American construction workers were standing on a raised metal platform, bare shouldered, wearing hard hats. Their platform was held in the air by a four-wheeled rig that had a long, telescoping arm. Heavily ribbed tires were dug into the mud at the base of the columns, a result of a rainstorm the day before. The men were installing a large wooden beam to span across the hallway between two columns. Floating in the air above the men, the beam dangled precariously from a construction crane cable. One man stabilized the floating beam into a horizontal position, grabbing it with his gloved hands and straining his big shoulder muscles. The other man held a large bolt, preparing to slide it into a pre-drilled hole. Engines of the throbbing big machines filled the air with background noise. The beam-and-column assembly was one of several large wooden archways to march down the entrance halls. Each raw wood assembly had a natural and honest, of-the-earth look and feel that seemed to match the spirit of these people.

As we stood in the mud, I explained to Karen that the Sisseton Wahpeton People have three sacred numbers. I had worked diligently to incorporate these numeric references into the building's design, recalling the guidance that Red Owl had given me:

"4 is the number of entrances into the Hoop of Life, the North, East, South and West."

"7 is the number of Sacred Rites. It is also the number of Dakota tribes."

"28 is the number of ribs in the buffalo, who has sustained and nurtured our people."

Becoming overly exuberant, I pointed out all the Dakota numeric references to Karen. "The central gathering space is twenty-eight feet tall. The diameter of the central skylight is twenty-eight feet. There are twenty-eight columns located around the edge of the main space." Karen recorded everything with her photographs. "There will be twenty-eight tribal departments occupying the building, and they will share seven receptionists and seven waiting areas. There are four entrances to the building…"

After our visit to the construction site, Karen and I drove to the home of Edward Red Owl and Chief Michael to talk about the project. As our car approached, we could see a small cluster of houses on a gravel road just north of the highway, out on the rolling hills of prairie-grass west of Sisseton. There were no trees and a distinct lack of farm fields. The houses were spread out, with empty lots between, seeming like extensions of the prairie. Their house was modest in size, a one-story ranch style with white lap siding, gray hip roof. Built in the '60s, it was a normal looking, anywhere USA house. The garage door was open, serving as the front door. Red Owl waved us in. A black-and-white cat brushed against my leg as we entered the garage and then went through to the kitchen door. Karen and I were greeted with smiles and introductions, then invited to sit down at the kitchen table.

Edward Red Owl and Chief Michael had been pivotal leaders during the project approvals and design. Red Owl, a historian and spokesman for the tribe, had served as head of the facilities committee. He was my principal contact during the building's design. Chief Michael had served as the chairperson of the tribal council and was a primary fund-raiser for the project. Red Owl and I reminisced about our first meeting at the tribe's facilities committee four years ago. He reflected on my vision that shaped the building into the sacred Hoop of Life.

Karen showed Red Owl and Chief Michael photographic images she had taken around the building's construction site. A band of white glazed block ran around the top of the building exterior, which was a design reference to the traditional white wedding dresses worn by the women of the tribe. The dresses were colorfully decorated with beadwork. Colored glazed blocks on the building mimicked the traditional bead designs. This decorative band was intended to greet visitors as they arrived, and to honor the women of the tribe.

Responding to Karen's photographs, Red Owl said, "Women are identified with all beginnings. It was a woman who brought the sacred pipe from the east, inviting the People to the first council."

At the inception of the building design, Red Owl had identified the four sacred colors of the Hoop of Life: black, which is associated with the west, yellow to the east, red to the north, and white to the south. The images on Karen's camera revealed that these colors were now visible in the building's block wall constructions. Each quarter of the building was built with a different color of burnished concrete block. The four colors would also apply to all interior finishes, including the carpets, wall paints, and furnishings.

As Karen showed her photographs, Red Owl offered a thoughtful refrain in his slow and reflective voice. "The colors of the Sacred Hoop are the colors of *all* people: red, white, black, and yellow. Inside all people, the color of their blood is the same."

A canopy was to be constructed at each of the four entrances to the building. In response to Edward Red Owl's guidance, each canopy would be built in the shape of one of the four sacred animals: the kit fox, the horse, the eagle, and the buffalo. I pulled four scaled models of the canopies out of a box and placed them on the kitchen table. "Each of the four animal figures will be quite tall, at twenty-eight feet." Red Owl and Chief Michael nodded their approval from across the kitchen table.

At a pause in the conversations, Karen asked if there was any spiritual significance regarding the number thirty-six. She had noticed that there would be thirty-six of the large wooden archways lining the entrance halls. I pooh-poohed Karen's observation, saying that there was nothing intentional about it.

"That's just the number of beams required to hold the roof up."

Edward Red Owl and Chief Michael exchanged glances. A look of surprise washed across their faces, and they straightened in their chairs. Red Owl leaned forward and asked Karen to explain again what she saw. Responding to the sharpness of his query, Karen flipped through the views on her camera to the images of the thirty-six entrance archways. Red Owl and Chief Michael studied the images and reflected for a moment. By reading their faces, it was obvious that Karen had stumbled onto something important. After a pause, Red Owl commented.

"That number is very close to the number of Warrior Chiefs who are honored in the history of our people."

I chimed in, "Wow! What a lucky coincidence."

Red Owl was quick to correct me. In his deep and thoughtful voice, he repeated a phrase that he had used in our very first meeting four years earlier.

"More than luck, Steve. There is a great mystery. That which is holy… is that which moves by itself."

I chimed in again, "Well… you could dedicate each wooden arch to a Chief… maybe put a name-plaque onto each column."

Red Owl raised his hand, gesturing me to stop. After a reflective silence, he spoke again.

"Uh… no. Don't need your help on that, Steve. Leave it to us. We'll follow it up ourselves."

There was a mysterious air of importance about Karen's discovery, filling us with curiosity, but our hosts weren't forthcoming with any further information.

Intentionally moving the conversation to another subject, Red Owl asked, "And how did you and Karen find each other?" Karen described how she and I had been high school classmates in Lincoln, Nebraska, and that she had moved away, living in France for the last thirty years.

Red Owl interrupted, noting that French blood ran in the Sisseton Wahpeton people. "French trappers were the first white men to come to the area, four hundred years ago, some taking Dakota women as their wives. French family names continue to this day among us. You, Karen, are from the east, like the woman who brought the sacred pipe to the first council fire of our people."

Karen continued, saying that she came to Lincoln last summer for a few months to take care of estate issues, after her mother's recent death, and that we became reacquainted at our high school reunion.

Red Owl knew that my wife had recently died. With a profoundness that I had grown to expect, he made an observation.

"A man loses his wife, a woman loses her mother, two people find each other, and there is a new beginning… This is the Hoop of Life."

Our visit to Red Owl and Chief Michael left us with new insight and with questions. Because of Karen's inquisitiveness, we knew now that the number of large wooden arches found within the new building approximately matched the number of warrior chiefs honored in the history of the Sisseton Wahpeton people. On the next day, back at my house in Omaha, Karen and I did an internet search to feed our curiosity about the Warrior Chiefs. We found a white paper on the history of the Sisseton Wahpeton Oyate that was written by Edward Red Owl himself. The number was not thirty-six. The exact number was thirty-eight Warrior Chiefs, who had been executed by the US government at the end of the Dakota War of 1862, in the small town of Mankato, Minnesota. This remains today as the largest single-day mass execution in the history of the United States.

CHAPTER 25
Run With Wind

Central Minnesota, August 1862

White man invaders are full of lies and broken promises. Large tracts of the Dakota land have been lost in exchange for promises of food and money that do not come. The Dakota have been evicted from their traditional homeland. The white settlers build their cabins and plow under the prairie, turning it into farmland. A small strip of open, empty plains is the new Dakota reservation, surrounded by a landscape that is parched, hot, and dry.

Over the past ten years, many of the Dakota people attempted to farm in the white man's manner, following the agency directives, but all crops failed this summer under the oppressive sun. Plowed fields turned to dirt and dust. The traditional source of nourishment for the Dakota people, the great buffalo herds, had disappeared, decimated by white hunters. The annual nomadic journey of the Dakota people that followed the buffalo migrations ended. Now, the last of the livestock and food stores are gone; plow animals have been eaten. Deer and game have disappeared from the countryside because of ten years of over hunting. The Minnesota River dwindles to a stagnant trickle and is fished out. One thousand tepees camp outside the agency compound on a disc of trampled dead grass. The encampment desperately awaits the agency's annual food allotment. It is a month late. Promises of food provisions are broken. Starvation is upon the people.

A white man trader throws an insult. "Let them eat grass."

There is no shade to fight off the onslaught of sun. A dejected young man walks through the dry and dusty prairie grasses turned to straw. A few tufts of brown cedar bushes wither on the horizon. Run With Wind, the young father, returns to his family from another failed hunt. He holds in his hand a dead muskrat that would provide only one meager meal to be shared by his mother, his wife, and himself. At least there will be a meal today. There is no game to hunt, no crops to harvest. Lack of food has brought the family to a state of desperation.

Tattered buffalo skins are thrown open onto the wooden ribs of their old tepee, inviting a breeze to waft away the oppressive afternoon heat. The breeze never comes. The worn-out tepee is a leftover from the good life of his father's time. Skins are necessarily still in use well beyond their lifetime, remnants of the bountiful past, the time of the buffalo herds, now gone. A thick layer of black soot cakes the hides on the top of the tepee.

The young father looks on helplessly as his wife struggles to breast-feed their newborn child. Starvation has brought weakness, sickness, and now, death. His mother sits motionless at the outer edge of the tepee. The woman's head is dropped forward. Hollow, sunken cheeks and deep wrinkles mar her face. Her toothless jaw is collapsed against her emaciated neck. Dull, lifeless eyes are drooped half-open, nearly dry. He goes to her, grabs her shoulder to arouse her, but gets no response. "She's gone," he says, more to himself than to his young, struggling wife. They knew that his mother's death was close. It is no surprise. Sadness and quiet acceptance, more than grief, is upon the young man.

Run With Wind turns to assess the condition of his wife and newborn child. The baby's fever raged for two days during his absence. Its crying had ended earlier this morning, followed by a series of convulsive heaves of the little body. Now, with the young father returned, there is only shallow, comatose breathing. "I can't wake him!" she whispers, fighting tears and terror. The young man draws close and drops to his knees, placing his hand on the baby's head. The young mother and husband huddle together, cradling their child. They watch the baby draw his last few breaths and go still. They surrender to failure and grief. The young mother hugs her dead baby and rocks back and forth. From deep within her torso, a quiet, long moan begins, interrupted by intakes of air. Her moan grows in volume and intensity, breaking into a wobbly wail. All that the young father can do is put his arm around her shoulder and match her rocking motion.

Run With Wind now shifts his worries to his young wife. She is withered, hollow-eyed, stretched skin clinging to her ribs, battered by starvation and sickness. And now, her heart is broken, lost in grief. Conflicted by his frantic urge to provide nourishment for his wife and stricken by his own grief, he carries his dead mother out from the tepee, places her body on a blanket, and covers her. The lifeless baby remains in its mother's arms. He makes a fire and cooks the muskrat. Pulling meat from the paltry animal, he pushes a strand of food into his wife's mouth. "Eat," he says. Her wailing diminishes to a mumbly moan as she chews. Dust clings to the streaks of tears on her cheeks. As he continues to get some nourishment into her, she calms. He gently helps her lie over on her side. Weakness envelops her. "Sleep now," the young man says as he softly removes the child's body from her grasp. The exhausted young woman quickly complies. She is stable for now, but tomorrow more food will be needed. There is none.

He quietly backs out of the tepee and lays the body of the baby next to the body of its grandmother. His mind races through practical issues. He has never organized a funeral before. There is a stand of saplings down by the river that can be used to build the burial scaffolds. *People need to be told.* Where should he locate the platforms? *I need to use the older blankets for the shrouds.* As he kneels to inspect the blanket laid over the bodies, grief catches up and washes over him. He slumps forward over his knees. Head dropped; his hair hangs down surrounding his face. He leans forward onto all fours. His chest heaves out a ragged moan. He breathes in and moans again. The young man's moans break into uncontrollable whimpers and tears. His spirit is broken, and he surrenders to the mourning.

The young woman doesn't sleep long. The meager nourishment revives her. She wobbles to a seated position, raising her emaciated torso onto her frail arm. She is fevered and shriveled by starvation. As she returns to consciousness, frantic fear wells up in her, and she tries to remember. With eyes glancing around the empty tepee, she blurts out a question in a broken, wobbly voice, "Where is my baby?"

The young man bolts to her side, yanking his mind out of his grief, thrusting his attention onto his wife. He rushes in and kneels next to her side, drawing her into an embrace, feeling her trembling body and the heat of her fever. "The baby has died," he reminds her, in a whisper, trying to find comfort in the tone of his words. Her memory returns, hitting her like a fist. She flinches, constricting her torso, under an upwelling of grief, clawing with one hand, grabbing forcefully at his leggings. Her heart is weak. She wrenches forward. Terrorized, the young man holds tightly onto his wife, fearing that she, too, is near death. Finally, she quiets, descending into a pit of despair. A shroud of mourning settles over the young couple. It is the end of joy, the end to all things good.

The saplings snap off easily as he swings his axe. He harvests another pole for the funeral scaffolds. *These will do.* While aggressively swinging his tool, a change wells up in the young man. *The white man did this to us. His stockade is full of our food.* Despair changes to blame. *They have no right to keep it from us.* Blame changes to anger. Anger changes to rage.

Friends from his hunting party gather to him and listen. They share the pain and rage in his words. "We can break the doors down and TAKE WHAT IS OURS." Other young men arrive. Without conscious intent, the Run With Wind becomes a leader. "THEY CAN'T STOP US!" He raises the broken spirits of his companions to fight. A war party forms around him and takes action. He has taken on the trappings of a Warrior Chief!

The small band of young Dakota warriors stealthily draws close to the agency outpost. Using a mixture of bows and arrows, axes and knives, the young Dakota men throw themselves into a silent, lightning-quick attack. The two young soldiers assigned to the store are surprised, overwhelmed, and killed. Two white traders inside the store are the next to die. The storeroom doors are smashed open.

It quickly becomes much more than the taking of food. Multiple war parties spontaneously form, swelling in numbers, scattering. News of the attacks spread through the Dakota camps. Broken promises of food and failed farming attempts have resulted in a summer of famine, starvation, sickness, and death for the Dakota people. Frustrations have turned to anger. Hatred is growing everywhere. Attacks spread out across the prairie like a wildfire enraged by the hot summer wind. The violence escalates into a war to take back the Dakota homeland which was stolen from them, to regain the good life that was lost, to protect, to defend, to punish, to avenge. The white man invaders must die.

CHAPTER 26

Cut Face

Central Minnesota, August 1862

A hollow popping sound surprises Cut Face as his war club impacts the farmer's skull. The warrior has crashed through the front door into the one-room log cabin. Immediately, the farmer is clubbed as he attempts to bolt from his chair at the table. A heavy, river-rounded rock, egg-shaped, as big as a fist, is the business end of Cut Face's club. The rock is lashed securely with buffalo hide to the molded *Y* cradle at the top of a cherry-wood shaft. A leather binding forms a grip around the lower shaft and the flared end of this powerful weapon, such that it can be forcefully swung. It is decorated with warrior trappings of colorful beaded strands and dangling feathers. A primitive stick drawing is scratched into the club's handle, of a face slashed across by a diagonal line, identifying its owner.

Before the farmer's lifeless body can crumple to the floor, Cut Face turns. In two lunging steps, he is upon the woman. The club is hoisted above the warrior's head with both arms. Backing into the corner in retreat, the woman raises her left hand to protect herself. Her mind flashes to the unborn child she is carrying. Cut Face powers the war club down onto her. The woman's arm is brushed aside like prairie grass in the wind. Just above the shoulder, the club smashes into her neck, collapsing her petite torso and tossing her head wildly sideways. The woman's body collapses limply to the floor.

A preteen boy, like a trapped wild animal, bolts from his hiding place behind a chair, stumbling over a cot. What the boy sees is a monster from hell. Below a diagonal scar, Cut Face's cheek and neck are painted red, resurrecting a vision of the blood that was thrown from the slashing cut across his face many years ago. The monster's eyes are wide open, his white eyeballs floating in black-painted socket surrounds. He spreads his arms into the air as he attacks, like the wings of a giant predator hawk. The long and ragged strips of hide that bind the seams of his leather sleeves fly behind like feathers, laced with tufts of black human hair from his previous murders, Ojibwe victims, trophies from his violent warrior past.

The boy knocks an oil lamp into the corner, shattering it and showering flames onto the wall of the log cabin. He makes it through the front door, bolting past Cut Face's two companion warriors, and out into the front yard. Cut Face, with several leaps of his tall and muscular frame, closes quickly on the boy from behind, the seven feathers of his head-dress lying back in the wind. A powerful horizontal swing of the war club hooks into the boy's ribs, stopping his run, knocking him sideways. His arms and legs flop forward in the air. A second crushing blow finishes the boy.

Cut Face dashes back inside the burning cabin and drags the farmer's body out. A strange, exuberant mixture of anger and joy, bloodlust, exudes from Cut Face as he grabs a fistful of the dead man's hair and knifes through the scalp. He raises his bloody prize in triumph as he turns and vocalizes a sound that is half scream and half song. "YAEuuuh-YAEYAE-YAEuuuh!" His two companion warriors are astonished by the viciousness and speed of Cut Face's violent acts.

Many more farms are attacked. The violence spreads to small villages of white settlers. In only a few days, the war escalates to large-scaled attacks on military outposts. Unable to defend against the onslaught, waves of white farmer refugees flee eastward in retreat toward St. Paul. The white man's army launches a frantic call to arms. Violence, terror, blood, and tragedy unfold over the ensuing month. In August 1862, the Dakota war parties kill hundreds of white settlers. In the whites' retaliation, hundreds of the Dakota people will die.

CHAPTER 27

Commemorative

Mankato, Minnesota, 23-26 December 1862

"Where you want 'em?" A burley and ungroomed worker brings a pair of planks to the platform, balanced on his right shoulder.

"Right there."

The boards drop, clunking onto the ground. Intermittent banging, hammering, and sawing are heard, the clattering of several carpenters busily at work, in spite of the crisp December air. The noise of construction echoes off the fronts of the new bank building and the hotel across the way. The carpenters are intent on completing their task. It is two days before Christmas. Lumber bounces on the back of a flat-bed wagon as it rolls by. Wooden wheels slowly turn through the half-dry soil, cutting new ruts into the dampened soft spots. Draft horses pull hard and breathe out puffs of mist into the cool air. A driver whistles and yells, "Whoa," as he leans back and pulls on the leather reins. The last batch of construction supplies arrive.

A raw wood gallows platform and its heavy timber frame are being constructed in the foreground of the frontier river town. The gallows' structure is centered in the wide and open area at the river's edge, back dropped by Mankato's line of newly constructed buildings along Front Street. Naked timber columns stand at each corner of the new gallows' platform, extending into the gloom of the gray winter sky. Hovering overhead, a thick beam is being lifted on the shoulders of four men standing on a wagon that serves as a makeshift scaffold. The men grunt and strain. Steam wafts from their backs into the cool air. Their words are few and short. "Almost. That's it. Yu'r there." One end of the thick wooden beam is eased gently onto the notches at the top of the wooden columns. A man on a ladder reaches quickly for a cinch rope.

The unusually large and robust gallows platform is nearing completion, twenty-eight feet square, surrounded by beams that are fifteen feet in the air. It must be sturdy enough to hold thirty-eight men, all to be hanged by their necks at the same time. Nooses drape from the beams, forming a dangling skirt around the edge of the gallows scaffolding. A heavyset worker conducts sandbag tests to ensure structural soundness and stability. The construction crew is a combination of blue uniformed soldiers and scruffy-looking local carpenters. A US Army engineer scrutinizes the operation to ensure that the platform will be completed by the end of the day and will function properly.

On the morning after Christmas, makeshift sales booths and display tables appear out of nowhere, scatter out along Front Street within view of the hangman's gallows. Sales agents stand on wooden boxes to get their heads above the gathering crowd. For sale are drinks, candies and confections, trinkets, blankets, bread and sausage in paper, gloves and scarfs, and medicinal remedies. A sales agent bellows out, "Get your commemorative spoons right here! A beautiful relief image of all thirty-eight Injuns, capturing today's event in history." Two wide-eyed boys watch with fascination as the panderer belches out his sales pitch. A wispy fog of breath emanates with each word from the man's mouth and fades into the crisp morning air. Hoping the sales agent will glance the other way, the two boys wait for an opportunity to snitch something from the sales table. The sales agent grumbles with a lowered voice, "Get out-a here, you little brats!" and threatens with a swing of his hat. He then continues, "Sterling silver, engraved with today's date and location. Freshly manufactured at the St. Paul Silver Works. Limited supply! THE END OF THE INDIAN WAR! Recorded right here on this beautifully detailed silver spoon. A real steal for two bits. A pictographic image of all thirty-eight Injuns, hanging from the gallows. In raised relief! This decorative collector's spoon is a novelty commemoration of this momentous day! Get yours now before they're all gone…"

The tiny frontier town of Mankato bustles with activity. Its two hundred residents scurry about, trying frantically to accommodate the gathering crowd. Visitors have been arriving by wagon and horseback for several days to view the big event. The stagecoach pulls in and another group of onlookers spills out, relieved that they have arrived in time. Store owners have hastily refitted floor space into make-shift sleeping arrangements for visitors. Homeowners have taken in strangers. Horse-drawn wagons loaded with beer, whiskey, and food from St. Paul pull up to the back doors of the local hotel, bar, and shops.

By noon, the number of people in the little town swells to three thousand onlookers. On hand is a wild mixture of thrill seekers, thieves, lawmen and soldiers, residents and visitors, mischievous kids, and salespeople. To get a good view of the hanging, a wrinkled old woman, draped in a blanket, jostles for position with farmers in worn-out overalls. People scramble up ladders; the canopies of stores creak under the added weight of spectators. Dignitaries and store owners stand with top hats, long dress coats, pipes in hand. Soldiers in uniform, shouldering long guns and bayonets, form into rows in the foreground of the gallows, to keep onlookers at a distance. Angry survivors of the attacks are present: vigilantes, loved ones, friends and families of the victims, full of hate. Screams for vengeance are heard. A regimented array of Army tents and corrals has turned up on the west edge of town. Five hundred soldiers and their horses are on hand to guard the prisoners and control the gathering crowd.

The event goes nearly unnoticed in the national newspapers. The public's attention is diverted away by the Civil War in the aftermath of the first bloody confrontation. Antietam has just claimed the lives of three thousand six hundred soldiers and wounded thousands more.

Despite this, the local and regional reporters hurry about their task, trying to capture the upcoming spectacle in words. "On this day, December 26, 1862, thirty-eight warriors of the Dakota Sioux will be hanged by the neck until dead. The hanging will take place here in Mankato, Minnesota. It will be the largest mass execution in US history. Under the leadership of Brigadier General Henry Hastings Sibley, one thousand soldiers of the US Army and the volunteers of the Minnesota state militia have hunted down and defeated the blood-thirsty Indians that attacked and killed nearly five hundred local farmers and settlers. The Indian attacks occurred all across south central Minnesota this last August. Three hundred and eight of the captured Indians were sentenced to death. President Abraham Lincoln himself has reviewed the judgment and granted a reprieve to all but the 38 warrior chiefs who led the uprising..."

The prisoners sit quietly on a dirt floor, constrained by heavy, metal ankle collars and handcuffs, elbows bound behind their backs. There is no detail in the dark half-light of the interior. Wisps of daylight sneak in through the slits around the door, revealing dark, slouching shapes seated with bowed heads. A thick chain runs between the legs of each prisoner and wraps around the sturdy center post of the makeshift brig.

The heavy wooden door bangs open. A soldier is silhouetted in the scorching bright light emanating from the opening behind him. Soldiers file in. The large central chain is unlocked and rattles free. Cut Face, one of the most violent of the prisoners, raises his head to face the light, embracing his death with pride and defiance. Run With Wind, the young warrior who led one attack during the first days of the conflict is lost in a blanket of sorrow, grieving over the death of his mother, wife, and child, welcoming his own death. Each of the thirty-eight prisoners is escorted by a pair of soldiers, one on each arm, out through the cheers and taunting of the boisterous crowd, past four empty horse-drawn panel wagons that were used during the previous days of the gallows construction, now ready to haul the bodies of the dead Dakota warriors away.

CHAPTER 28

Scout

Central Minnesota, February 1863

It was the end of a way of life for the Dakota People... the end of the good life, the beginning of a hard life. Most of the Sisseton Wahpeton Oyate were dead or interned. Eventually, some two thousand Dakota survivors would be moved to reservations to the west, on small confinements of land out on the harsh, treeless prairies.

In the immediate aftermath of the war, families were crushed, torn apart, scattered. Few men remained. Hardship enveloped the survivors. Women, children, and elderly were lost to hunger, exhaustion, disease, and exposure. Under the thumb of the white man's government, there was no choice but to accept it and try to survive.

Some Dakota warriors had escaped to the prairies, to the west and north. A new contingent of General Sibley's Army forms, tasked with helping to hunt down those who had escaped. These Scouts were Dakota men, paid by the Army to hunt down their own people.

One scout laughs boisterously, sitting at the white man's table and eating his fill. Drawing his cash from the paymaster, he is paid well to be savage. Wearing the white man's uniform, carrying a gun, he has his own horse, has his fill of whiskey and women. He carries out the white man's brutality. He knows how to succeed, how to get the information he needs. He knows his People. Making good use of his thick arms and big shoulders, the Scout holds a fearful child by a fist full of hair. He makes a demand of the grandmother, "Tell me now where he ran off to. Last chance, old woman."

Another scout is a broken man, desperate to save his family. The money he earns from the white man saves them from starvation, his wife, his two children, his father and mother. "Why did the warriors bring this hell down upon our people? Killing the white settlers was wrong. We are the good ones." Compliance. "We wish to live in peace before we all become dust. I will help you find them."

Out of anger, out of despair, the defeated and dwindling Dakota people were torn into two emotionally charged encampments: on one side are the warriors, and the others on the side are the peace seekers who reluctantly accept the new reality.

The spiritual scars of these deep wounds would linger and fester, continuing to divide the Dakota people into the distant future. A century and a half later, Red Owl offers an invitation to heal these old wounds.

"Now is the time for our people to return to The Hoop of Life."

CHAPTER 29

The Post-it Wars

Omaha, summer of 2011

Sharing our first summer together at my home in Omaha, Karen was pretty intent on enjoying quality time with her new man (me!) But having spent thirty years of her life as a single professional woman of the world, and not having experienced the "joys" of child-rearing, she was ill prepared to share my home with my two youngest sons, Matt and Mark, now young men, ages twenty-two and twenty-three.

The two guys had both left home and gone off to college but were still of the opinion that "Mi casa es su casa." In their minds, they felt completely justified in moving back home at any time for random stays. These return visits varied in length from days to weeks to months. In those instances when they were out of money, between jobs, with no place to stay, they would return home, bringing their extremely bad grooming and poor housekeeping skills, as well as their ferocious appetites and thirsts.

As an example of their questionable housekeeping skills, upon the occasional return of either young man, a most disgustingly bad habit would creep into "our" house: chewing tobacco. Half-full beer bottles containing a nasty soup of cigarette butts and brown-black spittle would sit around in the dark corners of the house, stealthily waiting as booby-traps, inevitably to be kicked over. Often these caustic messes were not immediately discovered, having a chance to soak into the carpet and distill down into sticky goo that harkened back to the Exxon Valdez oil spill.

Enter unsuspecting Karen. Luckily, the two guys never returned home for exactly the same period of time, giving Karen the advantage of dealing with each of them one-on-one. Even so, Matt and Mark were quickly identified as tag-team from hell!

Now, for you ladies who aren't familiar with this term, "tag-team" is a reference to an All-Star-Wrestling format whereby, like doubles tennis, a team of two wrestlers face-offs against another team of two wrestlers. But unlike doubles tennis, there is only one wrestler from each team in the ring at any one time. When the wrestler in the ring becomes exhausted from pummeling the other guy, if he can reach out and "tag" the hand of his teammate who is waiting outside the ropes ringside, then they can exchange places. The exhausted teammate will exit the ring, while the fresh and rested teammate will jump into the ring and take over the pummeling with vigor and vitality. If you have been paying attention to this detailed definition, you now understand how this is analogous to the Mark & Matt team facing off against the Karen & Steve team.

Karen was quickly identified as "the wicked stepmom," even though our marriage wouldn't occur for another two years. In the presence of either of these young men, it didn't take Karen long to conclude that it was futile to speak nicely.

"Please stop doing what you are doing… and thank you."

The politeness strategy failed rather quickly. Her next strategy was to wage a housekeeping war by weaponizing a pad of post-its. She began to stick messages on problem areas throughout the house. The bathroom became the first battleground in the Post-it Wars, where Karen launched a barrage of postings, including *PUT THE TOILET SEAT DOWN WHEN YOU'RE DONE*, and *WIPE YOUR PIDDLE OFF OF THE RIM*, as well as *WIPE YOUR PIDDLE OFF THE FLOOR*, and *FLUSH THE TOILET WHEN YOU'RE DONE*. I could never discern whether Karen intentionally chose to not write please and thank you on her notes or if there just wasn't enough room on the paper.

A secondary front in the Post-it Wars developed in the kitchen, where Karen attacked with postings such as *DON'T LEAVE DIRTY DISHES IN THE SINK and PUT YOUR DIRTY DISHES IN THE DISHWASHER.*

She left several defensive postings inside the refrigerator: *DON'T EAT THIS YOGURT,* and *THIS IS NOT YOUR BEER.* Occasionally, Karen lost skirmishes in the Battle-of-the-Beer due to sneak attacks launched under the cover of darkness.

The postings invaded the rest of the house, as well. *DON'T TRACK DIRT ALL THROUGH THE HOUSE. TURN OFF THE LIGHTS AND TV WHEN YOU LEAVE. PUT YOUR DIRTY SOCKS AND UNDERWEAR IN THE HAMPER. THROW YOUR EMPTY DORITO SACKS AWAY. DON'T LEAVE YOUR DORITO CRUMBS ALL OVER THE FURNITURE.*

In the spirit of exploring the newfound love that Karen and I shared, my personal contribution quickly evolved into that of a peacekeeper. I scurried around my house, wiping up piddle, flushing toilets, putting both lids and seats down, moving dirty dishes into the dishwasher, turning off the TV and lights, collecting dirty socks and underwear, picking up Doritos sacks, vacuuming up crumbs, and keeping the refrigerator stocked with a fresh tub of yogurt.

I soon took on the duty of an unexploded ordnance officer. Now, for those of you who are not familiar with military terms, unexploded ordnance refers to those bombs that were dropped but did not explode on impact. Like unexploded bombs, Post-its had to be carefully removed before their explosive potential was unleashed upon innocent dinner guests.

I also took on the responsibility of munitions officer. This is the important wartime task of keeping ammunitions resupplied. Why the Army doesn't call them "ammunitions" officers is one of those wartime mysteries lost in history. My duties involved the constant resupplying of Post-it packets, by purchasing them in the stationery aisle of the grocery store and placing them in the kitchen drawer.

Let's not forget my most dangerous task, which involved chemical warfare. Found in the deep recesses of the cabinet under the kitchen sink, I tested ancient, half-empty bottles of various caustic agents as to their efficacy in removing the sticky chewing tobacco goo from the carpet in the dark corners of the boys' bedrooms and TV room.

Luckily, I recognized the strange plant that grew to seven feet tall in the back patio area to be marijuana and yanked it out by the roots before any narcs caught sight of it. Whether it was intentionally planted or was an accidental result of an imprecise late-night roll-your-own effort was never clarified. I realize that this has no direct correlation to the Post-it Wars, but I have added this as background narrative to enhance your general understanding regarding the heightened anxiety level associated with unplanned returns of the boys to stay at the house.

Matt, my youngest, was the first of my sons to meet Karen. It wasn't the best of meetings. At the time, Matt was temporarily living at home with me in Omaha. Karen (Dad's hot new babe) had just arrived from Paris to spend a week in Nebraska. After picking her up at the airport, she and I made a quick stop at the house, specifically for Karen to meet Matt. We were there for only an hour before the two of us were to leave on a romantic out-of-town romp, capitalizing on a Special Valentine's Day Getaway Weekend offered by Arbor Lodge in Nebraska City. Karen proudly presented a special gift to me upon her arrival. It was a rather pricey bottle of her favorite Balvenie Double Wood twelve-year-old Scotch which she had purchased at a duty-free shop on her flight in.

Introductions were brief. "Matt, this is Karen."

"Hi, Karen."

"Hi, Matt."

After placing Karen's gift into my liquor cabinet, we were out the door.

Matt, having the house to himself, invited his college buddy, a member of the Creighton University baseball team, to stop by on a Saturday night. Two ladies tagged along. Matt's friends phoned some other friends, who phoned some other friends. Before Matt even knew what was happening (and without my permission!), the entire Creighton Blue Jays baseball team and a gaggle of ladies had piled into my house to party.

When Karen and I returned a few days later from our weekend of bliss, we discovered that my liquor cabinet had been completely cleaned out. A dozen full-size bottles of hard liquor had been killed. The only thing left was a pocket-size bottle of cheap Canadian whisky with only an inch of liquid in it. Most importantly, Karen's brand-new bottle of *special* scotch was missing in action. Karen had a conniption fit, which she directed at me, because it would have been inappropriate for her to yell at my son, Matt, whom she had just met. She left the yelling at Matt to me.

That summer, Karen visited Nebraska again, this time for a more extended stay of several months. This was an experimental new situation for the three of us—Matt, Karen, and me, living together in the same house. Matt had just graduated from college. He cocooned himself into his bedroom and the TV room in the basement, avoiding contact with Dad and Karen whenever possible. As he failed regularly at meeting Karen's housekeeping expectations, communications with Matt deteriorated quickly to Post-it note declarations.

On one occasion, Karen and I embarked on a housekeeping frenzy to get ready for a dinner party. We were intent on cleaning the entire house, top to bottom. Upon making our way to the downstairs TV room, we noticed a putrid smell, which we traced to Matt's bedroom door. Matt was not home, and like usual, his bedroom door was shut. I had not been in his room since he returned home from college to live with me several months ago. I opened the door and inhaled a waft of nasty-smelling stale air. What I discovered were wrinkled piles of dirty clothing strewn onto the floor, kicked to the edges of the room: underwear, T-shirts, sweatshirts, socks, and jeans. My impression was that I had walked into a giant nest. Matt's job bussing tables, washing dishes, and cooking in a hot and sweaty pizza kitchen had contributed dramatically to the odor clinging to his dirty clothes.

Karen and I threw the windows open, seeking fresh air. Empty chips bags, Jimmy John's sandwich wrappers, crumbs, and spoiled lettuce shavings were intermingled with the clothing. Since he had lived in bachelor pads with several other young men through his last three years of college, grooming and cleanliness had slipped well down on Matt's priorities list. Beer bottles half-full of chewing tobacco spittle and cigarette butts were tipped over onto carpet and clothing. "Jeezuz!" was my recurring comment with each new disgusting discovery in Matt's room. His desk was overrun with cans, plastic cups, bottles, fast food sacks and wrappers, all in various degrees of emptiness and moldiness. There was this especially bad smelling pair of old tennis shoes that he had been wearing around the pizza kitchen, which we immediately placed into a garbage bag and carried outside.

Karen and I threw ourselves into pickup/cleanup mode, vacuuming and scrubbing Matt's room. We did several loads of laundry, folding and placing clothes into drawers that, amazingly, were pretty much empty and unused. I taped labels onto the drawers: *socks, underwear, t-shirts*, etc. We discovered a baggie of marijuana mixed in with the clothing next to the bed, which was no surprise.

Karen and I were finishing up as Matt arrived home and walked in. Emotions contorted Matt's face, a strange mixture of surprise, embarrassment, anger, guilt, and humiliation.

"Are you OK with this?" I prompted, as he stood there in a funk.

Avoiding eye contact, Matt replied, "Well, uh... you went through my stuff."

I immediately spit out a barrage of fatherly advice. "Now that we've gotten your room clean, you need to..." Blah, blah, blah. "And leave the door open when you're gone to get some air in here."

Matt used this incident as an incentive to get the hell out as soon as possible. Within two weeks, with his new resume featuring his recent degree in environmental sciences, he found a job in central Nebraska working for the National Park Service. He and I conducted a weekend search and found a cheap used car, low mileage, not too old, which I bought for him, with his promise to pay me back at one hundred dollars a month.

Karen took Matt to the grocery store and gave him a seminar on home economics as they walked the aisles, discussing the cost of lettuce, lunch meat, cheese, and bread versus the cost of a Subway sandwich. They filled the trunk of his car with $250 worth of groceries, paid by Karen as a goodwill gesture and peace offering to Matt. The three of us moved Matt to Loup City, Nebraska.

Not long after that, Mark, my middle boy, showed up on the porch at the front door of our house in Omaha, with no car, no job, no money, and no place to stay. He had lost his job in Las Vegas and had failed in his attempt to play poker with the big boys in the casinos there. He had borrowed $200 from a friend to buy a bus ticket home. I took him in. Karen was nearing the end of her summer stay with me in Omaha.

Introductions, and Mark's entire short-lived stay, to quote Yogi Berra, were "déjà vu all over again."

"Mark, this is Karen."

"Hi, Karen."

"Hi, Mark."

We moved Mark into the downstairs bedroom, and TV room from which Matt recently had departed. Mark, like his younger brother before him, quickly exhibited the unique lifestyle of a young man (chewing tobacco spittle accidents, poor aim in the bathroom, partaking of other peoples' food and drink, grinding Doritos crumbs into the carpet, public aeration of smelly socks, etc.)

This quickly invoked a series of verbal requests from Karen, which quickly eroded into Mark becoming a non-communicative recluse, which quickly brought forth a barrage of Post-it directives from Karen, which quickly resulted in Mark finding a job far away, which quickly caused me to buy another son another car in a timespan of thirty days.

Karen was victorious in both Post-it Wars, defeating Matt in his short-lived occupation of the house and thwarting Mark's failed invasion of his old bedroom. My role as peace arbitrator diminished. In both campaigns, each young man rather quickly concluded, as opposed to surrender and submission to the enemy, that full retreat was the only viable option. Karen had survived her first skirmishes with my children. Our newly acquired love was still intact, though a bit war weary. And now, years later, the peace accord between the Post-it Wars participants is still being negotiated.

CHAPTER 30
Zina

South Bend, Nebraska, summer of 2011

Nothing like an old person talking about the old days. Here was Zina, ninety-some years old, her walker to the side, swallowed up by her recliner, afghan over her knees. "Mom, Steve Laughlin is here to see you," her daughter said. Zina remembered me well and perked up. Karen and I sat down with her in the sunroom porch of her cabin, now converted into a family room. Pictures of her kids, the grandkids, and the great grandkids were proudly displayed on the buffet. There was Ernie's WWII portrait and a box with his purple heart and another medal next to the newspaper article from the *Lincoln Journal Star* describing his heroics.

Me and my older brother were pictured there too, with the rest of the Pear Street kids in a Fourth of July photo from 1953. The picture showed us kids piled into a Radio Flyer wagon, dressed up in our Independence Day costumes. I was three years old, holding a stick with flag on it that was fashioned from an old pillowcase. Several of us kids had our heads wrapped in white rags smeared with ketchup. Zina's daughter, Bonnie, was standing in the wagon, banging on her toy cymbal, holding it high in the air. One girl was lost in the folds of her father's oversized WWII Army uniform, holding her hand up in a salute.

Zina and Bonnie were now living out at the lake at South Bend, an old clear-water sand pit on the shoulder of the Platte River surrounded by beaches and summer homes, under a stand of full-grown cottonwood trees. It was a place our family visited on weekends when I was a kid. I remember fishing from Zina and Ernie's dock as a five or six-year-old boy, catching a sunfish and showing it proudly to my dad. Their cabin was a wooden garage that had been converted into living space with bunk beds, a table, and a couch. The kitchen area consisted of a metal laundry tub and a drying board mounted to the wall. An old-style hand pump supplied water straight out of the ground. There was no ceiling, just exposed wooden rafters, and a corner draped with a fishing net filled with seashells and starfish. I remember the outhouse shack with its wooden seat, nasty smell, and collection of lazy flies down the hole.

So here we were, fifty years later. Karen and I were on a Saturday outing, biking on the sleepy little blacktop road that went around Zina's Lake. It was the same lake we had biked around the summer before when we were getting reacquainted. I struggled to recognize Zina's place. The little cabin I remembered had been swallowed by many additions and improvements made over the years. But I found it, thanks to the family name hanging on a plaque at the front door. It surprised me to have Bonnie greet us at the door, my childhood playmate, now sixty-six years old, living here with her husband and Zina. Bonnie invited us in. We had a joyful reunion and a round of introductions. Their family had moved from Lincoln and permanently moved out to the lake property many years ago.

Zina was quick to reminisce about the old days on Pear Street in Lincoln. When I was a child, Zina, Ernie, and their kids lived in the house next to mine. My dad and Ernie were good buddies, both WWII veterans. They were recently home from the war, raising kids and renting little old houses next to each other.

Zina's first story was about my dad. Pear Street was only half a city block long, running east from Twenty-seventh Street. It had virtually no traffic and was the perfect street for the kids to play on. The street dead-ended into a fence and hedge along an old lady's backyard, Mrs. Fowley. She was a widow living alone and didn't like us kids. Our football regularly bounced over the fence and into her yard. We would open her gate, hurry in and fetch the ball, while keeping an eye on Mrs. Fowley's back screen door. When the old woman caught sight of us, she would yell at us through her screen.

"YOU KIDS GET OUTTA MY YARD! AND KEEP THAT BALL OUTTA HERE, OR I'LL TAKE IT AND KEEP IT!"

On one occasion, she was in a really nasty mood. She ran out her back door and grabbed our football before we could retrieve it and took it inside her house. She then refused to give the ball back, yelling at us through the screen door. My father overheard the conflict and walked to Mrs. Fowley's fence line. He grabbed her gate, lifted it off its hinges and turned to walk away with it. Dad then yelled over his shoulder at Mrs. Fowley.

"YOU CAN BRING THE FOOTBALL TO MY HOUSE. UNTIL THEN, I'LL KEEP YOUR GATE."

Dad walked home with the gate and placed it in our living room against the wall. Zina recalled the gate sat there in our living room for several days. Eventually Mrs. Fowley's son, on the day he came to visit his mother, brought the football to our house and exchanged it for the gate. My father and Mrs. Fowley's son had a long, loud conversation on the front porch, using a lot of colorful language.

Zina's story gave us all a good, long giggle.

Zina's second story was equally entertaining. She recalled that there wasn't much space between our two houses on Pear Street, just enough to walk through, just enough so that the roofs didn't touch. This was before the days of air-conditioning. Open windows with screens kept the houses cool on hot summer nights. The bedroom window of Zina and Ernie was directly across from the hallway windows along the side of our house, so you could pretty much hear anything that was going on in the other family's house.

There were times when Dad's job with the railroad required that he work all night. On one summer night, at two in the morning, Zina was awakened by my mother talking loudly. Zina turned in her bed and looked out through her window screen and into our window across the way, to see my mother holding a double-barrel shotgun at her shoulder, cheek down on the wooden stock, aiming straight down our hall at eye level.

My mother's words were loud and clear, *"I SUGGEST YOU TURN YOUR ASS AROUND AND GET THE HELL OUTTA HERE BEFORE I DECIDE TO PULL THE TRIGGER."*

In the moment of silence following, she moved the gun's safety switch to firing position with a pronounced "*CLICK.*" Zina then heard someone clomping down the hall. The intruder banged the back screen door open and ran off.

After that, Zina and my mom shared some words through the window. Mom didn't recognize the intruder. "I couldn't tell if he was a thief, a drunk, a pervert, or what," she said calmly as she put the gun's safety switch back on with another pronounced click. She continued, "... Think I'll keep this gun close by, tonight… just in case."

Zina concluded, "Near as I could tell, your mother had things pretty much under control, so I rolled over and went back to sleep."

At the end of Zina's second story, we all had another good, long giggle.

Karen and I visited Zina again the following summer, on the next bike ride around her lake. On this visit, we were warmly received again, and Zina shared some of the old stories. Somehow, Zina contributed to the growing bond between Karen and me. We loved her memories about Mom, Dad, and us kids growing up on Pear Street and were blessed to have had the chance to reconnect with her. She's gone now.

CHAPTER 31
The '58 Chevy

Southern Minnesota, summer of 1958

Dad had just purchased his very first brand-new car, fresh from the factory. I was eight years old at the time. It was a 1958 Chevrolet Impala, four-door, two-tone yellow-and-white, with a turquoise-green interior, arguably the ugliest vehicle that ever came out of Detroit. Unlike the sleek '57 Chevy with the vertical fins above the rear fenders, the fins of the '58 Chevy were fat and flopped over onto their sides. They didn't look like fins anymore. They looked more like the curled-over ears of a plump puppy dog. Two more headlamps were added to the front of the car, such that each side now had double lamps, with a heavy metal eyebrow above. The car's front-end was extremely wide and heavy looking, with enough chrome added to sink a ship. The graceful and gazelle-like '57 Chevy had transformed into the lumbering hippo-like '58 Chevy. For some unfathomable reason, Dad loved this car.

 Mom, Dad, my baby brother, my older brother, and I were all piled into the new Chevy, headed north on a two-lane blacktop highway in southwestern Minnesota. It was the start of our family vacation, and Dad, filled with pride, was behind the wheel of his new car. Thanks to the long vacations that came with dad's Union job on the railroad, we spent two weeks every summer renting a cabin on a Minnesota lake. My older brother and I were in the back seat. Mom was in the front seat holding the baby in her arms. This was pre-Ralph Nader, before the time of seat belts and before car seats for infants. In the event of an accident, the plan must have been to launch the baby through the front windshield and hope for the best.

It was a boiling afternoon in early August, with the temperature hovering around one hundred degrees Fahrenheit. All four windows of the car were rolled down to keep us from being cooked alive inside the car. The triangular glass vents in the corners of the front windows were hinged into a partially open position, directing a strong backdraft of wind into the car and onto my brother and me in the back seat. "Why in God's name didn't you buy a car with air conditioning?" my mother asked, raising her voice over the sound of the wind whooshing by. In 1958, air-conditioning for a car was a fairly new idea that one could purchase as a "luxury" option. My dad, who grew up during the Depression and fought in WWII, had known hard times and was a bit tight with his money. "I'm out in the heat every day, and it doesn't bother me," he responded.

"I've got to pee," I announced from the back seat as we rolled down the highway.

"We're not stopping," Dad responded. His opinion was that if we stopped every time someone needed to pee, we'd never get there. He drove on in silence.

"Try to hold it for a while," Mom said, as she frowned at my father.

I held it for a few miles further before I repeated, "I've got to pee... bad!" Dad drove on without comment.

"You've got to pull over," Mom said, trying to come to my rescue.

"There's a coffee can under my seat," was Dad's response. "Have him pee in that. You can dump it out the window."

Mom directed my older brother to feel around under the front seat. He found the Folger's middle-size can with its rusted interior. By the looks of it, this can had been used for this task before. I stood up onto the floor mat. There was plenty of room. I dropped my pants and underwear down around my knees and grabbed the can from my brother. Dad issued a warning: "Get it all into the can. *DON'T PISS ALL OVER MY NEW CAR.*" His authoritarian tone made everyone nervous, especially me. After fighting off a nervous tremor, I held the coffee can carefully in front of me with both hands. I precision peed into it. The sound of the piddle against the tin

THE HOOP OF LIFE | 141

changed in pitch from higher to lower as I filled the bottom half of the can. My hands felt the heat from the warm urine through the tin.

"All done?" Mom asked. I nodded. She took the can from me and carefully hoisted it into the front seat. A waft of pee smell crossed my nose as she lifted the can. I pulled up my pants and sat on the front edge of the big bench seat next to my brother. We both focused our attention on our mother, who was preparing to pitch the pee out the passenger side window. While cradling the baby in her left arm, she held the can with her right hand above the middle of the front seat between herself and Dad. In a quick sideways motion, she swung the can across her lap, left to right, toward the open window, turning it over on its side in the process. At the open window, she halted the can's forward motion and launched the urine into the air. As the air whooshed by at 60 mph, the urine instantly atomized into a fine mist. The backdraft blew the cloud of urine into the back seat of the car, soaking my brother and me. Our faces were drenched. The urine left an unforgettable salty taste in my slightly open mouth and an intense stinging sensation in my eyes. The silhouettes of my brother and I were outlined on the back of the seat behind us by the darker damp fabric.

The bigger problem now was the urine in the new car! Dad blew a gasket. "You dumb broad! You don't throw it at the open window!" His thick neck flashed ruby red, and he yelled out a string of words that I had never heard before. "... *GAHDAM... SONVABISH... JEEZUZ-H-KRYST!*" He quickly slowed the car down, pulled it onto the shoulder, and stopped. "... What the hell were you thinking?" He frantically got out of the car, opened the trunk, and found his stash of rags. He then came around to the passenger side, opened the back door, and started sponging the urine off the upholstery in the back seat. His big torso and arms moved us two boys aside as if we weren't there. "Jeezuz! What were you thinking?" he repeated.

Silence and sternness washed across Mom's face. She set the can on the floor and tucked the baby into the portable crib, a small, white plastic tub with a tall handle, which sat in the front seat between her and Dad. Then she stepped out of the car and walked around to the driver-side rear door. Opening it and reaching in, she gently grabbed my brother and me by the arms and removed us from the car, without saying a word. After standing us up against the rear bumper, she reached into the trunk and opened one suitcase, where she found a clean towel, a washrag, and a bar of hand soap. She calmly pulled off our damp and smelly T-shirts. Using the drinking water from our travel bottle, she gave us each a quick spit bath and dried us. All this time, Dad was in a frenzy cleaning the interior and exterior of the car. Mom found two clean T-shirts in a suitcase. These were the extremely ugly, tight-fitting, horizontally striped, colorful variety of T-shirts that were popular in the '50s. She helped us pull the T-shirts over our heads and shepherded us back into the car. After that, she returned to the front seat, closed the door, picked up the baby, and waited, stone-faced.

Upon completing his grumpy last inspection, Dad returned his rags to the trunk and got into the car, and we headed on down the highway. A mile or so down the road, while keeping her eyes straight ahead and her head locked in vertical posture, our mother calmly and specifically spoke. Her comment threw Dad into another blast of colorful railroaders' language, spouting more words that I had never heard before. She said, "If you'd bought a car with air-conditioning, this never would have happened."

CHAPTER 32
Dog Hugger

Central Minnesota, summer of 1858

The grandmother gives a sideways glance at the boy as he walks past the tepee with his dog. The look on her face is somewhere between amusement and disappointment. The little boy has been hugging his dog ever since he first learned to walk. They are inseparable. His older sister has her doll to hug. Grandmother has her newborn baby brother to hug. The boy hugs the dog... always, ever since the dog was a little puppy at the time the boy was learning to walk. The boy is regularly seen standing with two arms locked around the animal's body, lifting it up against his chest. The puppy's head and front legs stick out above the boy's arms. Its plump little puppy tummy protrudes below the boy's arms, with its back legs dangling just above the ground and its tail curled forward.

Over the summer, the puppy has grown faster than the boy. The dog will always be small by dog standards, but even so, the dog's legs have doubled in length while the boy's hadn't grown much longer. Still, the boy hugs the dog. But now, the dog's back legs reach the ground. Using his hind legs only, the dog walks in front of the boy, his motionless front legs sticking out into the air above the boy's arms. The dog is happy to be part of it all.

"We should call him Dog Hugger," the grandmother says with a degree of sarcastic humor.

But there is a problem. Life out on the treeless prairie is a ceaseless struggle. The little boy is expected to help, even at his early age. His immediate task is to gather dry brush to be used as kindling for the family's fire. While gathering twigs, the boy continues to hug the dog. The boy and dog bend over forward together until the dog's front legs touch the ground. The boy then gathers a twig with his unused hand and stands up again while hugging both the dog and the collection of twigs in the other arm. It is a rather awkward arrangement.

The boy's father returns from a council meeting, walking with two of his warrior companions. The men take notice of the odd-looking mixture of boy, dog, and twigs walking on four legs toward the tepee. As the men part company, one of them offers a sideways comment, "You should call him Dog and Sticks."

The father, feeling slightly humiliated, moves towards the boy to take action and correct what is, in his mind, a ridiculous display.

"Put the dog down," he says, as a fatherly command. He then reaches toward the dog to remove it from his son's grasp.

The boy immediately draws back, yells, "NO!" in protest, and hugs the dog even closer.

The dog shows its canine fangs, growls, and snaps at the father's hand. As the man yanks his hand quickly away, the dog follows up with several aggressive barks.

The boy's grandmother, mother, and older sister witness the scene in its entirety. The three females are kneeling around a fresh hide that is stretched and staked to the ground near the tepee. They are scraping and cleaning it. The grandmother does not miss the opportunity to throw a sarcastic comment at the father, who is her own grown son.

"We should have named you Fast Hand."

The irritated father turns to the boy's mother and says, "When are you going to teach our son to stop hugging that dog?"

The mother looks up from her position on her hands and knees. She then sits back onto her heels, one hand dropping into her lap, the other holding the scraping knife. Her voice flares, "When am *I* going to do it?" She shakes her knife at the man, throwing scraps into the air. "I've been working on this skin of yours all morning, so you, the great and mighty warrior, can have a decent coat. I'm going to have to paint your war stories all over the coat, sew on the stinking scalps you've collected, and decorate it with

THE HOOP OF LIFE | 145

porcupine quilts." The anger in her voice peaks. *"NEXT TIME, YOU CAN CLEAN YOUR PORCUPINE!* Then, maybe I'll have time to teach your son the right way to pick up sticks!"

His daughter and mother look up and offer scowls in support.

The father quickly concludes that the situation is out of control. His mother, his wife, his daughter, the boy, and the dog are all giving him trouble at the same time. The only family member who isn't grousing at him is the papoose who is resting in his cradle that leans against the tepee. The baby wobbles his head and reaches out with his one free hand, trying to grab at the dog.

In silent frustration, the father waves a backhand gesture at them all, turns and walks off to find a sympathetic ear among his fellow warriors.

Red Owl explained to me that traditionally, a Dakota person was given a name at birth, and later received a final name derived from some outstanding thing that the person did that was memorable.

"The Dakota male received his second name at the time of leaving adolescence and becoming a man, through a Vison Quest. During this rite of passage, the boy, at the end of his youth, was isolated on a hill with his pipe. He remained by himself for four days and four nights, while praying for a vision to come to him. His vision would tell him what he should do as a man, and what his name would be."

CHAPTER 33

Larry

Colorado, summer of 2011

Continuing our newfound mission, two old people having fun, Karen and I drove eight hours west to spend two weeks in Estes Park, Colorado, to visit friends and do some hiking and sightseeing before her return to Paris.

I had one secondary aim for the trip. That was to take a day to find my long-lost older brother, Larry. His last known location was Denver, which was an hour's drive away from Estes Park. Larry was seven years older than me, making him about seventy years old. Every holiday season, I would receive calls from his children, who were now young adults, scattered around the country, getting married, having kids and raising families of their own. There was a sorrowful question that they would always ask me at the end of the holiday greetings. "Uncle Steve, do you know where my dad is?" I never was able to provide an answer. When Larry left their family twenty years ago, we all lost contact with him. I tried to reach out to him several times, unsuccessfully. Now, there was the distinct possibility that Larry was dead and gone.

I had collected all the old addresses and phone numbers I could find for Larry, using an old address book, Christmas lists, and torn envelopes with return addresses from my kitchen drawer. My younger brother, Dean, and my cousins were equally in the dark about Larry's location, but had some old addresses and phone numbers to add to my list. Most of the addresses were from the Denver area. On this day, I intended to drive to Denver and search for him. The last thing I did on my way out of Estes Park was to sit down in a local coffee shop with Karen and look through a missing persons search service on the internet, resulting in a few more possibilities in the Denver area. With all available locations for Larry in hand, I headed down the highway. Karen stayed in Estes Park to enjoy the day with our friends.

In the car, I started calling the dozen phone numbers I had gathered. "The number you have called is not in service" became a recurring recorded message. Twice, a real person answered the phone. The first one was polite. "Nobody here by that name. I've had this phone number for ten years." The second one was not. "Wrong number," followed by an abrupt disconnect. I called my entire list of phone numbers for Larry and found none to be correct.

Near the outskirts of Denver, I stopped at a convenience store and bought a city streets map. GPS service was not possible on my old flip phone. My address search had to make use of old-school methods. Near the northern outskirts of Denver, I turned onto Sagebrush Street, which was a gravel industrial road. The first address for Larry was nonsense. It was next to a metal salvage yard out in the middle of dry ranch land. Semi-trucks whipped by, kicking up clouds of dust that settled onto my car. The next address was in an aging neighborhood on the north side of the city, an apartment building where Larry had once lived. A middle-aged woman answered the door of the third-floor unit. Not recognizing my brother's name, she said that she had lived here for eight years and was not aware of any forwarding addresses. The third address was in a '50s-ish suburb on the west side, 1244 Linden Street. The trouble was that between 1200 and 1300 Linden Street, there was an entire city block occupied by a new grade school and playground. I drove into the midafternoon in search of more addresses. Near the city center, an area had been demolished and turned into an office park. There was a defunct trailer court address. I found another bogus apartment address where Larry and his fourth wife had lived long ago. That's right, his fourth wife.

Larry and I grew up together in Lincoln, Nebraska. I have a vivid recollection of a life-changing family conflict revolving around Larry. I was twelve years old. Recently graduated from high school, Larry was living at home and working on the line at a plastics manufacturing plant. I remember him looking like a "hood," wearing a greasy Elvis-style hairdo and rolling a pack of Lucky Strike cigarettes into the sleeve of his white T-shirt. On this day, Larry and Mom were shouting at each other in the kitchen. This was becoming a regular occurrence. Larry had done something terribly wrong, and Mom was well beyond mad. I did not understand what it was about. After screaming back and forth at each other several times, Mom slapped Larry hard across the face. Larry responded by swinging his fist and hitting her squarely on the cheek. She retreated backwards, holding her face, breaking into tears.

As I watched the violence exploding in front of me, my young soul was ripping apart. I reached out with both hands and screamed, *"STOP IT...STOP!"*

Dad had been in the backyard and was coming in through the kitchen screen door, drawn to the yelling. He saw Larry hit Mom. Dad, a tough blue-collar ex-WWII guy of few words and a big frame, outweighed my brother by more than a hundred pounds. Dad took several aggressive strides across the kitchen floor, accelerating like a freight train into Larry. He smacked Larry with a fist in his face that knocked him off his feet, nearly unconscious. Larry's thin and gangly frame flew backward, slamming into the wall and sliding down onto the floor. Dad leaned over, grabbing Larry with both hands by his shirt. He dragged Larry across the kitchen floor and threw him out the back screen door. The latch exploded into pieces as the door crashed open. Larry tumbled outside onto the driveway, arms and legs flapping wildly about, landing on his back. Dad stomped forward and hovered over Larry like a big grizzly bear. He yelled, *"GET YOUR ASS OUT OF HERE, AND DON'T EVER COME BACK."* Larry scrambled to his feet, retreated down the driveway, and ran off down the street. A shredded Lucky's wrapper and mangled cigarettes were scattered across the driveway, echoing the violence that had just occurred. The memory of this event seared into my brain. I never saw Larry around our house after that. Our mother died of cancer three years later.

So here I was, searching for my long-lost brother that I hadn't seen in some twenty years, driving around Denver for three hours or more. The six addresses that I had for Larry were all wrong. I had only one left to check. It was late-afternoon, and I needed to head back to Estes Park soon. Compared to the others, this one was a longshot. It was the address of Larry's fourth ex-wife's sister. If she was still there, maybe she could give me some information as to Larry's whereabouts. The phone number I had for her was incorrect. I pulled my car up to an address in Winchester, a suburb of Denver, in front of a small a one-story brick house with a hip roof, probably two bedrooms, '50s-ish. I walked up to the front door and rang the doorbell. A stocky, elderly lady wobbled to the door. Through the screen, she gruffly asked me, "Wuh duh yuh want?"

We were both probably thinking, "*This is going to be a waste of time.*" I said, "My name is Steve Laughlin, and I am trying to locate my brother Larry Laughlin. He gave me this address a long time ago. Do you know his whereabouts?"

She raised one eyebrow and dropped her chin to look at me over the top of her glasses. "Larry?" She paused after my question, then gut-grunted, "Humph!" and said, "He's out back working on the shed."

Needless to say, I was surprised. She opened the screen door and motioned for me to come in. We walked through the house to the back and stepped out through the sliding door onto the patio. The old woman moved to the right and backed up to lean against the house. She folded her arms as if to say to herself, "*This will be interesting.*" She yelled in the direction of the shed in the corner of the property. "Larry, there is someone here to see you."

Two guys in sweat-ringed baseball caps popped their heads out, one from behind the shed and the other through the shed's open door. I walked toward the shed, and they approached me. Both were skinny old geezers, stripped to their waists. Both had oversized guts, as if each had swallowed a basketball, suggesting long histories of beer drinking. It was a weird sight, these two half-naked string-bean guys with their bulging guts. Both had their mouths open as they approached. Between the two of them, only one tooth was visible. Neither one of them looked familiar to me. "Can I help yuh?" the guy with the tooth asked.

"Is one of you Larry?" I responded.

"That's me," the one with the tooth said.

"I might be your brother. My name is Steve Laughlin." We walked to within three feet of each other, leaned forward, and looked more closely. In a moment of mutual recognition, we saw something familiar in each other's eyes. "It *is* you!" I exclaimed.

Larry pulled his head back on his rather spindly neck, dropping his chin onto his protruded Adam's apple, and responded with a country-western twang, "I'll be damned. Well, hi there, li'l bruh-thuh! How yuh been?" He displayed a big, bare-gummed smile with his one tooth front and center.

After a handshake and a sweaty hug, we sat down together at the picnic table and chatted. As we got started, the older lady brought us a couple of cold cans of beer. Larry took off his baseball cap and exposed his balding scalp, which was dramatically different from my memory of him with his Elvis doo. He then gave me a rundown of the events in his life, and I did the same. Larry had led a colorful past. After being kicked out of my father's home, he had joined the Army and had spent four years as a private, stationed in Germany. Upon his discharge, Larry came back to our hometown, Lincoln, Nebraska, and, if my math is correct, he was married four times during the next eight years.

His first marriage was to Ruthie. She was a fairly smart and cute young lady, but she had a prosthetic leg, the result of a horrific accident as a child. The world can be a cruel place for a handicapped person, and I suspect Ruthie grew up feeling like a second-class citizen. She married Larry, despite his shortfalls, probably thinking that he was the best she could do for herself. Larry quickly drove her up the wall, and she threw him out.

In short order, Larry found another lady and was married for his second time. Mary was her name. She was tolerant enough of Larry, but was dramatically overweight and diabetic. They had a baby girl, and she quickly became pregnant again. Tragically, she died of a heart attack while giving birth to twin girls. Larry now had twin newborns, a toddler, and no wife. My father bluntly told Larry that he was "too dim-witted to raise three little girls." Dad demanded that Larry give the children up for adoption. Our cousin from Denver, who had driven in for Mary's funeral, threw Larry a lifeline. She invited him to come to Denver, where she would help him get his life in order. Larry, running away from Dad again, moved to Denver with his three little girls.

In Denver, Larry hired a babysitter named Caroline, a big bodied, take-charge woman who liked to wear bib overalls. She quickly became Larry's third wife. She was exactly what the three little girls needed, and they called her "Mom." But Larry was pushed aside.

It wasn't long after that he looked elsewhere for companionship. Caroline caught Larry fooling around with another woman. Larry was thrown out, again, and they divorced. Being thrown out was becoming a regular pattern in Larry's life. Caroline kept Larry's kids. Larry married Jan, the other woman. This was Larry's fourth wife. Next, Jan started fooling around with another guy and became pregnant, resulting in Larry divorcing for the third time. It was about this time that I lost track of Larry. Obviously, maintaining family ties wasn't his favorite thing.

OK. So here was seventy-year-old Larry, back together with his fourth wife, living in her sister's house, with her mother, and his ex-wife's brother-in-law, who was helping Larry fix the shed. Also living there was Larry's ex-wife's son, whom Larry had not fathered, now sixteen years old. The house was also the home to the sister's son and daughter-in-law and their two children, boys ages seven and nine. This brought the tally, near as I could tell, to ten people living in the two-bedroom house, which would have required some creative communal living solutions.

My guess was that Larry might have been the only sure-thing source of income for the group. Larry was a veteran and had become a lifer in the Army Reserve, which would have resulted in a pension. He had also worked over the years for Pinkerton as a night watchman, Barney Fife type; therefore, he had a check from Social Security every month. His stable income would have gone a long way towards explaining why Larry and his ex-wife had gotten back together again, with her clan of relations in tow.

As our reunion chat was winding down, I asked Larry, "Why don't you call your kids once in a while? You've got grandkids you didn't even know about."

He responded, "Those damn kids never call me!"

I explained to Larry, "They don't know how to! Your phone number has changed, and all your past mailing addresses are wrong." We rectified the situation on the spot, exchanging phone numbers, addresses, and email. I promised to pass the contact information on to Larry's children and keep in touch.

As our conversation ended, Larry put his sweat-ringed baseball cap on over his balding head. We stood up and pitched our empty beer cans in the garbage. Larry grabbed his western-style shirt from the back of a chair and slipped it on, pearl snap-buttons undone, bare gut protruding. We walked out front to my car, gave each other a sweaty hug, and said our goodbyes. I got in, rolled the window down, and started the car. Standing next to me in the street, Larry reached through the window and gave me a pat on my shoulder. He flashed his one-tooth, bare-gum smile and summed up the day in his twang, "Damn good to see yuh, li'l brother. Don't be a stranger, now."

CHAPTER 34

The Childhood Memory

Lincoln, Nebraska 1961

When I was an eleven-year-old boy, I had my first encounter with the Sun Dance. Remembering details from fifty years ago is difficult, but my youthful observations and emotions from this specific event are still vivid and riveting. I was on a school field trip to the museum of the Nebraska State Historical Society in Lincoln. The big yellow school bus stopped in the parking lot and opened its doors. The group of jabbering kids dribbled out onto the pavement and herded into the museum's front door.

As we shuffled into the exhibit area, I drew my youthful attention to a scaled model on display in the corner. It was about the size of a card table and was under a glass cover. A descriptive plaque was attached to the exhibit entitled *"The Sun Dance."* The model representation showed a ring of posts surrounding a flat area. Inside the ringed enclosure were scaled figures, several inches tall, not unlike the toy soldiers in my play chest at home. My interest changed to intrigue as I looked closer. These custom figurines depicted Indians. They were immaculately painted and attired in precise miniature detail. Each was half-naked, wearing buckskin leggings, breechcloths and moccasins. Their bare torsos and faces were decorated with body paint, and feathers were hanging from their hair. A tall post stood at the center of the circular area. Long lengths of rope were attached to the top of the post. Several figures were dancing at the ends of the ropes. My childish first impression was that the scene was festive, not unlike a Maypole dance. A group of Indians sat around a large drum at one side of the arena, and some spectators were at the perimeter.

I focused my attention more closely. Each strand of rope was pulled taught as the Indians danced in a circle. But the ropes were not held in the dancers' hands, nor were they tied around the dancers' waists. My perceptions changed from focus to surprise, then to shock. *The ropes were cinched into the living flesh of each dancer!* Two sharpened pegs were pierced through folds of skin at the top of each dancer's chest. Ropes were lashed to the blood-soaked pegs. Leaning backward, the dancers pulled the ropes taught. The flesh was pulled outward from their chests, stretching their skin into cone shapes. Blood streamed down each dancer's torso. "WHAT? OH MY GOD!" To this boy observer, having recently been traumatized by a bloodied finger caused by a wood-carving accident, this scene was incomprehensible and horrifying.

"Why are they doing this?" The dancers were intentionally leaning outward, inviting the pain, purposefully stretching the ropes, creating extreme suffering. This inquisitive boy made a frenzied attempt to read the description attached to the display and understand what he was seeing. "*Sacred ritual of the Sioux... outlawed by the white man...*" Nudged by the teacher to rejoin the students moving into the next room, I was pulled away before I could find an answer to my question.

This traumatic childhood memory lingered in the back of my mind for half a century. Over the passage of time, I overheard bits and pieces of knowledge, guarded and protected comments, hearsay and smatterings of descriptions. Recently, as I worked on architectural projects with the Dakota and Lakota people, I began to understand that the Sun Dance is a sacred rite that is cherished and protected. This sacred dance is conducted within a sacred circle and a sacred space, comparable, I guess, to the white man's sanctuary. I began to see the spiritual bond between the dance, the circle, the space, and these people. I began to understand my childhood memory. This seemingly unfathomable suffering that each dancer was imposing upon himself, this challenge to his own physical endurance, was a personal sacrifice for the spiritual benefit of his people, to help in the formation of a common vision.

In 2011, somewhere in South Dakota on a treeless hilltop, the prairie was hot and dry. It had been an exceptionally dry winter and spring. All green was purged from the grasses, replaced by the color of straw. The prairie had lost its fight with the heat. Rolling, parched hills ran as far as the eye could see. Knee-high whips of straw-grass lay over, nodding in an oppressively hot breeze. The treeless plain was broken only occasionally by a sprinkling of scraggly, browned-out cedar bushes struggling to survive.

Dark silhouettes of three men moved against a vast sky. Two of them sweated and strained to control the gas-driven hand-held auger, burrowing a hole into the ground, spitting out a nest of dry prairie soil. A log post was lifted onto a strong shoulder, then carried and end-dropped into a hole. Few words were uttered, short phrases, "Deeper... Over there... Drop it... OK." Backfill dirt was kicked by a dusty boot into the hole around the post, then tamped snug with a sledgehammer, head to the ground, held like a walking stick, lifted and dropped, lifted and dropped, *thump...thump*. Rivulets of sweat rolled down bronze skin, cutting channels through the coatings of dust on bare torsos. Logs, yet to be erected, were lying in a jumbled pile like giant pick-up-sticks.

When completed, the hilltop construction was an arena formed by a double ring of posts. Each concentric ring had twenty-eight posts, representing the twenty-eight ribs of the sacred buffalo. Each post had a *Y* shaped crutch-like top, symbolic of strength and unity, used to cradle the horizontal beams. Rope lashings held them together. Smaller-diameter branches spanned between the beams, forming a trellis. Dry, brown cedar boughs were stored in a pile, waiting to be placed over the top, to complete the sun-shaded perimeter. Four entry points into the circular arena were taking shape, at the cardinal compass points, each with a gate fashioned from a cherry wood frame stretched with a colored blanket. The trunk of a single cottonwood tree rested on its side, waiting to be hoisted into the center, to complete this sacred space.

The Sun Dance ceremony was outlawed by the US federal government as part of the assimilation of the 1800s. The failed white man's plan was that they would make the Sioux Indians into model citizens, dress like the white man, farm like the white man, speak in the white man's tongue, and worship under the white man's religion. It was against the law for these people to practice their own religion, speak their own language, or wear their traditional dress. Not until 1978 and the passage of the American Indian Religious Freedom Act, signed into law by Jimmy Carter, were Native Americans given their freedom back, freedom to teach their children to speak their native language and freedom to worship in their own way.

Red Owl explained to me, "After a century's passage of time, the People were given back their freedom to conduct the Seven Sacred Rituals, freedom to do their sacred Sun Dance, within the sacred Hoop."

CHAPTER 35

The Proposal

Omaha, October 2011

Throughout 2011, Karen and I were together the majority of the time, hopping back and forth across the Atlantic, in pursuit of our motto: two old people having fun. By the end of the summer, I had pretty much convinced myself that she was *the one*. In September, she was back in France for the month, while I remained in Omaha for work. Upon her return to Omaha in October, my plan was to propose that we get married.

OK... but how to go about it? First, I need a ring! I talked to my artist friend, Margie, who made custom jewelry. I came up with an idea for a wedding ring design and did a mock-up, using a beer can to mimic a finger, wrapped with a clay band in the shape of the ring and using a large marble to represent the diamond. She liked the idea I showed to her. Before she could cast the ring in gold, Margie would do a wax ring, actual size. It would be best if Karen could approve the wax ring design before casting it in gold. She could show Karen several diamonds to choose from. And she needed Karen's finger size.

OK... so, that means I can't do the traditional thing of popping the question down on one knee with ring in hand. Well, there's nothing "traditional" about us, anyway. Guess I could hold on to a bit of prenuptial surprise by proposing to her after we visit Margie, to size the ring and pick the diamond. But, to keep my intentions secret, I need a good lie to get Karen over to Margie's place.

Upon Karen's October arrival in Omaha, I announced the lie that we had been invited to dinner at the home of a friend whom Karen had not yet met. She and I dressed up for our dinner engagement in our fancy clothes and I opened a fresh bottle of Bleu de Chanel men's cologne that Karen had brought from Paris as a present. We walked over to Margie's house, which was a few blocks away, and rang the doorbell. Margie answered the door and invited us in while she yanked on the collar of her big dog to keep it under control. Margie was wearing blue jeans and a sweatshirt. My guess is that Karen was surprised. *"OK... apparently we have overdressed for the dinner."*

Margie said, "Oh, you two look so nice. Sorry I'm a bit grungy. I've been working in the garden today."

During introductions, as we stood in the entry hall, Karen glanced into the dining room to see that the old oak dining table was littered with books, newspapers, and garden gloves, and was definitely not set for dinner. Karen prompted Margie with a question. "Are we here on the right night?"

Margie said, "Yes, we were expecting you. The place is a bit messy, but come on in."

I imagine that Karen struggled to make sense of it. *"OK...maybe they have another room set up for dinner."*

Karen presented Margie a fancy box of French chocolates. Margie took them and said, "That's nice. You shouldn't have." We removed our dress coats. "Just set them over the chair."

There was a powerful aroma of barbeque sauce wafting through the house, and Karen commented, "Smells great!"

Margie responded, "Oh yeah, we just finished dinner with the kids."

At this point, I realized it was a mistake to not tell Margie that I faked the dinner invitation to get Karen over here. Karen, again, had to guess at an explanation. *"OK...Maybe they fed their kids early to get them out of the way."*

With Karen standing rather dumbfounded, I redirected the conversation to continue the illusion. "Margie designs and makes jewelry. She's got a neat workshop in the attic. Can you show it to us?"

Margie responded, "Sure, follow me."

We walked up three flights of stairs. At the top, we went through a door into the attic, which had a bare plank floor and gabled roof. The edges of the attic were lined with and shelves. Margie directed us to her main workbench and snapped on the overhead task light. She explained, "I do my preliminary ring designs in wax." She held a wax ring up for our inspection. "Once I have the wax ring in the shape I want it, I pour a plaster mold around it. Then I heat the mold in my oven and drain out the liquified wax. The next step is to pour molten gold into the mold to create the ring. After breaking it out of the mold, some trimming and polishing is required. The final step is to set the diamond into the ring with one of these little brackets."

Karen looked closely at the wax ring and the little brackets. "Fascinating!" she said.

Margie added, "I really like this design. When Steve asked me to make this ring for you, he brought this mock-up, which I used as a guide." Margie handed the beer can mock-up to Karen and mentioned my theme for the ring design; two hands holding onto something precious.

"For me?" Karen asked. She had to make another assumption at this point. "*OK...well, maybe Steve is giving me this fancy ring as a gift. Or, maybe...*" Karen was becoming suspicious, and raised one eyebrow.

Margie read the expression on Karen's face and blurted out a question to me. "Haven't you *asked her* yet?"

Feeling like I was being put on the spot, I sheepishly said, "Well, no."

Karen asserted the next question, "Asked me *what*?"

I paused and took a stab at inventing a noncommittal response. "Well, Karen... uh... would you like Margie to make this ring for you?"

Margie finally figured out what was going on. "*Ok... I get it. I'd better shut up, before I wind up being the one to make Steve's wedding proposal!*"

Karen, after reviewing the wax ring a second time, said, "Well, yes. That would be nice."

Margie went on. "Great. Now you need to pick a diamond. Here are the candidates." She spread three stones out onto the workbench. "This white one is two carats. This next one is bigger, but it has a yellow tint, which devalues it a bit. And this one has a unique oblong shape but is also less expensive because it has a gray hue." She ran down the prices on the diamonds, each being about the cost of a new refrigerator.

Karen said, "They all look great." Her next thought was "*Ok... but this is a heck of a lot to spend on a dinner ring.*"

I broke a long pause and pressed for my preference. "I think the oblong one would nestle into the 'hands' better." We all tentatively agreed, and I promised to phone Margie with a confirmation of our selection in the morning. The last thing was to size the ring. The finger that Margie selected to measure, which was reserved for wedding rings, was a huge clue, and should have revealed my intentions, but Karen missed it. After that, Margie said, "Well, I think we're done here." Her next comment was the understatement of the century. "It sounds like you two need to go somewhere and *talk things over*," she said, giving me a sly wink.

I responded, "That's a good idea. Thanks, Margie." We headed back down the steps. Margie lagged behind to shut off the lights, and Karen whispered in my ear. "Have they already had dinner?"

I whispered back another blatant lie to dodge yet another question. "Yeah, looks that way. I must have misunderstood. We can go to a restaurant." At the bottom of the steps, we grabbed our coats and thanked Margie again.

"Get back to me tomorrow morning, so I can return the other diamonds to the dealer. And good luck!" Margie said, throwing me yet another sly wink as we headed out the front door.

Out on the sidewalk, Karen turned to stop me. "What is going on, Steve?" she prompted.

Delaying my response, I said, "Let's talk about it after we get across Fortieth Street." I slipped past her and continued down the sidewalk toward home, inviting her to come along with a hand gesture. We crossed the street at a break in the traffic, which commanded our attention for a few seconds, and we arrived at the corner of Joslyn Castle.

"Why don't we walk through the Joslyn property on our way home," I said. Joslyn Castle is one of the most picturesque places in Nebraska. The old mansion was built of limestone in a heavy decorative style, with beautiful arches, balconies, turrets, and dormers. I threw in a few filler comments as we walked up to the front door. "The castle was built in the late 1800s by a wealthy railroad baron. It has recently been turned into a reception hall and state park." By luck, while overcoming a good measure of confusion on Karen's part, I had hesitated, lied, and delayed long enough. Standing in front of the castle's beautifully arched entrance canopy, I turned and drew her close. We looked deeply into each other's eyes.

At this point, I was guessing that Karen had connected the dots. "*OK...I think I have figured out what is going on here.*" With a sly half smile curling up the left side of her lips, Karen asked in a deep, Garbo-esque voice, "Do you have something to ask me?" She patiently waited for me to say something.

I paused for another few seconds, reveling in the moment, mirroring her lopsided smile. "Will you marry me?" I asked.

Her guarded response was "Well... Yes." We hugged and kissed. Then she added, "*But*... I need to think about it."

Slightly miffed, I turned to lead her with one arm down the sidewalk. "Come on, you can think about it at dinner. We've got a reservation at the French Cafe for eight o'clock." On the walk home and the drive to the restaurant, I explained that Margie hadn't really invited us to dinner. "That was just a ploy to get you dressed and over to Margie's to see your ring being made."

Karen chimed in, "Well, it was very confusing. Do you do anything normally?"

I responded, "Like asking a sixty-year-old lady who lives four thousand miles away to be my wife?"

Karen agreed, "It's not very normal, is it?"

At the end of our fancy dinner, I prompted Karen again. With lots of red wine as encouragement, Karen said, "Yes, I'll marry you," for the second time, and again she qualified her response, "*But* I'm not sure this is a good idea."

All I heard was "YES."

The following morning, Karen said, "Yes," for the third time, "*but* we've got a lot of stuff to sort out to make this work." I phoned Margie and gave her the go-ahead on the diamond ring.

Over the previous twelve hours, I heard Karen say, three times, "YES, YES, YES," but my guess was that Karen remained focused on her follow-up comments, "BUT, BUT, BUT." At this point, we were engaged... kind of, sort of.

CHAPTER 36
Positive

Omaha, April 2012

Six months had passed since Karen agreed we would marry. On this day, I was standing just outside the security lines on the ramp to Terminal A at Eppley Airport in Omaha. Karen had just finished another brief stay in France while I remained in Omaha to continue working. I held a bouquet, thinking that they were probably a waste of money considering the news I had received earlier in the day. I scanned the faces of the people arriving, trying to spot Karen. She was going to be staying with me in Omaha for two months. We caught sight of each other as she approached, with her backpack slung over her shoulder. She was not wearing her typical airport radiant face. We greeted each other with a hug and a kiss.

Immediately, she asked, "Did you hear on the biopsies?"

"Positive," I responded.

"Shit." Her concern deepened, and a grim expression washed over her face.

"We've got an appointment on Thursday with the doctor to discuss the options." I hadn't had a chance to give her the flowers and left them dangling upside-down in my hand as we headed off toward baggage claim.

On Thursday, Karen and I sat in the waiting room of the urology clinic. A scattering of occupants were sitting around, keeping their distance, a grim mix of older men, age spots showing on hands and faces, slouching in their chairs, one with an oxygen rig, another with a plastic bag peeking out from under his pant leg. A blanket of gloom seemed to fill the room.

They invited us into a private room to watch a monitor while we waited to see the urologist. It was an animated video clip describing how robotic surgery removes the prostate gland. Neither one of us had much knowledge of what we were walking into. The video frightened the hell out of us.

"Good God. Are they going to do that to me?"

The forthcoming answer would be "Yes, soon."

We were escorted into an exam room to talk to the doctor. He confirmed I had prostate cancer. They found two cancerous spots within my prostate gland. The results of the biopsy were ominous. The good news was that the spots were small, less than the size of a pea, and that we had found the disease early on. They discussed several strategies for attacking the cancer. All were wildly scary actions. One was to surgically remove a portion of the prostate gland. Another was to insert radioactive pellets into the gland, which would kill the cancerous areas. A third idea was to freeze the infected area. A fourth option was to adopt a wait-and-see posture, to determine how fast it grew. The fifth option was a total removal of the gland, called a prostatectomy, either by conventional surgery or by robotic surgery. The first four options sounded risky, leaving more of a chance that the cancer would return in the future.

Karen quickly agreed with me that the best option would be surgical removal of the gland in its entirety as soon as possible. We scheduled surgery for a month out. We chose the robotic surgery because it would leave less scarring on the abdomen, compared to traditional surgery, and was touted to be the "nerve-saving" surgery because of its improved accuracy.

Prostate cancer is not the problem one would wish on a couple who had just become engaged to be married. The prostate is a small gland, the size of a walnut, located immediately under the bladder. Its purpose is to manufacture the liquid portion of the semen. Nerves that operate the penis run through it. During the operation, these nerves can be irreparably damaged, and semen production ceases. After the operation, it was a genuine possibility that I could never have sex again.

Karen and I agreed that, over the past year, we had been having the best sex of our lives, better than anything either of us had ever experienced before. To have our joyful intimacies taken away from us so soon after we had found each other would be tragic. But that was the situation. We were already expecting that in our senior years, our sexual activity would decline.

"It was good while it lasted" was our refrain.

Our future together was thrown into jeopardy. There was the distinct possibility that we would cancel our marriage plans. Why should Karen get into a marriage where her sexual life was taken away, then be burdened with caregiver duties and eventually watch as her new husband died of cancer? Better for her to cut loose and return to the single life she was accustomed to. The one saving grace was that we could postpone our decision about marriage until after the surgery. Our planned marriage date was still a year away. There was plenty of time to make that decision later.

Also... there was an entire month of time left before the surgery—plenty of time to make up for all the lost opportunities for sex when we were separated by four thousand miles of ocean. During the month before my surgery, looking at the possibility of never having sex ever again, we had a *lot* of sex—every day, three times a day, between meals, during meals, in the morning, at noon, at bedtime and between times. A couple of sixty-two-year-olds were acting like twenty-two-year-olds. We had sex while she was brushing her teeth. We had sex while I was poaching eggs. (The eggs were overcooked, by the way.) During that month, Karen and I were living up to our motto, "two old people having fun." Who needs to worry about marriage when there was all this wild sex to be had right now? Holy cow!

The surgery went as planned, followed by a few days of recovery at the hospital. I came home with a plastic bag taped to my leg above my ankle to collect my urine. A catheter tube was inserted through my penis into my bladder, and my urine drained through a plastic tube down my leg and into the plastic bag. This was a temporary arrangement that was required during the week after surgery to allow healing. Part of the urine duct that ran through the prostate gland was surgically removed, and the two loose ends were spliced back together.

After returning home, I was feeling pretty good and could walk around comfortably. I walked out into the yard to talk to Ron and Gary, two of my neighborhood buddies who were standing on the sidewalk out front. As I approached, Ron said, "Jeemony, Steve, you are looking great. You are really fit and trim these days."

With sarcasm in my voice, I said, "Not bad for a guy who just had his prostate removed."

Karen and I had told no one about my situation until this moment. This was news. Pulling up on my pant leg, I proudly showed the guys the urine bag taped to my calf.

Through the week after surgery, I felt fine and adjusted to the new routine related to the urine bag. Karen was with me but planned to head back to Paris on the coming Sunday. I was in the hospital for another day on Thursday for the removal of my catheter. I came home wearing a pad in my shorts to collect any urine that I accidentally released. Because of nerve damage, I had lost some of my control. The pads would become a way of life for me, although I didn't know it. On Friday, one of our friends stopped by to see how I was doing, and all seemed to be well.

At bedtime, I confronted a powerful pain in my gut. The pain grew and persisted. I lay down on the bed and doubled over on my side. "Karen, something is wrong." The pain continued to grow, becoming aggressive and intolerable.

Karen rushed in and assessed the situation. "What is it, Steve?" she prompted.

"PAIN...in my gut!" I said, as my muscles cramped and I broke into a sweat.

"We're going to the hospital!" she said. Immediately, we were in the car, speeding toward the hospital.

The pain dramatically persisted at an intense level. "Karen! Pull over," I groaned. She stopped at the curb. I opened the door and vomited into the gutter. "Let's go," I yelled as I pulled the door shut, doubled over in pain.

In the emergency room, the terrible pain persisted. They placed me on a gurney and rolled into a curtained room. A doctor and nurse frantically tried to assess my situation. The high-intensity pain was nonstop and intolerable, causing every muscle in my body to constrict. Both Karen and I thought I was going to die. "Stop the pain! Stop the pain!" I pleaded. Karen frantically spouted information about my prostate surgery and the urologist's name and contact information. The nurse tried multiple times to find a vein in my arm to inject a pain killer. All my muscles flinched so tightly that she couldn't find a place to insert the needle into my arm. She tried several times and failed, missing the blood vessel each time. Her forehead broke into a sweat as she complained to the doctor that she wasn't able to do it. My body heaved with a long, continuous cramp. My blood pressure was through the roof. I was covered in sweat. Finally, a second nurse was called in, probably the old pro at injections, who quickly found the vein and administered the pain killer. As it took effect, my consciousness drifted away.

On Saturday morning, I awoke in an intensive care hospital bed and was told that a blood clot in my bladder had caused it to cramp. They had reinserted a catheter. I felt lucky that they had gotten it back in without ripping apart the urine tube that just last week had been spliced during surgery.

After three days in intensive care and three more days on the urology ward, I was home again with a bag strapped to my ankle and a batch of anti-cramping meds and pain killers. Karen was by my side. She had canceled her flight and stayed in Omaha for another few weeks.

Over the passage of this time, Karen and I became comfortable with the idea that we would proceed with our plans to get married, even though our motto, two old people having fun, was a bit compromised.

CHAPTER 37
The Pissers

Omaha, August 2012

Every first Tuesday evening of the month, the Prostate Surgery Recovery Support group would meet in one of the lounges at the hospital. This night there were about ten men in attendance. Borrowing from the acronym, the PSRS, we called ourselves "The Pissers." Our routine was sitting in an informal circle of chairs and having a talk-around, where each old geezer would give an update on the status of his pisser. It is amazing how at-ease a bunch of guys can be when talking about their pissers. It was an unwritten rule that wives shouldn't attend. MEN ONLY. I'd been to a half-dozen of these and never saw a woman in attendance, except that one night that a cute young lady came to give us a medical presentation on our pissers. There was always a rolling cart with plenty of coffee and sugar cookies to keep us all jazzed up.

ATTENTION WOMEN READERS! If you are modest or squeamish about sexual things, you'd be wise to skip this part of the book. Just flip to the next chapter. You guys, you can read on. You will probably enjoy it.

On this Tuesday, there was no formal program planned, just group discussion. I came prepared. When it was my turn to talk, I had a bag of show-and-tell items. I pulled out a contraption that vaguely resembled one of those newfangled fancy squirt guns, the oversize pump-action type. The device I brought had a barrel consisting of a clear plastic tube that was about ten inches long and two inches in diameter. The side of the tube had a measuring scale with a hash mark every inch. Attached to one end of the plastic tube was a gray plastic handle that kind of looked like a fat pistol grip, with a long plastic trigger. A pump mechanism hid inside the handle.

"I call this thing my pecker pump."

The parts broke down to fit nicely into a sexy black travel case with a molded foam liner, reminiscent of a James Bond briefcase with a fancy weapon inside. The kit included what I would describe as four thick rubber bands with varying diameters and thicknesses, each with a tiny number molded into the rubber. There was also a bottle of thick liquid lubricant in the kit, which I called my "love lube."

Ladies? This is your last chance to skip to the next chapter!

Now, you, the reader, need to understand what a prostate and prostatectomy are. As I said in the last chapter, the prostate is a gland that manufactures the liquid portion of the sperm. A prostatectomy is the removal of the prostate gland. Without this liquid for those little wiggly tailed sperm dudes, there is nothing for them to swim around in. As a result, there is no more sperm.

"What? Egads! No more sperm? This is like no more apple pie, no more rock and roll!"

Now, hold on, hold on. Things are not as bad as they sound. The prostate is just below the bladder with some pretty important plumbing going through it, including the sperm tubes, urine tubes and nerves that control your erection and urination. When your prostate is removed, all this plumbing has to be cobbled back together and doesn't work quite right. Nerve damage can be expected, which affects your ability to have an erection.

"What? Egads! My pecker and pisser don't work? No Hard-Ons?"

Easy, big guy, don't give up the ship just yet.

I had a robotic prostatectomy. The doctor who did my surgery sat in a console about the size and shape of a golf cart, located over against the wall of the surgical suite. His head was stuck in what looked like a full wraparound motorcycle helmet. The helmet was his display monitor. I was on the operating table with six jointed probes hovering over me like the legs of a giant metal spider. This was the robot. The probes inserted into my lower belly. The doctor operated with his hands attached to remote controls, kind of like a video game. Compared to traditional surgery, this was more akin to a robotic manufacturing plant. The robotic surgery is supposed to be more precise and minimizes nerve damage. This means that after your prostate is removed, you are more likely to control urination. Also, your chances of having an erection improve.

"WHOOPIE!"

And, instead of being left with a giant scar across your gut, you have some little pencil-size holes in your belly skin that heal up nicely. But keep in mind that your plumbing has been "cobbled together" and doesn't quite work the way it used to, resulting in some limp-and-drippy issues to deal with. Here's where the pecker pump comes to the rescue.

Now, back to my show-and-tell at the meeting of The Pissers.

"Using this contraption, my pecker pump, I can inflate my pecker and have an erection any time I want. And, it lasts up to half-an-hour, not like these two-minute up-and-down sessions you guys are used to. Women have a secret. They differ from guys. Duh! Now, what most men don't realize is that women can have multiple orgasms a lot easier than us guys can, and women can chain them close together into what comes close to the experience of having one long nonstop orgasm. Therefore, your long erection time makes your partner pretty happy. Not only that, but I can also pump my pecker up to a bit bigger than my normal size. You can make it longer and bigger around. This also adds to your partner's fun."

At this point, the coffee and sugar cookies were kicking in, and the old geezers leaned forward in their chairs to hear better.

"The first thing you do is slide one of these rubber bands onto the end of the plastic tube. You need to smear the end of the tube with the love lube to get the rubber band to slide easier. Next, you stick your pecker into the tube and pump it up. Your pecker fills with blood sucked from inside your body. After your pecker is erect, and just before you exit the pump, you slide the rubber band off the end of the plastic tube. The rubber band chokes down around the base of your pecker. This traps the blood in your pecker and keeps you erect. It also prevents any pesky urine drips or squirts from getting out."

The next part of my dissertation really got their attention. Up to this point, I had been talking about making their partners happy, but the next part was about the guys having fun too. "And believe it or not, *you* can have an orgasm too! It's kind of a dry heave. There is no semen, but the pleasure is still there. Remember when you were a young man, and you had three orgasms in an hour? Your fourth orgasm felt just as good, but it was a dry one because there was no semen left in you? It's sort of like that."

At this point, the old geezers were all smiles. They were giddy! One of the guys, named Charlie, had a mischievous smile and raised his eyebrows until you could see the whites of his eyeballs all the way around his pupils. He was the oldest of the group, being over ninety years old. I warned, "Charlie, you are too old for this. If you try it, you'll have a heart attack."

Charlie replied, "I can think of worse ways to die!"

We all had a good laugh. My presentation to The Pissers had been a success. I was the shining light in the darkness, the bringer of joy. If I was to run for mayor, all the old geezers would have voted for me. To celebrate the moment, we had another round of coffee and sugar cookies.

Ladies, Didn't I warn you? Don't blame me! I told you not to read this chapter… but you did it anyway, didn't you?

CHAPTER 38
The Wedding

Couiza, France, April 2013

During the past year and a half together, Karen had told me several times, "When I die, I want the money left in my accounts to be spent on a huge party for all my friends." Considering our recent engagement, I had a different idea for her to consider.

"Imagine a bunch of rickety old people, with walkers and wheelchairs, oxygen bottles and diapers, pacemakers and hip replacements trying to decide if they can even make it to your funeral party, let alone have fun once they get there."

My suggestion was that she should have her party now, while our friends still had some vim and vigor, since some of them were already dealing with age-related problems. Karen thought my suggestion was a good one, and we had a grand party related to our wedding. We planned to have two receptions, one in the south of France, and a second one in Omaha.

Her two closest friends, Paul and Philippe, suggested that Karen look into a place that they knew, in the far southwest corner of France, which might be a pleasant location for our reception. Its name was the Chateau des Ducs de Joyeuses, which roughly translated into the "Castle of the Dukes of Joyful Women." For us two old people having fun, this place sounded right. It was a five-hundred-year-old medieval stone castle in the foothills of the Pyrenees mountains near the Spanish border, on the edge of a tiny river town named Couiza.

In the 1500s, the castle was a garrison for French soldiers and cavalry, an outpost for the region. It had massive walls and round stone towers at each corner, reminiscent of the castle of the Wicked Witch of the West from the movie *The Wizard of Oz*. Three levels of rooms ran completely around the perimeter, with a spacious open courtyard in the middle. It was easy to imagine the place filled with knights on horseback in full armor, riding out through the heavy stone arches to pursue their campaign of subjugation of the people in the surrounding area.

They had skillfully refitted the castle to become a hotel with thirty-five guest rooms, dining, and reception hall, without losing its integrity as an old fortress. Tapered window openings of rooms poked through limestone defensive walls that were six feet thick and had crossbow slits in the old shutters. We invited 75 friends and relatives to come to our mid-April reception in France and stay in the castle for the weekend. A third of them came from the United States and the rest were from several countries around Europe, including Turkey. Karen, in fulfillment of her goal, had her big party for all her friends. She covered expenses for the lodging, food, and drinks (champagne!), while our guests handled their own travel expenses.

My oldest son, Dan, came a week before the reception to stay with us at Karen's apartment in Paris. He had been at his new job in Baltimore for a couple of years and had built up some vacation time and cash to make the trip. My two younger boys had just started new jobs and it would have been too awkward for them to get away, although they would attend the reception in Omaha later.

During Dan's stay in Paris, Karen was wildly busy organizing the wedding event. As a result, Dan and I were pretty much on our own. It was his first time in Paris. I was so proud to guide him around my second city, having spent a good amount of my time there over the past two years.

When Dan left home to go off to college, his primary goal had been to get out of Omaha. After college, he took a job in Baltimore. I had spent little time with him over the last ten years, except for his annual holiday visits and his return home for his mother's funeral. As fathers and sons go, we really didn't know each other very well. He had not seen me as the thinner, healthier guy that I had become. Dan and I had a good time getting to know each other again, two guys bouncing around Paris. One day, while the two of us were on a fast walk from Notre Dame to the Paris catacombs, I turned to Dan and asked him a loaded question.

"Dan, what do you think about Karen and me getting married?" His answer had the potential to be murky and dark, clouded by mother and stepmother perceptions.

He answered with a poignant one-liner. "Well, Dad... you sure are moving faster than you used to." Enough said.

The Chateau des Ducs de Joyeuses was under new management. A vibrant middle-aged couple had purchased the place and spent the winter on renovations. The people of our wedding party were to be their first official customers, and we had booked the entire castle for the weekend of April 19, 2013. Friday afternoon was sprinkled with arrivals, and we served a buffet dinner that evening. Our friend from Baltimore, Jerry, took over the DJ task of playing music in the lounge on Friday night, and we danced into the wee hours. Dan tried, unsuccessfully, to teach me the Macarena. With stone walls and big timber beams, they had renovated the original stables into a lounge that spilled out onto the courtyard. The guests ignored the chilly night air after the dancing and drinks kicked in.

After Saturday breakfast, a group of us took a mid-day train ride to the nearby medieval city of Carcassonne. I was the tour guide. Upon our return to the chateau in the late afternoon, we prepared for our wedding ceremony. The ceremonial room was tiny and was without the dramatic ambiance offered by the rest of the castle. At the very last minute, despite the cool temperature outside, I decided to move the ceremony out into the courtyard. Everyone gathered, dressed in their formal attire.

Our friend Paul began the wedding ceremony with an announcement. "We have a surprise for you this evening. It was not possible to conclude the marriage in Paris last week, because of a problem with Steve's passport. But, today, we have Philippe, the Mayor of Parnans, here with us to officially conduct the wedding. Let the ceremony begin." This was all a huge fib. We had already had our "official" marriage in Paris the week before, but we wanted to do a mock-wedding ceremony today, for its dramatic effect.

As the processional music began, the bridesmaids came down the central aisle. Just moments before, I had picked four of my Nebraska friends from the crowd to be their groomsmen escorts. The ladies, dressed in their formal gowns and enormous hats, holding floral bouquets, took their places up front. My son escorted Karen down the aisle. Karen looked beautiful in her new, flowing, white wedding dress. Philippe conducted his formal reading, speaking in French and looking very official with his bleu, blanc and rouge mayoral shoulder sash. Karen's friend, Thu Huong, translated the message into English, one paragraph at a time.

At the appropriate time, Philippe, the mayor, asked me, "Do you take this woman to be your lawfully wedded wife?"

My response was supposed to be the French version of the word "yes," which is "*oui*", which sounds like "we." I verbalized the "*W*" in English, but dragged it out, saying, "Ou-w-wait a minute. We *are* going to live in Nebraska, aren't we?"

Karen turned to me with an incredulous look and said, "*No*... we're living in France!"

Murmurs and whispers crept through the guests.

I responded, "Well... maybe *some*times we'll be in France, but *most* of the time we'll be in Nebraska."

Karen balked. "No, *most* of it will be in *France*!"

"OK, OK, how about 60 percent in Nebraska and 40 percent in France."

Karen made a counteroffer, "49 percent Nebraska and 51 percent France."

At that point, I reluctantly agreed, "OK, OK!" and mumbled under my breath, "I'm not so sure about this deal."

With impatience showing on the mayor's face, he repeated the phrase, "Do you take this woman to be your lawfully wedded wife?"

I began to say "oui," but it again came out as a question to Karen, "Ou-w-well, *I'm* going to wear the pants in the family, aren't I?"

Karen immediately swung her bouquet and aggressively swatted me on the back of my head, yelling, "*I'm the boss!*" Flower petals, leaves, and pollen dust flew into the surrounding air.

As I brushed floral remnants from my shoulders, I said, "No, no, I'm the boss, my dear, *most* of the time."

Karen agreed, "OK, OK, you can be the boss 51 percent of the time, my dear, and I'll be the boss 49 percent of the time."

I passively agreed. "I guess that's fair, but wait a minute." I turned to one of my groomsmen from Nebraska and said, "Bob? Got your notepad? Maybe you could write this stuff down. It's sounding like a pre-nup agreement." Bob nodded and pulled a pen and pad out of his vest pocket. "Be sure and write down that bit about who's the boss."

Again, I prompted the mayor to proceed. At this point, he balked, saying something in French that I imagined could mean, "This is highly irregular!" or maybe, "This is your last chance!" After a pause, he repeated in French, "Do you take this woman to be your lawfully wedded wife?" The guests were doubting the sincerity of the ceremony, seeing that there was too much drama and over-acting involved.

Their suspicions were confirmed when the four bridesmaids, standing as a backdrop for the ceremony, lifted flashcards, each having a big black individual letter and chanted, "O... U... I... OUI! O... U... I... OUI!"

Slowly, the guests joined in the chant. "O... U... I... OUI! O... U... I... OUI!"

I reluctantly acquiesced and turned to the guests. "All right, already! OUI! You happy, now?" Giggles and applause followed.

Then it was Karen's turn. The mayor said, "Do you, Karen, take this man to be your lawfully wedded husband?"

Karen said, "Ou-w-well... only if he stops slurping his coffee."

"OK, OK, no slurping of my coffee!"

Karen added, "And no clinking of your teeth on your fork when you eat!"

I baulked. "Jeez, Karen, I have these *big* issues like where we're going to live, and you have these shitty little gripes? OK, OK, never mind, no slurping and no clinking!"

Philippe did his best acting to look agitated and repeated his question.

Now it was Karen's turn to hesitate. The bridesmaids began again with the flash cards and the guests repeating, "O... U... I... OUI! O... U... I... OUI!"

After a pause, Karen turned to face the guests and announced, "OUI!" and made a wide, swooping gesture with her bouquet while taking a bow. We kissed as the audience applauded (probably because the ceremony finally ended, and they could go inside to get out of the chilly air and get on with the champagne and dinner).

It was not at all clear that this ceremony had been a spoof, performed as entertainment. Some of our guests required additional explanations to clarify that we had held our *official* wedding in Paris the week before. Luckily, our close friend, Philippe, was, in truth, the mayor of Parnans and had officiated last week's real wedding. He played this part well, convincing a few of our guests that Karen's blow to my head with her flowers was genuine.

I now can confirm that it definitely felt genuine.

CHAPTER 39

The Bass Dog

Omaha, June 2013

Karen and I had a second wedding reception in June, this time in Omaha for all our friends and family who hadn't been able to join us in France the month before. We held it in the backyard of one of our neighbors, behind their beautiful old turn-of-the-century mansion. We arranged a buffet line and dance floor in the large garage of their carriage house. Luckily, everything essential was protected from the weather. Typical of Nebraska in the spring, it rained heavily most of the afternoon and evening, forcing the hundred guests to crowd into the garage. One of our friends had a three-person band that played rock and roll oldies, and we danced into the evening. As we had requested, everyone came dressed in blue jeans, except for Karen in her wedding dress and me in my black tux.

Halfway through the evening, I grabbed one of the band's microphones. Having had a little too much bubbly, I was emboldened to tell one of my favorite stories. I had told this story so many times to my close friends, usually in light-headed settings, that several of the guests groaned and begged me to not repeat it. Not dissuaded, I told it again, with a few embellishments. (Every time I tell this story, there are a few more embellishments!)

It was early June, the prime time of the year for bass fishing. I pulled up to one of my favorite fishing spots, a half an hour east of the Missouri River, out on Highway 30 near Dunlap, Iowa. It was a fairly long drive from

Omaha but was usually worth it. There was a rather small farm pond and acreage that had been taken over by the Fish and Wildlife Department and made into a game preserve, mostly used by hunters and not very popular with fishermen. The pond was in the center of a two-mile square section of land, on the eyebrow of the Sargent River valley, a few miles south of the highway. I arrived towards the end of the evening, with only an hour and a half of daylight left...the ideal time of day for bass fishing.

Now I am not one of those sport fishermen catch-and-release types. I am DEATH TO BASS... HARVESTER OF FISH. I always thought it was rather stupid to spend all that money on fishing toys like boats, trailers, high-tech fish locators, electric trolling motors, only to catch a nice fish and throw it back into the lake. All those silly guys can do just that, and I will be waiting there with my waders and fishing rod, ready to continue my personal program, which I call catch-and-eat.

My loud-mouth younger brother Dean was at the wedding reception, standing near the back of the guests. Dean was a rather heavyset blue-collar guy and was a bit rough around the edges. He yelled, "Talk faster, Steve. We don't have all night." A giggle rippled through the guests. I did my best to ignore him and proceeded with the story...

On this day, I discovered that the access road down to the lake was blocked by a locked gate, due to the recent rain that had made it muddy and impassable. Not deterred, I parked on the grassy shoulder next to the gate. I accepted that I would have to walk down to the pond and was encouraged that I would be the only fisherman there. I opened the rear hatch of my Jeep Cherokee and put on my hip waders.

As I prepared my tackle, a young dog loped across the gravel road and snooped around behind the Cherokee. It was a medium-size hunting dog, with short, soft hair, white with black speckles and one brown ear, an Irish Pointer or English Setter or some such. It was attentive to my activities, wagging its tail. I greeted it with a few kind words, a friendly pat on its head, and an ear-scratch.

At this point, my story was interrupted by Mary, one of the wedding party guests, who was a good friend and neighbor. Standing stage left, she rolled her head back, and let out a howl, "OWU.. ou-ou-owu," in an attempt to mimic a howling dog. Apparently, she had heard me tell the story before. My wise-ass brother blurted out another comment, "That's it, Mary. Jazz it up. This story needs a little help." Another giggle rolled through the audience. I blew off the distraction and continued with the story.

After concluding my preparations, I locked up the Jeep and climbed over the cattle gate. The dog scooted through it, between the bars. There wasn't much of a road, not more than two muddy tire tracks in the grass, weaving down through a flat-bottomed gully full of brush and meadow. As I began my walk toward the pond, the dog ran fifty feet ahead of me and started to cross back and forth through the undergrowth. Apparently, the dog had mistakenly assumed that I was hunting. Not far down the trail, it froze into a pointer pose, one front paw raised, with a stiff vertical tail. I kept walking and flushed two quail from the bushes where the dog was pointing. Probably confused that I didn't shoot at the quail, the dog shrugged it off and ran out in front of me again to locate another covey of birds in the bush.

As I came within view of the lake, a breeze was wafting up over the small earthen dam. I could see a crescent of glassy calm water, protected from the breeze, running along the shoreline in front of the dam. Bass action was visible all along the shore, telltale ripples on the surface where nesting bass were moving about, in the middle of their spring spawn. During the spawn, the bass make their nests in shallow water near shore, by creating a depression on the bottom, using their tails to clear out mud and vegetation. They defend their nests aggressively from other fish but are easily spooked and will retreat to deeper water if they see a fisherman approaching. I believe they can feel the tremors from your footsteps vibrating the water when you walk too close. The trick is to sneak up slowly, stealthily, hiding behind vegetation, and stand back a few feet from the shoreline. I usually make my first cast from twenty feet away from the edge of the lake, to not disturb the fish near shore, and have often caught the best fish of the day on my first cast.

But on this day, this stupid dog was going to run in front of me all the way down to the pond and scare the fish away from the shoreline before I could even make a cast. As I approached the lake, I faked the dog out, turning left and taking a few steps, as if I was going to hunt in the field to the left. Sure enough, the dog scampered into the bush to the left. As soon as the dog disappeared into the undergrowth, I quickly crept down to the shore and made my first cast off to the right. It was a perfect cast, about three feet out from the shore. My lure hit the dead-calm water and sent out a ring of ripples.

The dog quickly realized that my attentions had shifted to the right. It did an about-face and ran at full speed past me, down to my right along the shore. It stopped exactly where I had placed my perfect cast, attracted by the ripples radiating out from my lure. "Gah-dam-it!" I told myself. The animal stuck its head out over the water, between tufts of grass along the shore. Its nose was within two feet of the floating lure. I was pretty sure that any fish that might have been interested in my lure had now been scared away by the dog. Typically, after the rings in the water settle, I would twitch the lure ever so slightly to attract a fish. My fear at this point was that the dog was going to attack the lure and get a mouthful of hooks. But I was so mad that I didn't care. So be it. "Go ahead and bite it, you stupid animal," I said out loud. I gave a gentle tug on my string, and the lure twitched in the water.

Instantly, a giant bass exploded out of the water, attacking my lure, going completely airborne, shaking its head side to side and splashing back into the lake, right in front of the dog's nose. Totally surprised, the dog jumped two feet vertically into the air. Upon returning to the ground, it had a conniption fit. I fought the fish for several minutes before I could bring it to shore. The fish violently thrashed around in the water, while the dog excitedly jumped and zig-zagged, running back and forth along the shoreline. As I lifted the fish out of the water, the dog timidly approached, bringing his jitters under control, and moving his nose to within an inch of the big bass. You fishermen know that bass have a peculiar powerful odor. The fish flipped in my hand, causing the astonished dog to jerk its head away, its two front paws leaving the ground.

I placed the fish on my stringer and walked down the shore to the right. I concluded that I was wrong about the dog scaring all the fish away and decided to ignore the animal and go about my fishing. The dog ran down the shoreline to the right and stopped at about 150 feet out. It stealthily leaned its head out over the water at the shoreline and lifted one front leg.

Then, it froze into a stiff pointer position with jaw set and white tail completely vertical; the tail having a very slight tremor. It took me a minute to realize what I was seeing... THE DOG WAS POINTING OUT INTO THE WATER, PRESUMABLY AT A BASS!

Mary, understanding that this was a high point in the story, stepped in front of me, attempting a pantomime, doing her best to capture everyone's attention by mimicking the dog on-point. Her movements were rather awkward. Remaining standing, she bent forward at the waist, placing one hand forward into a pose to mimic a dog's raised paw, and began wagging her tongue in the air while panting. But she wasn't sure how to mime the dog's tail. She fumbled around with the other free arm, waving her hand in the air behind her back. Settling on a rather pathetic presentation, while continuing to lean forward, she placed her hand, palm up, on her lower backside, then lifted her middle finger to vertical and wiggle it in the air, drawing a chuckle out of everyone.

"OK, OK, Mary, would you stop, already?" I pleaded.

She retracted her wagging tongue and protruding paw, then expressed her dissatisfaction by putting on her pantomime sad face, hands on her hips, elbows out.

Everyone booed me. Dean, attempting to live up to his newfound role as the heckler, blurted out, "Lay off, Steve. She's the best part of the story!" After the giggles quieted down, I returned to the storyline...

Having concluded that the dog was pointing at a fish, I tiptoed down the shoreline, sneaking to within casting range, not wanting to spook the dog and, more importantly, not wanting to spook the fish. I made my cast. The lure landed immediately in front of the dog's nose, out three feet from shore. A wave of excitement overtook the dog and a nervous tremor wobbled through its body. Then, the dog returned to its on-point stance, motionless except for an ever-so-slight nervous wiggle to its vertical tail.

After the ripples subsided around my lure, I gave it a twitch. Immediately, another giant bass exploded out of the water. I fought the fish to shore and landed it.

The dog was probably thinking that this was a pretty odd situation. This definitely was the strangest looking game bird that it had ever encountered.

It didn't hide in the grass, preferring to hide in the water. And the damn thing was not any good at flying, always falling back into the lake with each attempt to go airborne. This funny-looking bird's wings were too small. It was the wrong color, smelled bad and seemed to not have a neck, head, or beak. And... there was this hunter dude who had this strange looking skinny yellow shotgun.

As I placed the second big bass onto my stringer, the dog walked up to me, sat down on its hind legs and waited patiently. It posed, adopting the spitting-image of the RCA dog sitting next to the record player on the old-time advertisements, head cocked to the side. At this point, the dog knew what it was doing. And I knew the dog knew what it was doing. And... the dog knew that I knew the dog knew what it was doing.

I would not be up-staged by Mary this time. I had pre-arranged for the band to back me up. On cue, they played an old Danny Kay tune, "You say pot-ah-toe and I say pot-ay-toe," to which I sang, "I knew the dog knew. The dog knew that I knew. I knew the dog knew. The dog knew that I knew. I KNEW! THE DOG KNEW! THE DOG KNEW... THAT I KNEW!..." As the band played, and I sang, Mary jumped in for dramatic effect. She moved close and grabbed my hand. We danced, doing one of those cool, over-the-head arm-twirl moves. Mary finished with a graceful curtsy and more giggles came from the guests. I went back to telling the story...

At this moment of mutual recognition between me and the dog, I lifted my hand, pointed down the shoreline, and spouted a command: "*Go.*" The dog bolted to its feet, turned, and ran off, following the edge of the pond. It dropped its head and began a visual search, peering into the shallow water. Then, at fifty yards out, it stopped and pointed into the lake.

Filled with confidence that the dog had spotted another fish, I crept close to within range, placed a cast, and immediately caught another giant bass. The dog and I did this several more times until dusk. A five-pound bass is a once-in-a-lifetime fish for many fishermen... and I had three of them on my stringer, which would nicely provide six steak-size fillets. I began planning my next dinner party. Now, you lily-livered catch-and-release fishermen will be happy to know that I caught several more fish that night but released them back into the lake. As the last rose-colored light of sunset was upon us, with the three great big bass hanging from the stringer in my hand, the dog and I proudly strutted up the trail together, side by side.

On cue, the band played a Queen song, and I sang, "We are the champions, my friend..." Mary was quick to sing, "And we'll keep on fighting 'till the end." The reception party guests all joined in, "We are the champions, WE ARE THE CHAMPIONS..." Even my curmudgeon brother, Dean, made a failed attempt to carry the tune. Mary and I finished our duet, hugged, and raised our arms raised in the air. The crowd applauded as Mary and I took our graceful final bows.

To bring us back down to the truth, the story had a sad ending. Later that summer, I was back at the lake and talked to the owner of the farmhouse across the road from the wildlife preserve. The farmer's task was locking the gate when it rained. It was his dog. More precisely, it was the dog of his seventeen-year-old son, who was out back unloading some bales of hay from a truck. The farmer enjoyed my story about the dog's acquired talent for pointing at bass. He called his son over, and I repeated my encounter, slipping in a couple of opportunities to embellish the story.

"Yeah, she was a great hunting dog," the young man said, with some sadness in his eyes.

Then the father spoke. The dog had died, recently shot dead on a neighboring farm that had been losing poultry. His guess was that they had wrongfully blamed the dog for stealing chickens, which were more likely taken by the family of coyotes living on the wildlife preserve. I was saddened by the news, but felt blessed to have shared that one special evening with the bass dog.

Now, my good friend Mary is gone, too... another cancer victim taken away from us before her time. I felt blessed to have shared that one special evening with her, retelling "The Bass Dog Story," jumping on opportunities to add a few more embellishments.

CHAPTER 40

Bicycle

Paris, October 2013

Life in Paris was not yet routine for me in the fall of 2013, but it headed in that direction. Karen and I had been married for six months. Our plan was that we would use Paris for home base for nine months over the fall, winter, and spring, then return to Nebraska for the following summer. This would allow me time to jump through a series of bureaucratic hoops for the OFII, the Office of French Integration and Immigration. Since Karen had French citizenship, our marriage allowed me to process a resident visa, which would let me stay in France for extended periods of time without becoming a full-fledged French citizen. One requirement was that I had to learn the language to a minimum acceptable standard. The OFII offered a French language class, four hours each day, five days each week, which I attended in October and November.

    My choice of transportation for getting across Paris to attend my class was the bicycle. My ride took forty-five minutes each way. The location of my class was on the opposite side of the city. If you think of the map of Paris as the face of a clock, Karen's apartment was at eleven and my class was at five on the dial. This meant that I had to travel smack-dab through the center of Paris twice a day on my bicycle, once during morning rush hour and once during the after-lunch rush.

*   As I pedaled my bike into the heavy Paris traffic, my mind flashed back to a Sioux buffalo hunter out on the Nebraska prairie, riding his horse into a herd*

of stampeding beasts. The fast-moving mass of threatening dark bodies belched out plumes of hot breath. Hulking shapes with rounded black shoulders grunted and bellowed, enveloping me in a thunderous rumble, kicking up dust. It was exhilarating and frightening at the same time.

As I whizzed forward through moving traffic, next to a line of parked cars, I rolled into the narrow gap between the cars and a moving bus, its giant broadside like a wall. My eyes glanced left as I rolled past the bus's giant spinning rear wheel, clearing my elbow by inches. The bus moved closer. My left elbow brushed against the smooth metal body of the moving bus's midsection. Fear welled up in me, and I inched dangerously close to the parked cars on my right.

At curbside ahead of me were five black Mercedes taxi cabs, all immaculately polished, with their rooftop green lights on. The faces of the taxi drivers reflected in their mirrors as I approached from behind. All the while, the bus squeezed me ever closer to the parked cars. The side mirrors that protruded from the doors of the taxis were constricting my path, waiting to be impacted by me on my bicycle. *My mind flashed subliminally to the Sioux buffalo hunter upon his horse, galloping beside an enormous beast, trying to avoid the horn which protruded from the side of the angry animal's head.* As I rolled past the rear fender of the first taxi, the driver pulled his elbow in from the open window. He focused his eyes on my approach and, too late, reached downward for the control lever of his motorized mirror retractor. My right hand tightened around my handlebar grip as my glove slid across the taxi's protruding mirror. Immediately, the irate taxi driver began yelling obscenities at me in French, shaking his fist out the window as I passed. I was relieved that it was only a mild touch, with the fabric of my glove brushing over the top of the mirror. Maintaining my forward motion, I narrowly avoided what could easily have been an impact with the mirror and a lurch to the right into the side of taxi's front fender, followed by a bounce into the side of the moving bus. The taxi drivers ahead of me, watching the close encounter in their mirrors, quickly grabbed for their control knobs and retracted their mirrors, to a chorus of mechanical noises, *"BZZZZZZ, WHRRRR, ZZZZZZT, HMMMM."* I narrowly missed their retracted mirrors as my bicycle slipped by to a second chorus of shouted obscenities. More importantly, I avoided being rolled into a crumpled ball of flesh mixed with bent metal tubing. After the experience, I took up the habit of allowing plenty of distance between moving busses and parked cars before rolling into the gap.

Farther along, having not yet learned to slow down in traffic, I rounded a corner at a pretty high speed, my bike and body leaning left into the curve. Out front of Gare Saint Lazare, I straightened out and encountered traffic ahead of me, stopped at an intersection. I paid attention to the vehicles to my left and right as my bike shot through the gap between the two lanes of cars. I broke into the open and sped up, timing my move to catch the traffic light. Then, as I peered out from under my helmet visor, I was surprised to view five pairs of female legs scurrying through the crosswalk, moving directly into my path.

"Jeezuz!" I said out loud as I realized it was too late to apply the brakes.

These ladies weren't supposed to be there! The pedestrian traffic light had changed from a little-walking-green-man to a little-standing-red-man, signaling a do-not-cross message. This was completely ignored by these ladies, who were preoccupied with hurrying through the crosswalk at the last minute, presumably to squeeze three more minutes into the day's shopping. Slender legs, bare ankles, and stylish black shoes filled my cone of vision. *The sound of the clomping shoes sent my mind subliminally flashing back to Nebraska, to the sound of horses.* Noticing my bicycle hurling forward, the graceful flow of female legs was suddenly discombobulated. One pair of feet stopped abruptly, pigeon-toed, causing another to bump to a stop. Another attempted to move backward, stepping onto a toe behind. An elegant shoe plopped over on its side and popped awkwardly off a foot. A black purse and brand-name shopping bag dropped onto the street. Reaching toward the ground, a hand with an elbow-length black glove chased after the bag and purse.

A gap formed in the wobbling colonnade of legs. My foot powered down on my pedal, and I briskly rolled through the opening. In the clear, as I rolled away, I promised myself to slow down at the next crosswalk.

Further on, as I biked across a bridge over the Seine River, a beautiful, athletic woman, dressed in colorful skin-tight spandex racing clothing, whizzed past me at a fairly high speed, perched atop a sleek and expensive-looking racing bike. My eyebrow raised. Impressed by her grace and muscular physique, my eyes followed her, intently observing her passing. I tried to catch up with her and exhibit the idea that I was a biker from way back, with an abundance of manly stamina, worthy of her attention. Straining to increase my speed, my thighs and calves pumped, sprocket spinning. As I approached from behind, my view of the lady with the muscular legs and butt grew in size. As the distance closed between our bicycles, my shoulders and posture became erect, I expanded my chest and sucked in my gut.

Glancing over her shoulder, she caught sight of my approach from behind. Returning her head to forward, she tightened her grip on her handlebars and powered down with her muscular legs onto the pedals. In seconds, she spread the gap between our bikes from several feet to several meters and zoomed off into the distance, leaving me behind, huffing and puffing, woefully unable to keep up her pace.

The disappointing experience forced me into a self-conscious evaluation. I came to realize that, even though my self-image was that of a handsome twenty-four-year-old athletic dude with swagger, I was, in reality, a creepy sixty-four-year-old man in baggy street clothes, riding a stupid little folding bicycle with tiny wheels, my bargain helmet wobbling crookedly on my head, with my dress socks pulled up over my pant cuffs. These thoughts caused my chest to deflate. As my slouch returned, my gut swelled dramatically, assuming its familiar overhang of my belt.

My gaze drifted longingly down the bridge to the biker lady, now far off in the distance. Upon her disappearing from my view, I reduced my speed, which thankfully reduced my huffing and puffing down to a manageable level, such that my risk of having a heart attack or stroke dramatically declined.

I appreciated the way French people paid special attention to the first word of the French national phrase, *"Liberté, Égalité, Fraternité."*

Occasionally, this was interpreted as justification to take the *liberté* to ignore traffic rules. One rule I loved to ignore on my bicycle was "stay in your lane." Pedestrians occasionally would take the *liberté* to ignore another rule, "Cross the street only at the designated crosswalks." Unfortunately, two people taking the *liberté* to break these two rules at the same time would occasionally result in conflicts.

On one memorable occasion, I was speeding my bicycle between two rows of cars that were stalled in heavy traffic, when a jaywalker stepped out in front of me, attempting to cross the street. This was an elderly woman in a three-quarter-length beige coat, wearing a beige pillbox hat, with a beige purse, and holding a small beige dog in her arms. Her coat disguised the fact that she had a fairly stocky body and a heavy frame.

I immediately set my brakes, trying to avoid an eminent collision as she stepped in front of me. My front wheel grabbed the pavement and stopped abruptly. Momentum threw me forward, rear wheel flying up into the air. My torso launched over my front wheel, head and shoulders flying forward while I held onto my handlebars and brakes.

The short and stocky lady saw me careening toward her, out of control. Taking one powerful step in my direction, she turned her shoulder and rotated her dog away in a protective move. Lowering her head, she leaned into me, landing a perfectly placed body block into my shoulder and neck, stopping my forward motion cold. It was a move worthy of an offensive lineman on the New England Patriots football team stopping a blitz. I was knocked back onto my bicycle seat, and my rear wheel bounced back onto the ground.

Dropping my feet on either side of my bike, I looked up and attempted to speak in the French language, "Excusez-moi, Madame."

She straightened her pillbox hat and looked at me. Catching my accent, she replied in perfect proper English, voicing a masterful understatement, "You really should slow down, you know."

We both took the *liberté* to continue on our way, breaking the rules while weaving through the blocked traffic, me scooting between lanes on my bicycle and her jaywalking across the street while holding her little beige dog.

Upon arriving at my destination, I stood next to my mount. *My mind drifted back to the proud Sioux buffalo hunter, standing beside his horse, gazing out over the Nebraska prairie in contemplation of the challenges ahead.* In my case, the challenge ahead would be to make sense out of the conjugations of the French language.

CHAPTER 41
Fewer Problems

Paris, December 2013

Karen and I were leaving Paris for a week to Malta, an island in the Mediterranean. The trip was a continuation of our mission, two old people having fun, and was a combination Christmas visit and birthday present to me. We had been married for eight months.

While on the local RER train heading toward Charles de Gaulle Airport, I noticed a group of people at the back of the car. A young father was sitting by himself in a section of seats surrounded by a pile of suitcases and backpacks. Directly across the aisle was his wife, his three-year-old son, and another couple. The boy was dangling his feet above the floor. The father reached into his pocket and pulled out his white handkerchief. He leaned across the aisle and wiped his surprised son's nose. The father didn't quite get the job done, so he tried again. This time, the reluctant boy grimaced, let out a "Nuh!" and turned away. In an act of finality, the father reached across the aisle with his free hand and cradled the back of the boy's head in his palm. Suppressing the boy's resistance, he assertively placed the other hand and handkerchief over the boy's nose. He issued a fatherly command: "Blow!" The boy complied. The father completed wiping the boy's nose thoroughly, amid further squirming. At the father's conclusion, the boy, seeming to have resurfaced after nearly drowning, took a deep breath and returned to swinging his feet.

Having raised three sons myself, the scene reminded me of *me*, twenty-five years before. Attempting to telepathically send a message to this young father, I thought, *"When he gets older, you'll have fewer problems, but they'll be bigger ones."*

CHAPTER 42
Ninja

Omaha, July 1990

Many of the bigger problems that I encountered as a father involved Mark, my middle son. Even as a child, he had a tendency to get into trouble. I remembered one occasion when Mark was three years old. It was six months after we had moved into our new house. I was doing a few odd jobs through the summer to complete the house construction and had just finished installing six screen panels to enclose the porch next to the kitchen. Each panel was fairly large, as big as a door.

Mark was enamored with the Teenage Mutant Ninja Turtles, which were popular in the cartoons and toys of the time. As I was walking past the kitchen door, I heard a high-pitched gut-yell, "HEE-YAAAH," coming from Mark on the porch. Turning toward the sound, I saw Mark attacking one of my newly installed screens. He had a ninja "sword" in his hands, which was actually a long-handled sponge mop he had found in the corner. There was no sponge on it, only a bare plate of metal. It ripped completely through the brand-new screen. Mark had just finished his sixth Ninja swing, and all my new screens had long gashes in them. I gave Mark a fatherly talking to.

The following day, I was outside, in the process of removing the damaged screens (that I had just installed the day before!). Out of the corner of my eye, I noticed a yellow leaf falling onto my arm. I didn't give it much attention. Then I noticed several more yellow leaves quietly falling through the surrounding air. It was mid-July. The middle of the summer was not the time for the tree to be dropping its leaves. This was a huge tree, hackberry, fully grown, forty or fifty years old, 150 feet tall, with a giant over-canopy. It was the only full-grown tree on the property, the kind of tree that a person can be proud of... *Dropping its leaves in mid-July!* The bright-yellow leaves were falling like rain, half covering the green grass in my freshly mowed back yard. There was no wind, *just falling yellow leaves!* "What the hell?" I said out loud. I looked up. The entire canopy of leaves overhead was bright yellow. The tree was dying.

I went down the steps into the yard to investigate. My mind ran through the options. Insects? Disease? I walked closer to inspect the tree's trunk, looking for insect bore holes. What I found was a sticky ring of fresh sap around the base of the tree. There was a line of horizontal chop marks in the bark. I walked around the tree. The chop marks encircled the tree completely. The wounds were deep and oozing, at about two feet off of the ground... at "Mark height." Then I noticed my shovel lying on the ground nearby. The long side of the shovel's blade was sticky with sap and sprinkled with bits of bark. My mind raced back to the yell, "HEE-YAAAH," the sound of an attacking ninja that came from Mark as he chopped my screens to bits. "MARK!" I yelled out. "THAT LITTLE SHIT KILLED MY TREE!"

I didn't know where to throw my anger, at the Teenage Mutant Ninja Turtles or at Mark. Mark was within reach. I cornered him inside the house. In the presence of the wrath of Dad, he admitted to killing both the screens and the tree.

Only one time have I ever spanked a child of mine. One time. This was it! I sat down on a dining room chair, holding him at arm's length, rattling out another loud fatherly lecture. Then, I pulled his pants down around his ankles and put him face down over my knee. I raised my hand and slapped down hard, once, on the three-year-old's bare little butt with the palm of my hand.

Mark, who had been drinking apple juice all morning from his little sippy cup, immediately squirted urine down my jeans. I picked him up, my hands under his armpits, facing away, with his jeans gathered down around his tennies. He was launching a continuous stream of piss into the air, his bladder fully loaded. Urine arced out onto the dining room table, the chairs, the floor. Bolting to my feet, I carried him toward the bathroom, which was a few feet away, while Mark squirted a stream of urine across the buffet and stairwell. At the open door to the bathroom, the stream subsided.

Then, the teary-eyed boy turned his head toward me and said in a wobbly little voice, "Sorry, Dad."

I took a deep breath, calmed down, and after a long pause, I said, "I'm sorry too, Mark." I pulled his jeans up and gave him a good, long hug. We went upstairs together to get some fresh clothes.

Little did I know it at the time, but that phrase, "Sorry, Dad," would become Mark's mantra, to be repeated many times over the years ahead.

CHAPTER 43
Dead Cars

Omaha, 2005-2012

As a continuation of my narrative about sons having fewer problems, but bigger ones as they grow older, I am including here a series of incidents regarding cars, spread out over the seven years prior to Karen and I getting married. Now, I realize that a lot of you ladies are not terribly interested in car stories, and you might consider this upcoming chapter to be long and tedious, especially when the time wasted could better be spent on researching the internet for homemade bread recipes. Therefore, I invite you to skip this chapter. Now, you guys, who are more interested in car stories, and in eating homemade bread, can read on.

When Mark, my middle son, was in his last year of high school, I received a call from him. "Dad, I've got a problem."

"*Here we go again,*" I thought. "What now?"

"The Nova was stolen," Mark said.

This was not a baseball that ripped through the neighbor's flower bed or a jacket that was left at a soccer game. It was not even comparable to a bicycle stolen from the front yard. This was a *bigger* problem.

I prompted Mark for more detail. "Where are you?"

He replied, "I'm at the high school. I just talked to the super. The police are on the way."

As I drove over to the school, I said to myself, "*Who in the blazes would want to steal a twenty-year-old Nova? Surely a car thief could find a sexier car in the high school parking lot.*"

The Nova was already a rust bucket headed for the junkyard when I bought it secondhand (maybe or third- or fourth-hand) for the boys to drive to school. It also served as their knock-around-town car, with emphasis on the knocking around. The body and bumpers were pretty well beaten up. Dents and scratches were everywhere. It had cracked turn signals, rust around the wheel wells, a missing hubcap, a broken window crank, and cigarette burns on the seats. An oily film of finger smears coated the dashboard and interior of the windows. A layer of trash covered the floor consisting of wrinkled potato chip bags, crushed chips, squashed french fries, tennis shoe dirt, and several sticky soda-pop stains. Amid all this, there was one immaculately groomed part of the car that was in excellent working order, that being the giant custom array of speakers that lined the back window.

The call from Mark had come late Saturday afternoon. School activities for the day were winding down and the parking lot was almost empty when I drove up. A black-and-white police car was parked at the back door of the school. I made my way to the superintendent's office on the second floor.

Mark, the superintendent, and a police officer huddled over a monitor, looking at a security camera video. The super motioned me to come closer. "Take a look, Mr. Laughlin." He showed me the video. It was a series of still shots of the west parking lot. He explained that there was a ten-second gap between each photograph. His finger pointed to the car on the screen and said, "Now you see it...and now you don't." The car had vanished in the seconds between photographs. There was no evidence or clue given by the video as to what happened to the car. It just disappeared!

Mark and I escorted the police officer down to the parking lot. We talked to students and staff in the car's vicinity, but no one had any useful information. The theft wasn't noticed by anyone. As the officer filled out his auto theft report, he asked Mark, "Did you lock the car?"

"Uh-uh." Mark dropped his head in shame, looking at the ground as he replied.

"Did you leave the keys in the ignition?" was the officer's next question.

"Uh-huh," Mark mumbled, as his cheeks flashed red.

The officer then gave me a sideways glance. I glanced back. As we made eye contact, the officer and I telepathically transmitted a world of understanding to each other.

"Your kid needs some talking to," he said as he finished up. "We'll keep you informed."

Mark and I returned home. I gave him "some talking to."

Mark repeated his mantra, "Sorry, Dad."

It was late Tuesday afternoon when I received a call at my office from the super. "Some kids from the grade school found your car. It's in the trees west of the parking lot, at the bottom of the embankment."

The embankment had a dramatic slope and was overgrown heavily with mature trees and weeds. Down the hill, west of the trees, was a grade school and playfield. The wooded area was the perfect hiding place for the car. Between shots of the security camera, the unoccupied car had rolled backward across the high school parking lot, picking up speed as it went. It hopped the curb and rolled into the wooded side yard, picking up more speed as it rolled backward down the embankment. Near the bottom, the Nova impacted a large-diameter tree, hitting it hard, squarely in the center of the back bumper. The force of the impact folded the rear bumper in half. The tree pushed deeply into the car's trunk lid, such that the crinkled sheet metal lid took on a butterfly shape. When the downward plunge of the car finally stopped, the tree had crunched to within a foot of the Nova's rear window. The rear end of the Nova seemed to hold onto the tree like a clutching hand. The car sat there. Three days later, children discovered it as they peered through the chain-link fence at the edge of their grade school playground.

After calling for a tow truck, Mark and I stood and looked at the wreck. The Nova was a stick shift. I accused Mark, "You left the car in neutral, didn't you!"

"Uh-huh," was his sheepish reply, as he lowered his head to look at the ground.

"And you didn't set the emergency brake, did you!" was my next assertion.

"Uh-uh," he mumbled, his cheeks flushing red again.

As I had done the other day (and on many other occasions!), I gave Mark "some talking to."

And, the mantra, yet again, "Sorry, Dad."

The tow truck arrived. A cable reached the seventy-five feet down to the Nova's front end. The vehicle was rather easily dragged through the underbrush up the embankment onto the pavement. From the rear, the car looked like a blue Hollywood sea monster with gaping jaws that had just crawled up onto the beach to eat some unsuspecting sun-bathers. Mark climbed in behind the wheel and tried the key. We were amazed that the Nova started. We were even more amazed that the car survived a test drive around the lot. All four wheels seemed to be unaffected by the crash. There didn't seem to be any noticeable compromise to its drivability. The brake lights on the back end still worked, even though they had a cross-eyed look. The tow truck guy was paid and drove away. Mark drove the Nova home, and I followed in my car.

After some inspection and strategizing, I tackled the repair of the car myself. I was handy with tools and short on cash. With my toolbox in hand, I went to the U-Pull-It junk yard for cars on South Sixtieth Street. To my astonishment, I found four Nova junkers sitting side by side. They were exactly the same as our car, matching make, year, all four-door models, even the same ocean-blue color. The thought crossed my mind that there was probably good reason that so many twenty-year-old Novas were there in the junkyard. I found a rear bumper and a rear trunk lid to my liking and removed them. The total bill for the two parts was fifty dollars. Now, for me, being cheaper than a sparrow in heat (cheep, cheep, *cheep*!), this fit my repair budget nicely.

The next scene was the Nova at the end of the driveway, rear end to the street, with me standing on the floor of the open trunk, one foot either side of the gaping jaws of the monster, banging on the rear panel with a sledgehammer.

Amazed and concerned onlookers from the neighborhood formed a semi-circle around the car.

"Stand back!" I naively joked as I swung the sledge into the metal. "If the gas tank catches a spark, you don't want to be close by."

The crowd of kids and parents immediately backed away to a safer distance. Luckily the Nova didn't blow up, and Mark drove it to school the next day.

Although the Nova was miraculously brought back from the dead, it didn't live long. Mark called a month later. "Dad, I'm stalled on Dodge Street, west of Thirty-Ninth."

Dodge Street is Omaha's main east-west arterial. It was rush hour. I arrived to witness a very long line of cars backed up behind the Nova, which was blocking one of the westbound lanes. There was an odd mixture of oil and radiator fluid draining profusely from the underside of the engine compartment, which ran out from under the car and into a large puddle in the gutter at the edge of the street. We pushed the vehicle by hand around the corner, out of traffic.

I imagine now, rest in peace, that the car is back in the U-Pull-It yard next to the other four Novas with matching make and year, all four-door models with the same ocean-blue color, with one of them missing a trunk lid and back bumper.

THE NOVA WAS DEAD CAR #1.

Later in Mark's senior year, I received a report from Jim, my neighbor, while I was out of town on a business trip. He had received a call from Mark requesting a ride home after being involved in a fender bender. Jim drove out to Ninety-Sixth and Maple to pick Mark up.

Jim described to me the scene as he approached in his car. A bright and glowing visual show reminiscent of a Pink Floyd stage emanated from the flashing emergency lights of a dozen fire trucks, police cruisers, ambulances, and tow trucks huddled around the intersection of the "fender bender." The Jeep and the other vehicle were sitting in crumpled piles on either side of the street. Mark had attempted a left turn and hit an oncoming vehicle head-on.

They sent the other driver to the hospital with a broken arm, cuts, and bruises. Mark was standing by, dressed in his soccer uniform.

He had been desperate to attend one of his team's soccer games. To learn from the Nova incident, I had left specific directions that Mark could *not* drive my car while I was out of town. To enhance my directive, I confiscated his driver license when I left. As a further preventative measure, I had hidden the car keys in my dresser drawer, upstairs in my bedroom. But Mark snooped around until he found them and killed my Jeep.

THE JEEP WAS DEAD CAR #2.

Four years later, during the week before their mother's funeral, Matt and Mark were leaving with the second family car. I was outside doing yardwork when they backed into the neighbor's driveway to turn around. It was their mother's Nissan, taken over by the boys during her declining health. Matt was behind the wheel, and Mark was shotgun. I had mistakenly assumed that Mark, the middle boy, having worked in a gas station for seven years, would know the basics of car care... you know, check the oil, check the tires, listen for the chirping noise when the brake pads are thin. During their mother's sickness, I had paid little attention to the Nissan. As Matt backed into the driveway and slowed to a stop, the Nissan made a sound something like a cast-iron tub being dragged across cobblestones.

I yelled, "Jeezuz! Can't you hear that?"

Matt saw me running up to the car, stopped, pulled his ear pods out, and grunted, "Huh?"

I took the car in to have the brakes looked at. The shop manager showed me a picture he had taken of one of the brake assemblies. The picture was going to be framed and placed on his Hall of Fame photo wall. It was absolutely the worst case of brake damage he had ever seen. The brake pads had worn off and the metal shoes had been grinding against the brake drums for a very long time. One pad eventually wore completely through the drum wall. The shoe pierced into the drum interior and broke off, looking rather like a scene from *Star Wars* when the Battle Cruiser pierced into the Death Star.

"They didn't hear this?" was the attendant's familiar question.

And this was just one wheel. It was going to cost more than what the car was worth to replace all four brake shoes and drums. The boys had killed the Nissan! Like the Nova and the Jeep Cherokee before, "rest in pieces", this was the third family car that they had sent to the grave within four years. The chronology of our family history was becoming a series of dead car events.

THE NISSAN WAS DEAD CAR #3.

Then there was the dead bicycle incident. This might not be appropriate to include in the dead cars chapter, but one could argue that it has a literary weight that results in a meaningful contribution to the descriptive background and essential chronology of the narrative.

Matt worked at a pizza parlor near home while he was in high school and through college. He would finish Creighton University with an undergraduate degree in environmental science but needed an extra semester to graduate. After all his roommates at their rental house graduated and moved away, he moved back home for the first time in four years. With his mother having recently died and his two older brothers off on their new lives, it was just me and Matt at home. Thanks to the dead Nova, the dead Jeep and the dead Nissan incidents, the young man had no car. His situation compounded because he had no money to purchase another means of transportation.

But his job was nearby, so I bought him a bicycle. Having previously had access to a family car, Matt was initially insulted and embarrassed to be bicycling around, but he eventually accepted it. In fact, this twenty-two-year-old guy quickly turned into an aggressive biker. I often saw him zipping through the neighborhood with speed and impunity, blowing off safe biking and road rules such as stop signs, lane markers, sidewalk edges, curbs, and helmets.

Matt's phone call came to me at the office. He *never* called me at the office. "Dad, I've got a problem. I had an accident on my bike."

Matt was flying down a sidewalk at top speed when he T-boned a car that was crossing an intersection. He slammed into the rear door behind the driver, at 90 degrees to the car. He didn't have a helmet on, and luckily, his head and body skimmed behind the rear window. Coming to a stop lying on the trunk of the vehicle, he suffered only bruises and minor cuts. But the bike crumpled into a heap of metal tubing. The car had a dented rear door and a broken window. Matt received a traffic ticket for failure to yield right-of-way.

"On a bicycle?" I pondered.

I met with the car owner, a Latino, fiftyish. His car was an older four-door Toyota. He had an estimate from two body shops to repair it for about $1,500 dollars. I offered him on-the-spot $750, cash, and said, "If it was me, I'd go to the U-Pull-It yard, yank a window off a junker for thirty dollars, install it myself, and push out the dent by hand." He took the cash. Matt was on foot after that.

THIS WAS THE DEAD BICYCLE.

As you recall, in 2011, Matt had a short-lived and ill-fated encounter with Dad's new roommate, Karen, involving a bottle of scotch and a barrage of Post-it notes, resulting in his exit. He took a new job working with the Park Service in Loup City in central Nebraska. Matt made it through his first season there, but the problem was that the job was only for nine months of the year and shut down over the winter. He found a filler job nearby working for a beef auction house, shoveling cow shit out of open-air stalls in freezing conditions. Early in February 2012, Matt had enough and was out of work again.

I received a call from him at my office on a Friday afternoon. I hadn't heard from him since Christmas. This was only the second time, ever, that he had called me while I was at work.

"Dad, I've got a problem," he said.

"*Shit... here we go again,*" I said to myself.

Matt was fifteen miles south of Loup City on the highway, in the middle of nowhere, surrounded by fields of corn stubble dusted by snow, standing next to his car with its hood up. A highway patrolman had just covered his engine compartment with spray foam from a fire extinguisher to squelch the flames that had been erupting from the engine. After Matt and I discussed our options, I said, "I'll be out there around five o'clock. I'll call to find you when I get close." Acting on fatherly instinct, the last thing I did on my way out of Omaha was to stop at my bank and draw out $1,000 cash in hundred-dollar bills.

My drive from Omaha to Loup City took about two and a half hours. Loup City is a stereotypical small town in central Nebraska, with a population of about a thousand residents. At dusk, I picked Matt up at the police station lobby on Main Street. The car was across the street at a filling station lot, next to the tow truck. "How much was the tow?" I prompted.

"A hundred bucks," Matt said.

"Is it paid for?" was my next question.

"Uh, no," Matt replied.

The filling station was closed. "Do you know how to contact the tow guy?" I asked.

"I got his number," Matt replied.

It surprised me to see that this car was not the Mazda I had bought for him ten months before, for which he still owed me $4,000. He had driven the Mazda into a tree a few months back and decided not to tell me. He wasn't hurt, but the Mazda was totaled. I guessed that alcohol was involved.

THE MAZDA WAS DEAD CAR # 4.

After some fatherly discussion, we inspected the latest casualty. The fire-damaged car was an old Subaru. The engine compartment was completely burned out and the finishes on the hood, fenders, and front end were torched. Luckily, it hadn't blown up.

THE SUBARU WAS DEAD CAR #5.

I ran through some options as to what to do with the car. "It's not worth anything," I concluded. "They'll charge us a parking fee if we leave it here. We need to tow it somewhere. Maybe we can sign the car over to the tow guy. He can probably haul it to a salvage yard and get some cash out of it. Do you have the title for the car?"

"Uh, no," Matt replied.

"Where is it?" I asked.

"The farmer I'm buying the car from has it," he said.

"Uh-huh." At this point, I realized I was talking like Matt, borrowing from his repertoire of finely tuned communication skills that he learned in college. "How much do you owe?" was my next question.

"Five hundred dollars," Matt said. "I've paid him two hundred so far."

I was relieved that it wasn't another $5,000. We drove to the farmhouse on a hill just outside of town. The farmer's wife was unloading a horse from a trailer, and we watched while she led it into the barn and put the animal into a stable. As dusk was deepening, the fixture hanging over the barn door came on and threw a pool of golden light onto the surrounding ground.

"What's up guys?" the lady asked as she took off her gloves. She recognized Matt. "Rita," she said, introducing herself to me and shaking my hand.

After explanations, Rita stepped inside the house to grab the title for the car. She returned, and I gave her five hundred-dollar bills out of my billfold. She pulled an envelope and pen from the front pocket of her bib overalls. The envelope was an unopened bill from the propane company. Rita tore it open and took the bill out, placed the bill back in her pocket. She scribbled out a receipt for the $500 on the back of the empty envelope and handed it to me. Then she signed the title and handed it to Matt. At this point, Matt officially owned the junked car.

I suggested to Rita that if she could get some salvage value out of the derelict Subaru, she could keep the car. Rita said, "OK, there's a salvage yard over in Grand Island. We'll take it." I directed Matt to sign the title and hand it back to Rita. She now owned the Subaru again.

"Now we've got to find the tow guy and pay him for the tow," I said.

Standing with us was the farmer's teenage daughter. She chimed in, "I just saw Charlie down at the restaurant." Charlie was the tow guy.

Matt still needed to get his stuff out of the car, so we kept the key, promising to return it. Rita said, "Just leave the key with Charlie. Good luck." Our eyes made contact, and Rita gave me an all-knowing parental wink of understanding as we left.

Matt and I drove the mile back to the main intersection of town. The restaurant was catty-corner from the police station and across from the gas station and lot where the Subaru was parked. We walked in.

THE HOOP OF LIFE | 205

"Can I help you?" the server asked.

As Matt scanned the supper crowd, I said, "We're looking for Charlie, the tow guy."

The server turned to the table in the corner where four rough-looking overweight men sat in their dirty work clothes. "Charlie," she said in a rather loud voice, over the top of the dining room chatter, "these guys are looking for you."

Charlie turned and recognized Matt. "This is my dad," Matt said, as we approached the table.

Charlie remained seated and gave me a handshake. I asked, "How much do we owe you for the tow?"

"A hundred bucks," Charlie replied.

"Pay you now?"

"Sure," he said. I pulled a hundred-dollar bill out of my billfold. Charlie scribbled out a handwritten receipt on the back of his cafe bill. I explained that Rita owned the car now and the plan to leave Rita's key with Charlie after we grabbed Matt's stuff. Charlie handed me the receipt and said, "Sounds good. I'll be here for a while." He gave me an old guy's man-to-man look and wink that, like Rita's wink, transmitted yet another dose of mutual understanding.

Matt explained to me he was moving to Kearney when his engine caught fire. He was planning a short-term stay with his cousin until he found a new job. All his possessions were in the car's trunk. Translated into Father language, he had no job, no car, no money, and no place to stay. We decided it would be best if he came home to Omaha to stay with me until he found another job, hopefully one that was full time, year-round, and not involving shoveling shit while standing outside in the middle of winter.

We returned to his car and unloaded all Matt's stuff into the back of my car, with emphasis on the word *stuff*. We returned the key to Charlie at the restaurant and drove away, with Matt leaving Loup City for good, or so I thought. As we headed south on the highway, I asked Matt if everything was closed out at the house he had rented.

"Uh, no. I owe some rent."

"Still owe some rent?" was my fatherly question.

"Uh-huh," was his reply.

I turned the car around and headed back to town. The landlord's place was three blocks north of the town's main intersection. His little old house was next door to the little old house that Matt had been renting. It was well after dark, but the lights were still on at the landlord's place. We walked to the front door and rang the bell. The landlord and his wife came to the door. They recognized Matt and invited us in. John and Helen offered handshakes and introductions.

I asked, "How much does Matt owe you in rent?"

"Two hundred bucks," the landlady said, "for last month."

"Was there was a deposit?"

Helen replied, "Another month's rent. We are going to have to keep it to replace the carpet—tobacco stains and cigarette burns."

Apparently, Matt hadn't changed his housekeeping skills much. I pulled two hundred-dollar bills out of my billfold. Helen grabbed her little booklet and scribbled out a receipt, which copied through the waxy blue transfer paper onto the next page. Helen handed me the receipt. As we headed out the front door, Helen said, "Good luck." In a repeat of Rita's and Charlie's parting gestures, I received a compassionate look and wink from Helen, which transmitted a world of mutual understanding. We drove home to Omaha in the dark.

Over the next few weeks, Matt conducted a job search on the internet. He was able to find an opening for a job in his field. The new job was in the small town of Niobrara, which has about 350 residents, in north central Nebraska, on the Missouri River, across from South Dakota. The job was a good one for Matt. He would be in a five-person office, which was an offshoot of the Environmental Protection Agency, conducting soil, water, and air quality tests on the Santee Sioux Indian Reservation nearby. The Santee are part of the Dakota Nation. The town of Niobrara is a four-hour drive northwest of Omaha.

To move there, Matt would need another car. The two of us went through the newspaper and identified several cars that were worth looking at, all for sale by owners, middle-aged cars with medium mileage, in my price range. After looking all weekend, we settled on a ten-year-old Nissan Altima with twenty-three thousand miles, a granny's go-to-church car being sold by her son. It was a full-sized four-door sedan and was pricey at $10,000, more car than Matt needed, but it was our best option out of the ten cars we looked at. We decided I would buy the Nissan for myself and sell Matt my car. I was driving a 2003 Honda Civic with sixty-thousand miles. It was a smaller car, which seemed to better fit his needs. I would sell my Honda to him for $6,000.

I was less inclined to be the great provider again since Matt still owed me $5,000 on the defunct Mazda and another $800 from the Loop City fiasco. This time I took Matt to my bank so he could secure a loan to buy the car from me. I had been with this bank for twenty-five years, with all my credit accounts and my home loan. My assumption was that my history with them would help. We sat down at the bank with a young lady to process Matt's car loan. Upon placing Matt's name into the computer, she said, "Matt, your credit check shows that you currently owe $1,675 on a Cabela's credit card and that you are six months delinquent."

I blurted out, "Jeezuz! Really?"

Avoiding eye contact, Matt fessed up, "Uh-huh."

The bank attendant said, "I'm sorry, but Matt's credit rating is too low for us to consider your loan request."

After a pause, I asked, "What if I co-sign on the loan?"

The bank lady said, "Let me get this straight. You want to co-sign on Matt's loan so that he can buy *your* car?"

Like father, like son, I said, "Uh-huh."

She said, "Uh...Let me review this with my boss." Upon her return, she repeated that Matt's credit rating was too low to allow the bank to process the loan.

I responded, "Even with his father's co-signature, with my twenty-five years of excellent history with this bank and my home equity line with $150,000 available credit?"

Her simple comment was, "Sorry about that." We left.

As luck would have it, that evening I happened to be talking to Gary, my friend and neighbor. He was a senior staff member at a local credit union. "Let me talk to my loan officer, Steve. Maybe she can help."

Sure enough, we talked to the credit union, and Matt got his loan. Besides the $6,000 to purchase the Honda from me, they paid off the Cabela's card, gave me $800 for my Loup City expenses, as well as $4,000 for the money Matt still owed me for the Mazda, the first car I bought for him. Matt's loan was for $12,975. Welcome to the adult world, Matthew.

CHAPTER 44
The Radial Café

Omaha, March 2012

I need to revisit the situation with Mark, my middle son, now twenty-five years old. After a year and a half trying to survive in Las Vegas, he was home again, between jobs, living with me for a month, in March 2012. Karen and I were engaged, planning to get married early in the following year. She would be in Paris for another month and planned to be in Omaha during the late spring and early summer.

For the month before Karen's arrival, Mark and I treated our home like a bachelor pad. We had a good time together. He was free labor, and I could use a little extra help. He used his time at home to do a major project in the house, almost single-handedly installing an oak floor on the main level, which kept him busy for the month.

I had a routine of eating at the local beanery, the Radial Cafe, on Saturday morning. My buddies from the neighborhood and I would have breakfast together—bacon, eggs, toast, hash browns, and coffee... lots of coffee. Unofficially, we had a reserved table, the "old geezers" table in the corner, thanks to our reputation as heavy tippers. On any given Saturday, out of the group of ten guys, it was a good bet that six or seven of us would show up at the table at any one time. We were all empty nesters. Our kids had all grown up together and had left home to pursue their new lives. The group of guys welcomed Mark to the breakfast table as if he was just another old geezer. We had great fun rolling out the bullshit.

But on this specific Saturday, it was different. Karen had arrived. Mark and Karen had just spent most of the previous week together at my house, new roommates exploring ways to get along, and concluding that it was *not* possible. Mark's smoking, drinking, tobacco chew, and general lack of interest in keeping the house tidy didn't sit well with Karen. She resorted to her barrage of Post-it messages to express her concerns. This incited Mark to conduct a frantic job search to get the hell out as soon as possible. Mark's job hunt was the focus of the conversations on this Saturday around the old geezers table at the Radial Cafe, with Mark and me in attendance.

Jim said, "The *Wall Street Journal* reports a boom on, up in Williston, North Dakota."

John followed with, "Mark, you ought to go up there and get a job."

Brad chimed in, "Guys bring in the big bucks—$100,000 a year on starter jobs."

Gary said, "Unemployment is a half a percent up there, best in the nation."

Ron remarked, "My nephew works up there right now. Give him a call."

Dan added, "You need some dependable wheels to get around up there in the winter."

Karl concluded, "Good ol' Dad needs to buy Mark a four-wheel drive."

At this point, all the old geezers stopped talking and stared at me, waiting for me to respond. I scanned around the table at the gallery of goofy, big grins. Feeling like the group was ganging up on me, I stood up, signaling that I was done. "Well, it's time for Mark and me to be leaving. See you guys." I dropped a twenty on the table as Mark slid out of his chair. The guys started spitting out another round of chatter, hounding us all the way to the door.

Jim said, "Come on, Steve, don't leave grumpy."

John remarked, "You can handle it. You got deep pockets."

Karl inserted, "Besides, you can't buy a car without our input."

Brad continued, "You need us to help you choose the right vehicle."

Dan added, "You're used to buying cars by now, aren't you, Steve?"

Gary offered, "The credit union is probably good to give you another loan."

Ron spouted, "Don't buy a bicycle this time."

As we walked out the door and headed toward home, Mark turned to me and said, "I feel like I have eight fathers."

Mark gave Ron's nephew a call in Williston, who reported that companies up there were not accepting mail-in or email resumes and were not taking job interviews over the phone. "There are too many no-shows. You have to come here and apply in person. There are a lot of losers trying to hire on—guys who didn't graduate from high school, ex-cons, boozers, and the like. With your college degree in business, there is a good bet that you will be hired by somebody right away."

Even though, on principle, I was reluctant to lower myself to the level of accepting the advice of those hardheaded old roosters at the cafe, they came up with two good ideas. Mark liked the idea of going up to Williston to find a job. And the other idea, which was for me to purchase him a vehicle, seemed to be the best way to get him up there quickly. Mark had no credit history, no cash, and wouldn't be able to swing a car loan, so I cut him a deal. I bought my brother's used Chevy Dakota pickup truck for $10,000 and gave it to Mark, on the promise that he would pay me back within the first nine months of his new job. I was planning to join Karen in Paris in early December and needed to be repaid by then at the latest in anticipation of our upcoming wedding expenses.

Mark drove up to Williston and found a job. Nine months came and went. Karen expressed her dismay that Mark was not paying me back. He's twenty-five, for God's sake. "When I was that age, I had been on my own for five years, married and had my own house. He needs to row his own boat. How many years are you going to provide for your sons?" It was a good question.

Mark had talked to me only twice during the nine months. I hadn't seen any cash from him, just vague promises. I pretty much accepted the idea that I was not going to see the money Mark owed me anytime soon, and possibly never. I made one last attempt to reach out to him by phone and email but received no response. My flight to Paris was scheduled for a Saturday afternoon departure. Karen was already gone, having taken a flight earlier in the week. My phone rang on Friday evening, 7:00 p.m. It was Mark. He gave me a brief message.

"Hi, Dad. I'm driving down to see you. I've got your cash. I should be there early tomorrow."

I reminded him of my travel schedule, and he hung up. At 7:00 a.m. Saturday morning, the front doorbell rang. It was Mark. I invited him in. He had been on the road all night. Mark walked directly to the kitchen, reached into his pocket, and pulled out a thick wad of cash, folded in half. He unfolded the money—all hundred-dollar bills—and started laying them on the kitchen table. He counted out ten of them, stacking them neatly into a pile. Then he started a second pile, placing ten more bills onto it, then a third pile, a fourth, and fifth. To my surprise, he finished with ten piles of hundred-dollar bills, ten per pile... $10,000 total, in cash, on the kitchen table, the entirety of what he owed me.

At 7:30 a.m., we walked over to the Radial Cafe for breakfast with the old geezers. They were all happy to see Mark again. He gave an update of his life in Williston, working as a dispatcher for a pipeline supply company. It sounded like a boom town from the Old West. One of Mark's stories impressed the guys. He remembered walking into a bar on his first night in Williston. He noticed that the room was full of men.

"Where's all the women?" he asked the bartender.

Without looking up, the bartender replied, "Dorothy left six months ago."

Mark concluded that in the last six months, there had been only one woman in the bar, and you made assumptions as to what type of woman she was. The old geezers got a good chuckle and concluded that Mark had turned out to be an OK guy.

Jim said, "Found work up there, did yuh? The *Wall Street Journal* is never wrong."

John responded, "Your dad bought you that truck?"

Luther added, "You had him worried whether he'd see that cash again."

Dan chimed in, "You're hauling in big bucks if you paid him back in cash."

Gary said, "Can't deposit that much. The bank'll think you're a drug dearer or mafia."

Ron asked, "My nephew helped you find that job up there, did he?"

Karl said, "Best to listen to us old guys. We're right once in a while, yuh know."

I was reluctant to admit it, but yes... the hardheaded old farts were right. Even though it left a pasty taste in my mouth, we gave them a round of thank-you's. This time, Mark dropped a twenty on the table as we left. He hopped back into his pickup and headed north toward Williston, which is about a twelve-hour drive from Omaha. He's still up there, ten years later.

One last little glitch occurred before I could hop on the plane and fly to Paris. I stopped at my bank to put the $10,000 cash into my savings account. The lady behind the counter raised one eyebrow and called a manager over, who escorted me to a private office. They proceeded to do a security check on me to see if I was who I was supposed to be. Eventually, they took the cash. As our meeting ended, the bank manager confided in me.

"When someone walks into our bank with that much cash, we get suspicious, thinking they must be a drug dealer or mafia."

I hurried off to catch my plane, wondering where Mark got all that cash, whether he had a lucky streak at the casino or if he was bringing home the big bucks with his job... or maybe he was a drug dealer or mafia.

CHAPTER 45

Rehab

Niobrara, Nebraska, September 2013

It was early September 2013, and I was in Omaha, booked to fly to Paris for an extended stay. Karen had already left, after spending the summer in Nebraska at my house. We were newlyweds, married just a half year. Our plan was to live six months in Karen's Paris apartment through the winter and six months in Nebraska at my house over the summer.

Matt, my youngest son, called from Niobrara, a small town in north central Nebraska where he had his job. I hadn't talked to him since the wedding last spring.

"Hi, Dad. It's Matt."

"Hi, Matt. What's up?"

"I got a problem."

"Oh, shit. Here we go again," I thought.

"I've been drinking a lot lately and doing meth. Nothin' else to do around here."

My mind flashed back to Matt's previous alcohol and drug problems in his college days. I tried to offer some understanding. "Yeah, you're pretty isolated out there."

He continued, "My boss has been talking to me about it. They want me to attend a rehab program. If I do it, I can keep my job."

"I see. Have you had some difficulties?" I prompted.

"Yeah, well, things haven't been the best," was his guarded response.

"Well, Matt... What do you think?" I asked as I tried to fill in the gaps in his truncated comments.

"I don't know," he said and then paused.

After a quick analysis of his situation, I asked, "Well, Matt, do you like your job?"

"Yeah... pretty much."

Doing my fatherly thing, I said, "Well, they must like having you around. Otherwise, they wouldn't be giving you the chance to get straightened out. Sounds like you need to look into it."

"Yeah... guess I gotta to do that."

"You need to know that I'm only here for three more weeks. Let me know how it shakes out as soon as you can, hopefully before I leave for Paris."

"OK. Talk to you later."

Matt was quick to start the rehab program in a small town in north-central Nebraska. He would stay there for six weeks, in a lockdown setting, every day full of intense counseling and activities. They offered a low-interest loan. Matt would pay for the program himself.

Toward the end of his first week, I drove there and stayed overnight, attending "family day" activities. I felt lucky to still be in the country to offer Matt some support. The place looked like a renovated one-story motel, with thirty rooms arranged in a *U*-shape that opened onto a tree covered lawn and courtyard. The day included breakfast and a long private meeting with Matt and his counselor, followed by an in-the-round group therapy session, lunch, and a couple classroom-type work sessions in the afternoon. Matt talked about his problems several times throughout the day, breaking down into tears. I cried with him.

It became clear that Matt had a long history of alcohol and drug abuse that had started in his early college days and continued over the past seven years to the present. He faced big challenges to overcome, including addictions to alcohol and meth. The good news was that he admitted his problem to himself and to everyone and was taking part in an intensive rehab program. After detox, recovery, and graduation from the program, he was going to have a long-term maintenance routine, including weekly meetings with the counseling staff. He identified a core group of alcohol-free and drug-free friends to socialize with. And he kept his job. Matt was surviving a dramatic brush with fate.

Fingers crossed, knock on wood. I was hopeful.

But there was a weirdness about the relationship between Matt and me. He was always closer to his mother. Through the years, now with his mother gone and me off to a new life with another woman, a communication barrier had developed between us. Matt and I were totally disconnected. My authoritarianism had always been at odds with Matt's self-conscious and reclusive nature. Our communications distilled down to me calling him twice a year, on Christmas and his birthday, resulting in simple conversations and short phrases.

"How's it going?"

"OK."

These white-label updates contrasted against those outrageous phone calls from Matt when he had some enormous problem and needed my help, a "Jeezuz" moment. There was no middle ground.

We both had working relationships with the Dakota people, me with the Sisseton Wahpeton and Matt with the Santee, two Sioux groups who share the same language, culture, religion, location, and history. Matt had been invited by his first boss, a Native American, to attend their annual Sun Dance. He has become part of the Dakota community, working with them, socializing with their young people his age. But Matt and I could not talk to each other, about the Dakota people, or about anything else, for that matter.

During our family day group therapy session at the rehab center, there was a moment of connection between Matt and me. I was invited to tell my story. When I was his age, I had a problem similar to his. I was probably an alcoholic as a young man, but never admitted it and was arrested for DWI. During my fourth year of college, while in London on a study-and-work program, I smoked opiated hash nearly every night and was very close to using heroin, only to be saved by fate. The drugs were no longer available to me in Nebraska when I returned to complete my last year of college. As I talked, I felt that there was some measure of understanding transmitted between Matt and me - "a Jeezuz moment" in reverse.

"I didn't know," was Matt's simple response. He couldn't have known. Fathers don't talk about these things with their sons.

My thoughts flashed back to my father. Dad and I talked little, which mirrored my inability to connect with my own sons. My dad was a gruff, old, blue-collar railroad man, and I was a hippie college kid. I remember standing next to him in the driveway at our home one afternoon, looking out over the grass in the backyard. It was the only time he confronted me with my drinking problem. There were twenty tufts of grass that stood in the yard. They were the spots where, after a night of heavy beer drinking, I often relieved my bladder before coming into the house and going to bed. The urine acted like a fertilizer, causing the tufts of grass to grow taller and darker green than the surrounding lawn. My dad recognized them for what they were.

"You been pissing here? Son, you're drinking too much. It'll get you into trouble. Slow down on the booze."

They were wise words, but I blew them off as "stupid Dad talk." Then, when I was arrested for DWI, I called and said, "Dad, I got a problem," which had now become enshrined as perhaps the most recurrent phrase in the Laughlin family history.

A week after my visit to Matt at the rehab center, I flew off to Paris. But Nebraska was giving me guilt pangs. My three sons had become young men, now ages twenty-six, twenty-eight, and thirty, college graduates, off on their own careers, scattered around the country. Even though their mother had been dead for four years and even though Karen and I were now married and beginning our new life together, Nebraska was tugging at me, pulling at my desire to provide a home, to be there for my children, to be a father when they needed me.

CHAPTER 46
Muskie Lure

Central Minnesota, 1983

Dean, Dad, and I were fishing in Dean's new boat. We were on Little Boy Lake, in central Minnesota, just south of the small town of Longville. It was reminiscent of all the summer vacations of my childhood. But this time was different. It had been a dozen years since the last time we were fishing together. In the past, our family vacationed every year on Little Boy Lake for two weeks in August. These family vacations generated some of my fondest childhood memories. Mom was gone now, having died while I was in high school, after an extended struggle with breast and colon cancer. My older brother had left the family circle long before. I was in my early thirties and had drifted away from dad, distracted by college, summer jobs, a new career and married life, in Omaha, fifty miles away from my family home in Lincoln.

But here we were, again, what was left of the family, three guys out on the lake together. Dean and Dad had continued the fishing trips to Minnesota through the years of my absence. Dean's new boat had all the bells and whistles, including fish locator, big motor, soft chairs on swiveling posts, and electric trolling motor. He was pretty proud of it. Dean was my younger brother, in his mid-twenties, still living at home with Dad, two gruff, blue-collar railroad guys. Dad had retired from Burlington a few years earlier, at sixty-two, having been a freight conductor. Dean had hired out for the railroad immediately after high school. He had concluded several years of apprenticeship and was now a carman, repairing box cars in Havelock

Shops, making pretty good money, a single young man on a union salary. He had just bought the bass boat and trailer that Dad could never talk himself into buying.

Dad had grown up during the depression, was a sergeant in WWII Europe, and had seen some tough times. Now, in retirement, his physical condition was in decline and he was always in a cantankerous mood. Most of his days were spent in his lazy-boy recliner with his TV remote control in hand. He suffered from rheumatoid arthritis and was dramatically overweight. His backbone and neck had pretty much frozen solid, so that if he wanted to look left or right, he had to shift his whole body. Due to lack of dental hygiene and missing teeth he had a real Jack-o'-lantern smile. Hard-headed old geezer that he was, he refused to go to a dentist to get fixed up. His mobility was diminished to where, at lakeside, both Dean and I had to put our muscles into the effort of getting him safely from the dock into the boat and onto a chair. Even though he was getting old and rickety, he still was Dad and still the boss!

Out on the lake, Dean motored over to Musky Bay, and we pulled our heavy tackle out to do some casting for muskies. In all the years of fishing, no one in our family had ever boated a big musky, although each of us had hooked one, providing some thrills and excitement before breaking the line and leaving us with some great fish stories. The bigger ones could weigh forty pounds and be forty inches long. It was an obligatory family ritual that we had to spend at least one afternoon out casting for muskies.

Dad had a tackle box dedicated to big musky lures. They got little use and looked like new, with brilliant colors, giant hooks, sparkling big spinners, and buckskin tails. Dad grabbed a lure that was about the size of a hot-dog bun. He hooked it onto the steel leader at the end of his line. The lure mimicked the markings and size of a big bullfrog, with olive-green back, yellow belly, and two goggle eyes popping out of its head. It was a top-water floater with propeller spinners, one forward and one behind, to churn the water and make noise as it was retrieved across the surface.

Most important to this story is that the giant lure had two huge treble hooks along its body, each the size of a shot glass. The hooks were needle-sharp and heavy-duty. Just down from the point of each hook was a mean-looking barb that pointed backward. Once the hook was stuck a half-inch into the flesh, past the barb, it was very hard to rip it back out again. Now, imagine three guys in a boat whipping these things around at the ends of their fishing lines.

Dad had been casting for years and perceived himself to be an expert fisherman, but he hadn't come to grips with the idea that his physical skills had dramatically declined in recent years. The rheumatoid arthritis had deformed his fingers, bending them sideways at the joints and causing him pain. He sat in the captain's chair facing out one side of the boat. There was a spot on the water, near a bank of weeds, where he wanted to place his first cast. He lifted his rod and giant musky lure straight back over his head to a horizontal position behind his back, wanting to get a full 180-degree over-the-top swing. In doing this with his handicapped fingers, he accidentally released a couple feet of line behind his back. Dad was not aware that the musky lure was dangling precariously near the surface of the water behind the boat. Proceeding with the cast, he stretched his arms back and started a strong overhead swing of his rod. The lure inadvertently touched the surface of the water and came rocketing forward at the wrong trajectory. With a loud whack! The heavy lure slammed violently into the back of dad's head, knocking his baseball cap forward into the lake.

"GAH-DAM-IT," he yelled.

Dean and I were astounded to look at Dad and see the musky lure on top of his head, perched rather like a bird in a nest.

He reached up and grabbed the lure, discovering that it was attached to his scalp. "JEEZUZ H-KRYST," he bellowed out as he tugged at the lure, then barked at me, "STEVE! GET THAT GAH-DAM THING OFF ME!"

I closed my gaping mouth, dropped my rod, and jumped to his side. Immediately, I grabbed the lure with one hand and carefully lifted. "There is only one hook in you," I said with relief.

"GET THE FUHKUN THING OUT, GAH-DAM-IT," was dad's command.

With my other hand, I carefully grabbed the treble hook and sheepishly pulled on it. "The barb is buried," I said with a cringe.

THE HOOP OF LIFE | 221

"I DON'T GIVE A SHIT! YANK THE FUHKUN THING OUT," he yelled.

I pulled harder on the hook, but it was deeply buried. A cone shape of thick, rubbery scalp lifted off of Dad's skull as I pulled. I stopped, let go, and sheepishly said, "It won't come out."

My dad blew a gasket. "DON'T BE A CHICKNSHIT. YANK THE FUHKUN THING! GAH-DAM PIECE OF SHIT!" As he yelled, his neck turned red, and he flung his head left and right. The big lure flopped this way and that, bouncing against the sides of his head, causing the propellers on the lure to clatter.

"Dad, Dad... settle down. Let's take a minute to get the string off of it," I said. "Hold still."

Dean sat at the bow of the boat with his foot on the control for the electric trolling motor. He was happy to not be involved, leaving his big brother to handle Dad. His strategy of avoidance didn't work.

"DEAN," Dad yelled, sending Dean's body into an uncontrolled flinch, "GET YOUR ASS OVER THERE AND NET MY FUHKUN HAT OUT BEFORE IT SINKS!"

Dean was quick to comply.

I removed the string from the lure.

"NOW YANK THE GAH-DAM THING OUT!" he bellowed.

I cradled the big lure in the palm of my hand, and reached around it with my fingers, grabbed the hook firmly, then pulled harder. The cone of rubbery scalp appeared again. This time it rose to a half-inch tall, to where the skin on his forehead lifted. His eyebrows and ears rose involuntarily. I backed off, saying, "I can't do it."

Dad blew a gasket, again, yelling, "YOU GAH-DAM CHICKNSHIT! I'M A WAR VET. I'VE BEEN THROUGH WORSE SHIT THAN THIS. SHOW SOME FUHKUN BACK BONE."

Then he turned to my brother again. "DEAN," Dad yelled, causing my brother to flinch uncontrollably again in his chair. "GET THE GAH-DAM FILLET KNIFE." Dean was quick to comply again, rustling around in a tackle box. In silence, he handed me the rusty old fishing knife and retreated to the bow of the boat.

"NOW, CUT THE FUHKUN THING OUT!"

I started to cuss, "Jeezuz, Dad. The fillet knife? It's dirty!"

Undeterred, he said, "BULLSHIT! WIPE IT OFF."

I complied. "OK, OK." After dipping the knife in the lake, I wiped it off with the boat rag. The cone of rubbery scalp reappeared as I pulled again on the hook. Placing the blade on the hook's point of entry, I cut. The dull blade rubbed against his scalp with a squeaky sensation, kind of like trying to cut through thick rubber. I balked again. "I can't do this."

This threw Dad into a cussing fit of several more sentences, using further variations of colorful railroad language.

I suggested we need to find a doctor in Longville or Walker to remove the hook.

While listening to Dad's retorting on this idea, I discovered that there were three kinds of doctors in his experience: "SONZA-BISHES, MUHTHUH-FUHKUZ," and "CAH-SUHKUZ." Dad extended the conversation belittling me, his "CHICKNSHIT" son, while exuding editorials about doctors. But he eventually agreed to have a doctor remove the hook.

We arrived back at the boat dock and unloaded. As we were helping Dad climb onto the dock, he dragged his leg across my fishing rod and musky lure that was lying against the inside wall of the boat. A hook from this lure stuck deeply into the calf of his leg, resulting in yet another round of cussing. I cut one leg of his trousers off at the knee.

The two lures, one dangling from the side of his leg and the other perched on the top of his head, wobbled from side to side as we slowly walked to the car. The cussing diminished probably since, in Dad's mind, there was some sort of economy involved. We had already committed ourselves to visiting a doctor, so it would be kind of a two-for-one bargain on hook removals.

After our thirty-mile drive into Walker and fifteen minutes searching around town, we were lucky to find a clinic that was open in the late afternoon. The hook removals and tetanus shot went quickly and without incident. It surprised me that Dad kept his cussing under control while in the doctor's presence. At the end, the doctor walked us to the front door and gave us a few parting words, trying to compliment me on my triage skills.

"I see you tried to cut out the one that was in his scalp. You almost got it."

That comment threw Dad into yet another cussing tizzy that lasted the entire drive back to our cabin at Little Boy Lake, railing about the wasted time and money and his "CHICKNSHIT" son.

As I write this, I realize I am sixty-six years old, the same age that my father was when we took this last trip to Little Boy Lake together as a family. He died two years later, weakened by congestive heart failure, and finished by pancreatic cancer, a battered old man, worn down by life.

I am living longer than my father did, thanks to my new life with Karen. I am thinner, eating better, and keeping active in my senior years. But there are a couple of things that Dad and I have had in common. Like me, Dad had raised three boys, and like me, he lost his wife in her fifties to cancer. I understand now that I had some luck that eluded my father. He gave me a college education, an opportunity that he didn't have. When he was a teenager in the early 1930s, his father died, an event that put his family into a downward decline from which they never recovered.

Also, finding Karen and finding love again late in my life has given me a new vitality, a new life, a second go at it, that my father never had…another roll of the Hoop of Life. Thanks, Dad. Thanks, Karen.

CHAPTER 47

Five Ribs

During visits to far-off places, from 2010 through 2014

When Adam had humankind's very first rib injury during the creation of Eve, he probably was in a lot of pain that you have heard little about. Before Eve, I'm guessing that Adam must have been a lonely and miserable dude. But he did not know the pain that would come his way with the arrival of a female companion. Not to be confused with the emotional pain that always arises from male/female interactions, what I am referring to is real physical pain. You know, the "OUCH, THAT HURTS!" type of pain. It usually takes six weeks for a rib injury to heal. Since rib injuries rarely result in hospitalization (and since quality health care wouldn't arrive on the planet for another twenty thousand years, depending on who you listen to), he would have suffered on through the pain while continuing to perform his manly duties. One should factor in that when Eve came along, Adam was love-struck, which had a lot to do with his ability to tolerate pain. From my personal experience, I've had several opportunities to contemplate his situation.

Flash-forward to Omaha, Nebraska, in the late summer of 2010, when I was love-struck. I was on my crash weight loss program to impress this lady. Karen and I had only one intimate night together before she returned to her home in Paris. It would be four months before we saw each other again. We were planning to rendezvous in New Zealand for ten days of bliss, to explore our newfound love. But before that could happen, since I was weighing in at the boxing category of heavyweight, my plan was to peel off twenty more pounds of baby fat by jogging. Unfamiliar with my new jogging shoes and after a lifetime of dragging my feet, I tripped on a crack in the sidewalk and fell. Having worked forty years behind a desk in a sissy architect's job, my wimpy arms had about as much muscle mass as you would find on a pair of chopsticks and were absolutely no help in catching my fall. Comparable to a beer keg rolling off the tailgate of a pickup truck, my torso bounced down onto the sidewalk. I heard a popping sound and immediately winced in pain. I had broken a rib. Now, besides pursuing my weight loss program, "The Joy of the Pain of Hunger and The Joy of the Pain of Exercise," I could now add the pain of a broken rib.

The doctor said, "There is nothing we can do. Just rest and wait six weeks for it to heal." So, owing to my love-struck status, like Adam, I suffered on through the pain while continuing to perform my manly duties.

THIS WAS BROKEN RIB #1.

In December 2011, Karen and I were committed to each other and conducting our long-distance dating routine. During this time, she developed an interest in my personal health. Karen had worked in Germany for several years and subscribed to certain exotic health maintenance routines that Germans regularly use, namely massage, yoga, and Ayurvedic medicine, practices that are rather foreign to men from Nebraska. She arranged we spend two weeks in an Ayurvedic spa that was on the southern tip of the Indian subcontinent. It was a quaint little compound of aging one- and two-story stucco buildings with red tile roofs. The property was covered with palm trees and was above the cliffs overlooking the Indian Ocean. We spent our time there in the company of ten others, all Germans, doing exotic health things. On my first day, the therapists requested me to remove all my clothing and wrap a towel around my waist, after which I was laid face down onto a special wooden table, bathed in hot oils, and massaged by two rather muscular male attendants. Another treatment involved lying on my back while a pea-green paste was spread on my face, and they placed two cucumber slices over my eyes. A third novel treatment required that a half-inch thick layer of clay mixed with herbs be troweled onto my scalp and held in place for the day by a large banana leaf wrapped around my head and tied with twine. The assembly resembled a bright-green football helmet and had a jello-like jiggle. Needless to say, good ol' Nebraska Steve was disoriented through all this.

On the second morning of our stay, we attended a one-hour yoga class before breakfast, held in an open-air pavilion in the center of the compound. After several warm-up exercises, the yoga instructor asked us to lie face down on our mats and bend at the knees to lift our feet backward into the air. Next, he directed us to reach behind our backs and grab our ankles, which I accomplished with some difficulty. They then asked us to arch our backs upward and backward, lifting our chins and knees above our mats and raising our feet and hands toward the ceiling, adopting the classic yoga onion pose. At that point, there was a loud popping sound, similar to a champagne bottle being uncorked, which everyone in the room heard clearly. It was the sound of one of my ribs breaking under the stress. The pain was immediate and excruciating. This turned out to be my first and last day of yoga class. We visited the hospital in Trivandrum. After tests, we had an extended discussion with the doctor, not about my rib, but about the status of his alma mater's football team, Oregon State. He concluded with a comment that was becoming one of the recurring themes of my time with Karen.

The doctor said in his distinctly Indian version of English, "Dere ees nossing we can dew. Just rest and wait seex weeks for eet to eel."

THIS WAS BROKEN RIB #2.

The following winter, during the week after Christmas, 2012, Karen arranged a stay for us in the Trois Vallées in the French Alps. She had decided to introduce me to skiing. My oldest son expressed concern that I was too old, at sixty-two, to learn to ski. I pooh-poohed his comment and reiterated our mission: two old people having fun. The Trois Vallées is a classic Alps ski area, with several resort communities nestled into the valleys as the base of snow-covered mountains, with ski lifts running to the summits. Young people were everywhere, on the slopes and at outdoor bars that overlooked the ski lift access points.

My oldest son was correct to be concerned. I was distinctly frightened of losing control when skiing, having recently heard that Sonny Bono had died of head injuries when he skied into a tree. Add to that, my lack of muscle strength when bending my knees. After taking a private two-hour beginner's lesson in skiing, I went with Karen to the "baby slope" to fine tune my skills. I had a rather stiff posture and imagined myself to look like a fence post nailed to skis. Remembering the old news clips, my style of skiing would have made Gerald Ford look like an Olympic ski champion. After building my confidence, Karen and I moved to the "infant slope." At the top, thinking that I'd pause for a moment to scan the situation and build my confidence, I stood with my skis pointing sideways to the slope. The snow was compacted and icy. To my surprise, I started sliding sideways down the slope. Completely out of control, I picked up speed during my sideways slide, and at about one hundred feet out, I blindsided an elderly lady who, like me, was foolishly trying to learn how to ski. The two of us tumbled down the slope, skis and sticks flying in all directions. I fell forward and landed hard, jamming one elbow into my ribs. Recognizing the now familiar popping sound and excruciating pain, I slid to a stop. The rest was a blur of walking and sliding to the side and down, while Karen retrieved my equipment. I have no idea what became of the lady I collided with.

The doctor at the clinic, speaking English with his distinctly French accent, said, "Dere ees nossing wee can dew. Joost rrrest and you weel ave to wait seex weeks forrr eet to eel." After two hours and fifteen minutes on skis, I concluded that I'd had enough and spent the rest of our trip sitting at the bar, in the classic role of a creepy old guy flirting with the young snow bunnies while Karen was gone - skiing on the slopes.

THIS WAS BROKEN RIB #3.

The following year, 2013, Karen showed me Laos and Cambodia. We were newlyweds, and this was our honeymoon trip. My impression was that Laos had only one blacktop road running through the jungle from the south to the north end of the country. After a rather sweaty and crowded bus ride shared with Laotian natives and chickens in cages, we arrived at the small community of Vang Vieng on the Nam Song River. The town was a destination for adventure seekers, young people who enjoyed remote jungle hikes, zip lines, all-terrain vehicles, rock climbing, kayaking while cranked up on marijuana. We two old people... What were we thinking? Anyway, we rented a motor scooter for a day, and the two of us toured around the area. I had owned a motorcycle in my college days and had confidence that I could handle the machine safely.

Thirty miles north of town, we concluded our road trip through the jungle and head back. The highway was devoid of traffic, so I slowed down to nearly a stop to execute a *U*-turn. At that moment, Karen shifted her body weight from right to left. The motorbike lurched over to the side. Compared to when I was a skinny college kid with lightweight damsels hopping onto the back of my motorcycle, Karen and I were quite a bit heavier. Our combined body weight overpowered my left leg as I tried to catch our fall. Meanwhile, Karen incorrectly remembered a Harley Davidson rule from the old days that passengers should never put their feet out. The motor scooter fell in slow motion onto its left side, spilling Karen and I out onto the blacktop highway. Karen was unhurt by the fall. She had a soft landing... *on me*! As I fell face down onto the pavement, Karen drove her shoulder into my back. I heard a now familiar popping sound and felt that now familiar excruciating pain.

Luckily, there was a rudimentary little clinic back in Vang Vieng specializing in adventure injuries. We arrived late and were the only people at the clinic. After checking in, I was escorted into a room by a technician of diminutive stature who spoke no English. He gestured I remove my shirt. Holding my elbow, he guided me over to stand in front of a wall with my shoulder blades touching a panel behind me. He then dramatically took a pose, standing at attention in front of me, suggesting that I do the same. Using his forefinger, he raised my chin slightly. Bringing both his hands forward, he grabbed my shoulders and squeezed them, giving me a slight jiggle, as if to lock them into position and to suggest that I not move. In the center of the room, he stood next to a machine that reminded me of an old-style photographer's stand. My memory next is of the technician removing a cover from a box and exposing a large X-ray lightbulb. Standing to the side of the machine, without the presence of any lead protection panels that I could see, he turned the brilliant X-ray bulb on while timing the exposure on his wristwatch. It was quite a long exposure time. As I listened to a loud buzzing sound, I had the distinct fear that the credit cards in my pocket were being erased, but luckily, this was not the case. The result was an extremely clear X-ray negative of my rib cage.

Two Laotian doctors placed the film on a back-lit panel and looked at the film, as Karen and I stood by. In a back-and-forth exchange of broken English, the message we received was, "Bad break. Loook eere. Velly bad." While one doctor pointed at the break, the other doctor touched his two forefingers together and folded them, miming a break while vocalizing a cracking sound. He then said, "Do no-ting. Rest. Wait to eel." The second doctor said, "Seex weeks." Raising his forefinger in the air and waving it back-and-forth, he said, "No temple climbing."

A few days later, while climbing a temple at the border between Laos and Cambodia, we ran into an American emergency room doctor and his partner, who was a nurse. We were the only four people at this pyramid. Their words were encouraging. "If you haven't been coughing up blood by now, then you haven't punctured your lungs, and you are probably out of the woods. On the off chance that this happens, you would need to fly to Bangkok for intensive care. Otherwise, there is not much that you can do. Just rest and wait six weeks for it to heal." We headed south and spent the next five weeks climbing pyramids and riding around in bouncy tuk-tuks.

THAT WAS BROKEN RIB #4.

In 2018, on her suggestion, Karen and I toured Argentina and Chile. We camped out at the base of Torres del Paine, in southern Chile, which I refer to as "The Towers of Pain." Our attempt at the day long climb to the summit through the Patagonian wilderness was cut short by a massive rainstorm. As we retreated down the mountain, the trail turned to torrents of water running over slippery mud and rocks. Even with the help of two walking sticks, I fell five times. Having had previous opportunities to memorize the standard medical recommendation for a broken rib, this time I chose not to see a doctor.

THIS WAS BROKEN RIB #5.

In case you haven't been paying attention to the timeline, the first five years I shared with Karen resulted in five broken ribs. To satisfy your curiosity, each time was a different rib. Now I had firsthand knowledge of the pain that Adam suffered during humankind's original rib injury. With my having gained empathy for Adam's situation, I wondered if he, like me, eventually developed skepticism when contemplating his female companion's next suggestion for having some fun.

CHAPTER 48
Karneval

Cologne, Germany, January 2014

Newlyweds, married for nine months now, Karen and I were out to enjoy life. We drove her old BMW off to Germany, or Allemagne, as the French call it. Karen had worked in Cologne for several years when she first moved to Europe in the late '80s. She had several friends to see and some old watering holes to revisit. It was Karneval week, and she wanted to introduce me to the festivities. She had picked a hotel that was near her old stomping grounds. We brought along two bicycles. They were rail bikes, designed to fold up to the size of suitcases to fit onto the baggage rack on a train. The two folded bikes fit neatly into the back seat of her BMW. The assumption was that the bicycles would solve the expected lack of parking and transport during Karneval, and that Karen would most likely be too drunk to drive her car. *So, we'd pedal our bikes drunk instead?* Good thinking!

After checking in at the hotel, we pedaled to the first of Karen's old Kneipe (pub) hangouts in Lovenich, a suburb of Cologne. It was closed, possibly out of business; we couldn't be sure. A few blocks further down and to the right, onto a side street, we approached her second choice. It was on a corner lot, a two-story building, three or four hundred years old, stereotypical old-world German construction, timber with brick infill, with residences above and the bar on the main floor. In the early evening darkness, its open-shuttered windows with their small panes of glass glowed warmly from the activity inside. Karen and I walked into the boisterous interior, sidestepping around people, tables, and stools. Hand-cut columns and swayback beams of the dark, old, timbered interior were wooden-pegged together overhead.

As we moved toward the serving rail, Helmut, an old buddy that Karen hadn't seen in twenty-two years, started yelling, "Karen, Karen," from across the room. Helmut's face was lit up upon spotting Karen, and he motioned us over with his free hand, beer in the other. He was sitting by himself on a stool at a plank table that was attached to the wall. Karen gave him her typical French double-cheek kiss and blurted out a happy burst of greetings in German. In fact, her German was better than her French. The two of them had been bar-room buddies for several years before Karen had moved to France. We grabbed open stools and joined him. Helmut immediately caught the barmaid's attention, and we had beers in our hands before introductions were over. Helmut had done pretty well for himself in the leather industry and, apparently, was needing some company to help him enjoy the evening. He wasn't about to let us buy any beer. He couldn't speak much English, and I couldn't speak German, but that didn't stop us from having a fun evening and drinking a lot of Kolsch beers from Cologne. I tried to buy several times but was roundly discouraged every time, to where the barmaid scolded me when I tried to sneak a purchase in while Helmut was gone to the WC, reminding me that, "Nein, Nein... Helmut kauft es." I lost track of the number of beers Helmut bought us, but there were too many. At the end of the evening, we thanked Helmut and bid him a long, blurry-eyed goodbye.

Then we were confronted with hopping onto our bikes and pedaling back to the hotel. It didn't occur to us that walking the bikes was an option. Karen luckily knew the way back to the hotel, because I was having great difficulty finding the pedals, let alone finding the hotel. My memory was a bit compromised, but I remember having difficulty with the telephone poles and buildings that kept moving out into my pathway. Somehow, we made it to the hotel with only a few abrupt, unplanned stops.

The next day, we were invited to the home of one of Karen's old friends again in Lovenich. A small group of friends were there in the mid-afternoon, celebrating Karneval. After some drinks, snacks, and conversation, we all stepped out onto the corner to watch the neighborhood parade come by.

The neighborhood seemed to be a wholesome place to me, similar to a typical neighborhood in Nebraska, with single-family houses, gabled roofs and dormer windows, front yards with white picket fences, a sprinkling of over-canopy trees, driveways with cars and garage doors. The parade was small-townish, with high school marching bands, tractors pulling flatbed trailers that were hand-decorated into floats. Impressive old vehicles from the antique car club drove by. Local dignitaries waved at the crowd from the back seats of fancy convertibles. There was a '57 Chevy and a two-tone '58 Cadillac with big tail fins.

One float stood out to me in the parade. It was a flatbed truck, decorated around the edges with a split-rail fence that was draped with hides and colorful blankets of Native American design. A tepee mock-up stood on the deck, next to a full size-plastic horse, painted with white-and-black splotches and war-paint markings on its cheeks and hind end. There were eight or ten teenage girls on the platform, dressed like Dakota warriors. Several of them wore full feathered headdresses of the Sioux chief variety, while others had headbands with a single feather sticking up in the back. Instead of the traditional white feathers with black tips, these girls had feathers that were all dyed to match their school colors: white with bright-blue tips. I couldn't read the name on the side banners of the truck, but it probably was a reference to their mascot, the Chiefs, or the Warriors, I supposed. Their costumes included war paint on their cheeks, frilly edged skirts and vests to mimic deerskin vestments, spears, hide-stretched shields, bows and arrows with rubber suction points.

As the "warriors" reached into their pouches and threw sugar candies out into the crowd, I was dumbstruck by the irony. Here I was, some five thousand miles away from the land of the Sioux, in Cologne, Germany. The ghosts of Dakota warriors from 150 years past were still stirring, yelling war whoops and shaking their bows in the air, spreading defiance, evoking the drama of their life-and death struggles of years gone by.

CHAPTER 49

TV Box

Istanbul, Turkey, September 2015

Continuing our quest as two old people having fun, Karen and I toured around Turkey for three weeks in a rental car. Istanbul was at the top of our bucket list. Karen had worked there several times over the previous ten years and was familiar with the city. We met two of her colleagues for lunch. Their office was in a slick new tower, one of three office buildings surrounding a vogue shopping center lush with plants and fountains. Slim businessmen in black suits and model-esque females were everywhere. In terms of its modernity, the complex competed with anything that Europe or the US offered. My impression of Istanbul was that of a vibrant, modern metropolis. The atmosphere was contrary to my preexisting imaginings of Turkey as an arid, primitive place lost in the past. We had a pleasant lunch with Karen's two lady friends and had a tour of their office. Afterward, Karen and I walked to the subway station to catch a ride back to our hotel in the old town.

The train platform was deep underground. We had to go down several flights of crowded escalators, as the afternoon rush was in progress. At one landing, two guys joined us from a connecting hall. They were carrying a very large box with a new flat-screen TV inside. One guy was leading, the other behind. As they turned onto the down escalator ahead of us, the broadside of the big box became visible, displaying a photograph of the flat-screen TV, slightly skewed for dramatic effect. A close-up of a Sioux warrior was featured on the screen, with the eagle feathered headdress of a chief atop his paint horse, war-paint on his grimacing face, feathered spear—the whole bit. It was nearly a life-size image, riding right out of Hollywood into the underground metro station in the middle of Istanbul. Depending upon the success of sales, this image of the Sioux chief was possibly seen on a hundred TV boxes today on the streets of Istanbul, enough to create a sizable war party.

My mind quickly ran through the sights we had seen as we drove around Turkey, including Crusader castles, Greek amphitheaters, the troglodyte cities of Cappadocia, the graveyards at Gallipoli, the ruins of Troy, the Hagia Sophia, Roman temples, and a Neolithic city that was possibly the oldest on the planet. My conclusion was that, in competition with all these remarkable images from the past, this Dakota Sioux chief was putting up a pretty good campaign to hold the attention of people in Istanbul. And at this moment, since it was a popular brand of TV, a Sony, Toshiba, Hitachi, or the like, the chief was winning his war for the hearts and minds of people all over the world.

CHAPTER 50

The Yellow Chain

Paris, 17 November 2015

It was strange to be bicycling through Paris, just days after the horrific tragedy. One hundred and thirty people had been killed and some three hundred more wounded, all gunned down in Paris by terrorists in a monstrous act of brutality. News channels were showing cell phone videos of the carnage: people spilling out onto a side street from the Bataclan theater while the killing was in progress, wounded people collapsing to the pavement, a man hobbling to safety on one leg, another dragging a limp body away leaving a streak of blood, a woman hanging from a third story windowsill to escape the line of fire. A horrific, never-ending moment showed terrified people hiding under tables in front of a sidewalk cafe, while a man hovered over them, pointing his automatic weapon, trying to fire, but unable to because his ammunition was spent, or his gun was jammed.

Three days of national mourning had just passed. This was the first day, a Tuesday, when Paris was supposed to go back to business as usual. Paris was not back to business as usual. A hush blanketed the city. The tables and chairs on the sidewalks in front of cafes and bistros, which usually were bustling with patrons, now were sparsely occupied, a few wary attendees nervously throwing their gazes to the left and right out onto the streets. Gatherings of candles, flowers, and messages were spontaneously appearing, informal memorials in front of the sites of the tragedy. Pride of the place was trying to show itself, with *Bleu, Blanc, et Rouge* displayed along the public ways. Most notable was the Eiffel Tower, brilliantly lighted by the nations' colors but paled by the lack of tourists in the nearly empty plaza at its base. Police and armed soldiers in camouflage were visible everywhere, in front of prominent buildings and at major intersections, their black automatic assault rifles displayed chest high, downward pointing, trigger fingers laid straight against gun stocks, on the ready. Sirens and blue lights flashed as police vehicles rushed to the next alarm location. Criticisms were being leveled at the government, either for responding too strongly with knee-jerk bombings in Syria, or for responding not strongly enough after the *Charlie Hebdo* attacks earlier in the year.

It was at this time that, surrounded by the aftermath of the attacks, Karen and I had a startling experience. We had just returned with our bicycles from an evening event and were in the courtyard of our Paris apartment building. I had just placed my bicycle on the bike rack. Pulling the gray anti-theft chain from my handlebars, I stood behind the rack, preparing to lock up the bikes. Karen was waiting to park her bike next to mine.

"Do you have the yellow chain?" I asked.

"No," she said, "you did all the locks." Her voice flared. "What did you do with it?"

I looked around at all the usual places it could be - on the handlebars of the bikes, on the bike rack, on the floor of the courtyard, draping over the adjacent bikes, in my shoulder bag.

"It's not here. Maybe it fell off my handlebars."

Karen's words turned to fire. "You lost the fucking chain? You *idiot*! I spent *fifty fucking euros* on that chain!"

My thoughts went into memory recovery mode, and I sheepishly replied, "Maybe we left it over there."

"No, *you* left it over there, you *stupid asshole*!"

Karen was standing next to her bicycle, with one hand on the handlebars and the other gripping the seat. She spontaneously went into an act of rage. With a lunge, she lifted her bicycle and hurled it at me. It flew forward, its front wheel bouncing on the pavement, the bicycle lurching onto its side, wobbling out of control. Too late, I thrust my hands outward, trying to protect myself but missing. The bicycle's frame hit me hard, below the knee, in the middle of my shinbone. Sharp pain was instantaneous and intense. The bicycle collapsed to the ground.

Anger immediately welled up in me, overshadowing the pain in my shin. I aggressively bolted over the bike with a long single stride, lunging toward Karen. My right arm shot outward and high. As I took a second attacking step toward her, I grabbed her shoulder and shoved. She recognized my anger and my attack. Her facial expression switched immediately from anger to fear. She scrunched her shoulders up around her ears and retracted her head in a protective ducking move. As I muscled forward into her, she lurched backward, her fearful retreat matching my angry attack.

At that moment, both Karen and I recognized the violence that was upon us. I disarmed, halting my attack, letting go, backing off. She recovered her balance and regained her composure. Our emotions quickly subsided, and discussion followed. We had been at each other like this once before, in the kitchen in Omaha, which resulted in a pot bouncing off the microwave.

After we both calmed down, we decided I would get back onto my bike and retrace our path through Paris, keeping an eye out along the way for the lost yellow chain. As I was leaving, we apologized to each other for blowing up, and there was forgiveness. I never found the chain.

We both realized how quickly we had descended into genuine acts of violence and how easy it was to release the anger. It was part of us, hidden, locked away, a monster waiting to get out. Not far away. Close. Too close. Anger turning into rage. Rage turning into violence. In November 2015, in Paris, the monster got out, like it had done many times in the past, in many other places… like it did in central Minnesota in August 1862.

CHAPTER 51
John Lennon

Southern Spain, May 2016

I read the messages written on the plastic back of the seat in front of me. *Life Vest Under Your Seat. Fasten Seat Belt While Seated.* The phrases were repeated in Spanish. *Chaleco Salvavidas Bajo Su Asiento. Mintengo et Cinturon de Seguridid Abrochado.*

Karen and I had just left Malaga and were flying back to Paris after spending a week at one of those fancy resort hotels on the beach of the Mediterranean Sea, east of Gibraltar. We were now in the economy seats of a Boeing 737. Karen had the window seat with the view. I was feeling a bit like a sardine sandwiched between her and the big guy in the aisle seat. The seatback in front of me was too close to let me use my laptop. Out of boredom, and needing something to ease my claustrophobia, I dug into the vinyl pocket in front of me, looking for a magazine to read, or, if it was in Spanish, something just to look at. A slick travel magazine titled *Europa* was tucked away, waiting for me. Flipping through the first few pages, I discovered the magazine had several interesting articles, all written in Spanish on the left half of the page and in English on the right half, intermingled with some nice photographs. The articles were a mixture of human interest, travel, and cuisine, splashed with fashion, people, and destinations: LeBron James, Santiago, Harrison Ford, the wines of Mallorca, Salma Hayek, Times Square.

Between articles on Seoul and the Ice Hotel, there was an article about John Lennon's time in New York and his murder thirty-five years before.

The opening lines read, "It was 10:50 p.m. Only one fan lingered in the doorway of the Dakota building: Mark David Chapman, who pointed his revolver and fired five shots." A large aerial photograph of the New York home of Lennon and Ono was featured, with the caption, "The Dakota building today with its magnificent views of Central Park." I repeated to myself, "Dakota building."

As I read the article, the building's name distracted me from John Lennon's story. It was repeated, again and again, "Dakota building." My mind wandered into the past, thinking that the building probably received its name when it was built in the late 1800s, after the Dakota Indian Wars had become part of the national conscious. The article's author, Rodrigo Palilla reduced the phrase to its essence, *the Dakota*, and repeated it yet again. Incredible, it seemed to me, as I counted the five times the author used the word *Dakota* and could only count four times that the name *New York* appeared in the text. There was something about it. Even here, flying over southern Spain, 150 years later, four thousand miles away, on a Spanish airline, reading in a Spanish magazine an article about John Lennon, there was DAKOTA.

The word is branded into our brains. It is recognized anywhere on the planet. How appropriate to use this word for its dramatic effect when writing about John Lennon's murder. It is a word synonymous with American history, and with violence, anguish, and brutality. What is incredible is that the Dakota waged their war at exactly the same time that the US was in the throes of the horrific Civil War that took some 650,000 lives. Somehow, despite that, this small culture of nomad buffalo hunters, the Dakota have imprinted onto the minds of people the world over.

As we bounced around Europe on our quest of two old people having fun, Karen and I regularly observed references to the Sioux people. On the island of Malta in the southern Mediterranean, we ran across dream catcher hoops with feathers and beads hanging from the rearview mirrors of two cars nosed into a curb in front of an ancient church. In Florence, we found a carved wooden Indian, a Sioux chief, standing in front of a restaurant, holding the menu in his arms.

We found many references to the Sioux people sprinkled around Paris. On the way to our favorite farm outlet vegetable store, Karen and I regularly walked past a small storefront gallery off the beaten path. The gallery windows displayed several female mannequins glued, painted, beaded, and feathered in an outlandish style that harken back to traditional Sioux clothing but faithful to the rhythms of Paris, contemporized into sexy fashion statements.

In Paris, the Musée du quai Branly, on the left bank of the Seine near the Eiffel Tower, which specializes in "dialoguent les cultures" had an amazing temporary exhibition entitled "*Plains Indians*," which we visited in the summer of 2014. The artistry and clothing of the Sioux culture was displayed. Karen and I had failed to pay much attention to these sorts of things during our previous lives, growing up in the homeland of the Sioux. Yet the world seemed to pay attention to these Sioux people, confirming that their struggle of 150 years ago was meaningful.

But something was missing, something beyond the museum exhibits, the commercialized Sioux warrior images, the Hollywood myth, the corporate branding, the children's toys, the dramatized symbols seen everywhere. These people remain out on the rolling hills of prairie grass NOW, laughing with joy, grieving for lost loved ones, spouting angry words in disagreement, suffering through difficulties; young people falling in love, parents wishing for better lives for their children, making ends meet, old people fading away. Amid all this, they are struggling to hold on to their culture, their spirituality, and their language, to own and protect their identity, living with the ghost of the good life that was taken away, reaching out to capture it back. The Dakota, Nakota and Lakota people, the real people that I came to know, like me, were experiencing all the things of life, the good things, the bad things, and the strange things. But unlike me, surrounded by my comfortable trappings of the white man's world, these people seemed to have had to reach out farther and hold on harder.

CHAPTER 52
Bathtub

Paris, February 14, 2016

It was Valentine's Day. This is the day when guys typically feel uncomfortably guilty for not doing something special for their lady and when women wait around expecting some gesture of endearment to come forth from their man to profess his love.

On this occasion, Karen had her typical hour of grumpiness at the start of the morning, which never matched well with my typical hour of dullness. I usually watched an hour of news while sipping that first cup of coffee and returning slowly to consciousness. Karen usually started her day by hovering over me while blurting out a barrage of honey-do items like take the clean dishes out of the dishwasher, or put the dirty dishes in the dishwasher, or take all the dirty dishes to the kitchen, or clean the drips of coffee off of the kitchen floor, or all of the above. My vegetative state in the early morning typically resulted in very few of her honey-do items being accomplished. Her typical fit of hovering and spouting commands resulted in my having great difficulty hearing or comprehending any of the latest news headlines. We had been married just shy of three years. This was what our love had distilled down to. Our motto of two old people having fun needed editing by the addition of the word "*not*."

After an hour of this on Valentine's Day morning, the coffee and my guilt kicked in. Here we were, retired and living part-time in Paris, the City of Love. There ought to be something special we could find to do. I was considering optional ideas. Interestingly enough, Karen had not pre-planned anything special to do, either. I decided that, whatever we did, I would need to clean up a bit, so I walked down the hall to the bathroom to shave, brush my teeth, do my toenails, and take a shower. At sixty-six years old, one thing that still had some special-ness was sex! Now, there was an idea, especially appropriate as a jump-start to Valentine's Day.

"Karen," I yelled from the shower, "why don't you come in here and take a shower with me!"

Karen thought this was a good idea and postponed my morning kitchen duties. Adding momentum to the moment, she showed up naked in the bathroom with two champagne glasses and a bottle of bubbly.

"How about a bubble bath, instead," she suggested, radiating a big grin.

I agreed, posting a mischievous one-sided smile.

"Bubble bath and bubbly," I proclaimed with a giggle, "Double bubbles!"

Now, Karen and I are not what you would call petite people, being both about six feet tall and weighing in at the next higher boxing category above middleweight. Combine with that the European space standards for bathroom design, which are smaller than those you would find in the wide-open spaces of Nebraska. The result was two rather large people shoehorning into the rather small tub. We definitely needed the extra soapy-slipperiness provided by the bubble bath to fit into the tub together. I'm guessing that bubble bath is a French invention, with their propensity for fancy aromatic toiletries. Both ends of the tub had a comfortable back-rest slope, making me think that these free-spirited Frenchies had two people in mind when they designed the tub, albeit two smaller people. Facing each other from opposite ends of the tub, we found there was just enough tub length for the two of us to submerge into the water so that only the top half of our shoulders were above the waterline, with neck and head resting comfortably back on the built-in rim. Karen, being genetically well-endowed, reclined while her boobies bobbed half-sunken in the water, rather like a couple swimming pool floats. Our legs folded into a pose that you might see on a downhill skier, fully bent at the hips and knees. With our knees poking up out of the water, it seemed like there were too many legs in the tub with us. But our feet were comfortably down at the bottom of the tub, well placed to enhance our mission, with a little wiggle room.

Believe it or not, it was pretty comfortable. The goose-neck Roman-style spigot was well clear of my shoulder and swiveled a bit to the right, such that it was out of the way. I could add hot water into the corner of the tub, missing a direct hit on my body. A long-handled body brush held in my left hand, used like a paddle, moved the hot water along the side of the tub, towards Karen. The force of the hot water jetting from the spigot now and then created a steady batch of bubbles on the surface of the water.

Fulfilling my manly duty, I popped the champagne cork and poured the two glasses. As a rather strange turn of events, we were so damn comfortable in the hot, bubbly water that we completely blew off our mission, which had been to have sex. We stayed in the toasty warm bath for two hours, giggling and chatting. It felt like when we first had first fallen in love six years before, with our endless talks on the telephone. We each had three glasses of champagne, completely killing the bottle before leaving the tub.

Even though we missed our initial chance for hot sex in a hot tub, we accomplished our mission a little later, two squeaky-clean old people with wrinkly prune skin. We sat around the rest of the day reading, pecking on our laptops, and warming up leftovers for supper, followed by watching an old George Clooney movie, sipping on our gin and tonics while snuggling under a warm quilt on the couch. Let's not forget those all-important kitchen duties, which I accomplished, albeit later in the day than usual. All in all, it wasn't a bad Valentine's Day, re-discovering our motto, two old people having fun, even though we completely blew off all those romantic opportunities that Paris offers, out there in the City of Love.

Somewhere between the second and third glasses of champagne while soaking in the tub of bubbly hot water, my mind drifted five years into the past, back to the time when Karen and I were new to each other, two sixty-year-old people, surprised to have found love late in our lives. I remembered our visit to Red Owl, our Native American friend, at his little house out on the Dakota prairie, sitting around his kitchen table. Karen and I listened intently to the words of this wise old man as he described our newfound love in his low and slow voice: "A man loses his wife, a woman loses her mother, two people find each other and there is a new beginning... This is the Hoop of Life."

CHAPTER 53
The Knot in Time

While rough hands snag the silk, while a youthful encounter is the beginning of a bond, while we see a place for the first time all over again, while Abraham Lincoln issues pardons, while the good life ends, and a hard life begins while a protective mother points a shotgun, while dirt is tamped snug with a sledgehammer, while a nurse can't find a blood vessel to insert a needle, while knights in full armor ride out through stone arches, while a father wipes the nose of his young son, while a thick wad of bills is pulled from a pocket, while old men chuckle, while a dozen teenage girls throw sugar candies, while John Lennon is gunned down, while a man and woman find new love late in their lives, while running hot water creates a steady batch of bubbles,

> VISION: evoked by the search to know the old ways.
> VISION: evoked by a sacred dance, within a sacred circle, within a sacred space.
> VISION: evoked by image makers, movies, advertising, toys, TV, blah, blah, blah.
> VISION: evoked by seeing what is in front of you after a lifetime of looking past it.
> VISION: evoked by great loss and the rediscovery of joy.

END

About the Author

Steve Laughlin was born in Lincoln, Nebraska, in 1949. He is a graduate from the University of Nebraska, College of Architecture and has a master's degree from the University of California, Berkeley, College of Environmental Design. A professional architect in Omaha until his retirement in 2013, he and his first wife Sharon raised three boys and shared thirty-five years together until her death in 2009. He married his second wife, Karen, in 2013, who is a French citizen. Mr. Laughlin now lives part-time in Omaha and part-time in Paris.

"*The Hoop of Life*" is Mr. Laughlin's first novel, which is a collection of stories inspired by his family life. Also featured in the novel are the Dakota and Lakota people, who Mr. Laughlin came to know through his architectural work.

Note from the Author

Word-of-mouth is crucial for any author to succeed. If you enjoyed *The Hoop of Life*, please leave a review online—anywhere you are able. Even if it's just a sentence or two. It would make all the difference and would be very much appreciated.

Thanks!
Steve Laughlin

References and Sources

Berg, Scott W. (2013). *38 Nooses: Lincoln, Little Crow, and the Beginning of the Frontier's End*. Vintage Books, New York.

Jensen, Richard E., Paul, R. Eli & Carter, John E. with Introduction by Richardson, H.C. (2011). *Eyewitness at Wounded Knee*. University of Nebraska Press.

Torrence, Gaylord (Curator) (2014). *The Plains Indians, Artists of the Earth and Sky*. Editions Skira, Paris.
From the Exhibition April-July 2014. *Plains Indians*. Musée du quai Branly, Paris, France.

Exhibition: *Commemorating Controversy: The Dakota-U.S. War of 1862*. The National Museum of the American Indian, Washington DC, January 2012
Produced by students of Gustavus Adolphus College, in conjunction with the Nicollet County Historical Society, Minnesota.

Discussions with the Lakota people of Pine Ridge Reservation, Pine Ridge, South Dakota during school renovations and the design of their dormitory, circa 1995.
Architect of Record: Leo A Daly, Architects and Engineers, Omaha, Nebraska.

Discussions with the Dakota People of the Sisseton Wahpeton Oyate Reservation, Sisseton South Dakota during the design and construction of the Sisseton Wahpeton Administration Building, circa 2010.
Architect of Record: Leo A Daly, Architects and Engineers, Omaha, Nebraska.

We hope you enjoyed reading this title from:

www.blackrosewriting.com

Subscribe to our mailing list – *The Rosevine* – and receive **FREE** books, daily deals, and stay current with news about upcoming releases and our hottest authors.
Scan the QR code below to sign up.

Already a subscriber? Please accept a sincere thank you for being a fan of Black Rose Writing authors.

View other Black Rose Writing titles at www.blackrosewriting.com/books and use promo code **PRINT** to receive a **20% discount** when purchasing.

www.ingramcontent.com/pod-product-compliance
Lightning Source LLC
Chambersburg PA
CBHW071957070526
44583CB00015B/1227